People *of the* Latchmere

(an ancient watercourse that connects the districts of Canbury, Tudor, Ham and Petersham)

From the early to mid - 20th century

by Gordon Elsden

Written by

Gordon Elsden

Published by

Phoenix Endeavour, Hong Kong

Layout and design

Lindsay Birch
eight one five design 07914 941249
www.eightonefive.co.uk

9 781527 278271 >

Images/Photographs:

Every effort has been made to identify the owners of the photographs used in this book, to gain permission for their use with reasonable payment when required and recording of the correct accreditation. The difficulty is that local history groups on Facebook and other internet sites are awash with historical images, many times repeated, yet there is no clear indication of their origin or ownership.

If it is discovered that appropriate accreditation has not been made on any of the images in this book, please contact the author at remarkableham@yahoo.com to rectify for future print runs and general use.

It would also be really useful if owners of any such photos which are now repeatedly seen on local history Facebook groups and other internet sites could register their ownership with the local history centres in Kingston and Richmond. In this way they are more likely to get appropriate recognition for their ownership.

Previous page: October 1922 – A Dicks family wedding

Opposite picture: October 1955 – Building a bonfire on Ham Common for Guy Fawkes Night
(Photo by Hulton Archive/Getty Images)

People *of the* Latchmere

From the early to mid- 20th Century

by Gordon Elsden

To Claire, Tom, Sophie & Harry

**and the children of the Latchmere,
past, present & future**

*"Twenty years from now you will be more disappointed by the
things that you didn't do than by the ones you did do.
So, throw off the bowlines. Sail away from the safe harbour.
Catch the trade winds in your sails.
Explore. Dream. Discover."*

Mark Twain

Maps and photographs

List of Aerial Maps

List of Aerial Photographs

Contents

Foreword

History was a subject I loved at school, but it was clearly focussed on great people, great buildings and great events. I grew up in New Malden, amidst the endless suburban sprawl that had followed the railways out from London. For entertainment, there was nearby Kingston with its old market centre, the Thames, Canbury Gardens and Richmond Park as well as the shopping centre including the Bentalls department store and, of course, the theatres and cinemas. I also loved family stories but did not think of these as history. Some of my earliest memories are of catching the 213 bus to Kingston with my grandmother. There was afternoon tea in Bentalls Silver Café (for us children, ice cream) while a piano was being played. There were picnics in Canbury Gardens or a boat trip up the river to Hampton Court. There was even a brief theatrical appearance! My sister and I were taken to ballet classes when very young, and sometime in the early fifties, Miss Hayman's Ballet School gave a show in the Empire Theatre. We both remember the smog that day. My mother and grandmother had made tutus for us and these had to be taken into Kingston on the bus through the smog, the tutus finishing up grey rather than white after the journey!

I moved away from the area during much of the sixties and seventies but then returned to live in the middle of the area described in this book. As I have explored the area I have become intrigued by the sources of the street names and by the local geography. And I began to ask questions, many of which are illuminated by "People of the Latchmere". Gordon Elsden has taken the family stories of people living in this small area to the north of Kingston and the east of the Thames in the first half of the twentieth century, and woven them into a tapestry which is local and intimate while also reflecting the great events of the period such as two World Wars. I have been fascinated to read how the British aviation industry was born and built up within a mile or so of my house, and to picture Harry Hawker trying out early seaplanes along the river just outside my windows more than 100 years ago!

I hope other readers enjoy his book as much as I have and thank Gordon for providing so many fascinating stories and introducing us to so many ordinary people living through periods of extraordinary change.

Julia Higgins

In 2020, Dame Julia Higgins was awarded the Sir Frank Whittle Medal for her sustained excellence in polymer engineering

People *of the* Latchmere

From the early to mid- 20th Century

This is the story of a remarkable group of people who lived, went to school or worked in the vicinity of the Latchmere Brook in the early to mid 20th Century. The Latchmere Brook was an ancient watercourse that threaded its way through the Canbury district of Kingston and Ham then changed its name to the Sudbrook as it passed under the wall into Richmond Park. It then continued on a north westerly course through Sudbrook Park and Petersham Meadows before greeting the Thames at the end of River Lane.

These people, many of them children at the time, personally experienced the devastation caused by the 2nd World War and the long period of rationing both during and after the war. Those, who I personally interviewed, are remarkable in that at the time of interview about their experiences they had an exceptional recall of names, places and incidents that happened so long ago.

They are the last of a generation that could comfortably live without computers and they took austerity in their stride. They lived in a period where material possessions had less value than personal relationships and the intimacy of a good time together, whether out and about with friends, down the pub with mates or playing games and singing songs with the family at Christmas. For their entertainment, they were skilful users of their imagination.

VE Day Celebrations at the vicarage of St Luke's Church,
Courtesy of Owen Walter

Through the retelling of their stories we have an invaluable insight into a turbulent period characterised by a scarcity of "comforts" and a group of resilient people who made the most of what they had. Perhaps in a period when we are also faced with uncertainty, fear and sacrifice we may take some inspiration from them.

Gordon Elsden, December 2020

The Latchmere Brook, alias Sudbrook, connected Kingston, through Canbury, to Ham and Petersham. The route of the original brook has been overlaid on the streets and landscape that we know today.

© Gordon Elsden

The Mysterious Latchmere Brook

It is with the benefit of the findings of an archaeological excavation of a small Agricultural Roman settlement (dating from the 1st to 4th centuries) that we now have evidence of the southern end of the Latchmere Brook as it entered the Thames.

If we travel back in time, just under two thousand years, we will find a stream three metres wide and one and a half metres deep, leisurely making its way in a south westerly direction from what is now the junction of Kings Road and Acre Road running at the end of the back gardens of Elm Road and Acre Road along the north boundary of St Luke's Secondary School to Canbury Park Road, just east of Kingston Railway Station. It then headed directly west, followed many years later by the railway line, until it met the Thames. The stream is sustained by a multitude of smaller streams tumbling water down the slopes of the high terraces from Kingston Hill to Richmond Hill.

Shortly before the stream enters the Thames, we find a small Roman settlement based on its northern bank. The Canons of Merton Abbey, Lords of the Manor of Canbury, would later build a grange holding a huge tithe barn just along from the Roman settlement, also on the north bank of the Latchmere. (Canbury derives its names from Canonbury, associated with its long period under Merton Priory).

At one time the Latchmere Brook was lined with osiers that were used for making baskets.

Unfortunately, as our population increased, humans fouled the stream and later when they discovered it was carrying disease, they incarcerated the stream deep underground, away from the human settlements that were progressively migrating north out of Kingston.

In ancient times a natural feature in the landscape such as a brook would often be used as a boundary. As such it would define the borders of plots of land. Although the Latchmere Brook has long since disappeared in Canbury, north of Kingston, its location can still be seen by the configuration of plots of land in the landscape which effectively mark out its course. This explains why in this 1924 aerial photograph, the former roller rink extends at an angle from Canbury Park Road, its eastern wall following the line of the former brook. The brook then establishes the boundary of the grounds of St Luke's Secondary School and the fence line of the end of the back gardens of the houses of Elm Road and Acre Road until they converge at Kings Road. Further north, the brook can be seen clearly defining the eastern boundary of the East Surrey Barracks and the Latchmere Recreation Ground. © Historic England

But here's the strange thing; the same stream also runs in a north easterly direction underground from Kings Road, defining the eastern boundary of the former barracks of the East Surrey Regiment and Latchmere School. It then continues underground marking the eastern boundary of the Latchmere Recreation Ground before crossing under Tudor Drive.

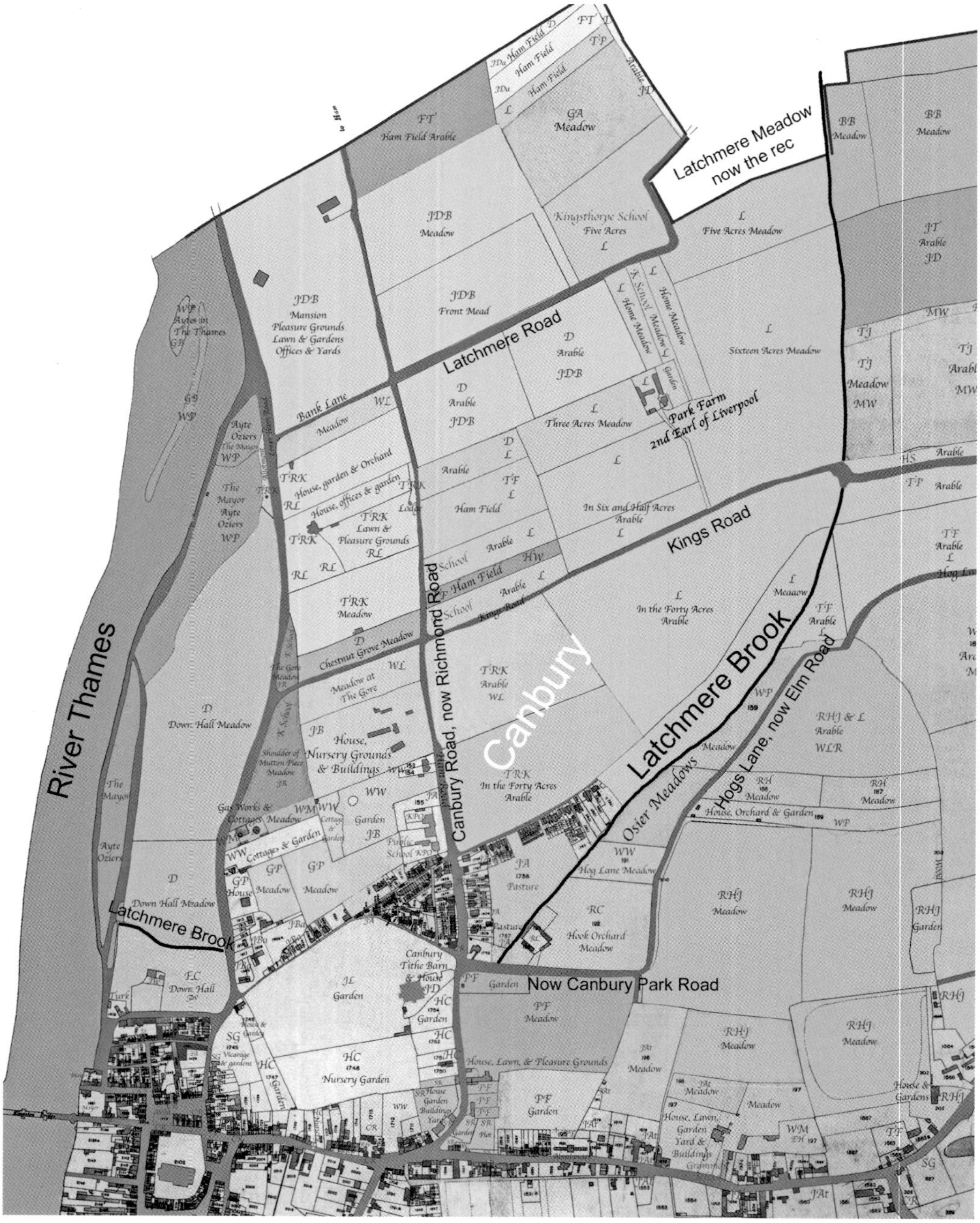

1841 Tithe Map showing the progress of the Latchmere Brook though Canbury and Ham. The Brook was lined with osier beds running parallel with Hogs Lane. GE

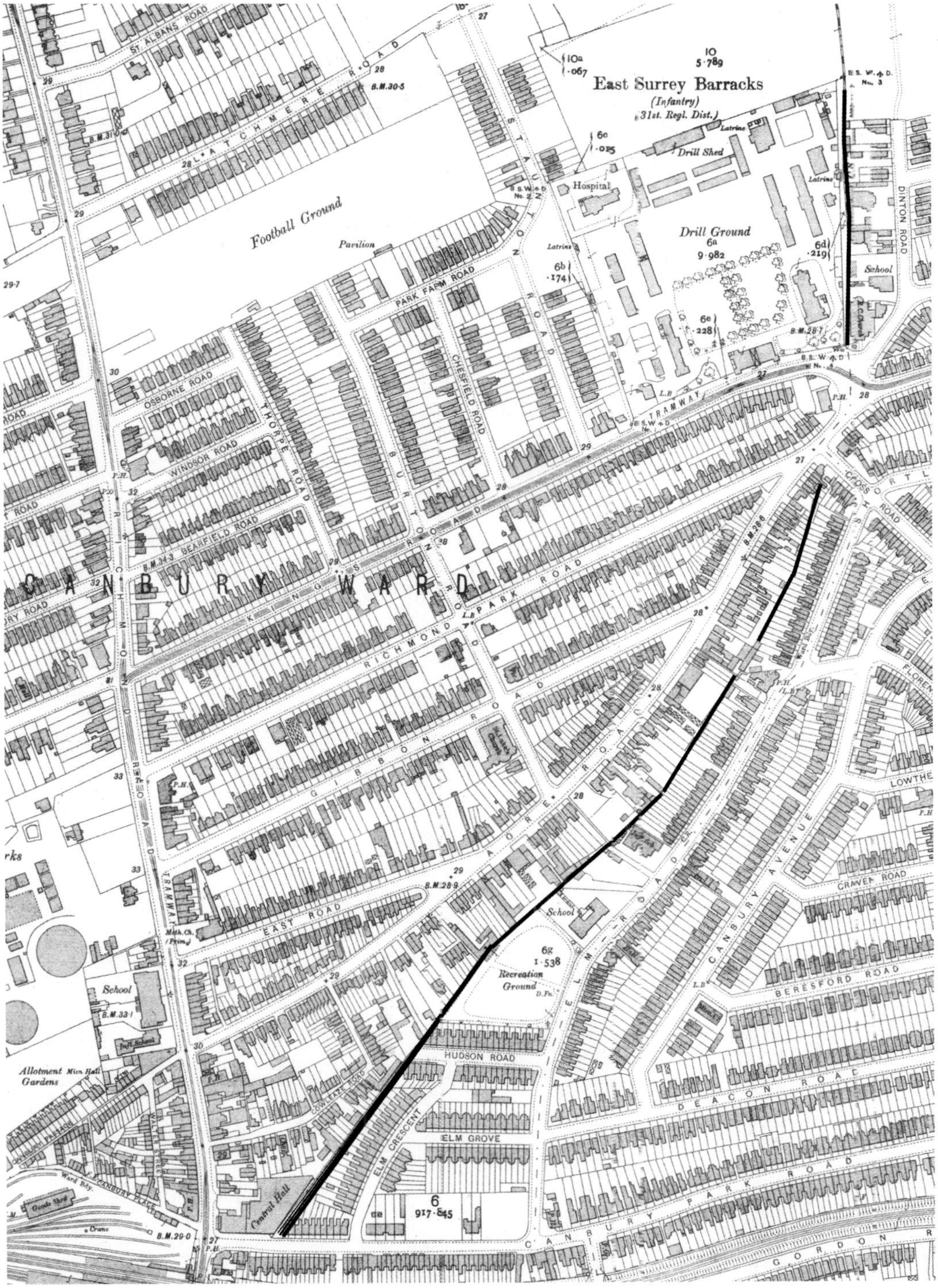

The route of the Latchmere Brook overlaid on a 1913 Map. It shows the brook running down the eastern side of the Barracks, between Elm Road and Acre Road along the northern boundary of St Luke's Secondary School then down the eastern side of the roller rink that faces onto Canbury Park Road. NLS

The marker stone shows the location of the Latchmere Brook, deep underground. It can be found next to the south eastern corner of the wall of the East Surrey Barracks on Kings Road GE

The Brook then passes under the back gardens of numerous houses until it reaches Ham Common woods. Finally, just outside the park at Ham Gate, the Latchmere is allowed to breathe again and take back its natural form as it comes to the surface. It has been helped considerably by the members of the Ham and Petersham Association, who realising its value, have provided a carefully tended natural environment around the brook before it flows through a hole in the wall of Richmond Park. If you are lucky you may even see the flash of one of the kingfishers that occasionally visits. As the brook enters the park, it changes its identity to the Sudbrook and by this name it is known, until it finally greets the Thames at River Lane in Petersham. The brook has effectively travelled across the lower terrace (the Latchmere Terrace) that lies between the high ground of Richmond Park (from Kingston Hill to Richmond Hill) and the River Thames.

Latchmere Brook runs under the junction of Kings Road and Acre Road. In the distance is the steep slope of Kingston Hill before it was covered with houses Courtesy of Owen Walter

So why does the Latchmere Brook flow in two directions?

Early farmers, wishing to use the brook as a catchwater to both prevent flooding of their fields and as a source of water for their fields during drier periods, may have canalised existing streams into a single catchwater running along the base of the hill, through the lower Latchmere Terrace. This was then fed by the small streams running down from the upper terraces from Kingston Hill to Richmond Hill. One of those small streams can still be seen on the northern edge of Dinton Sports Field. The blocking of many of these streams has resulted in routine flooding along the Latchmere Terrace.

Victorian surveyors in 1894 were good enough to do a detailed survey of the Latchmere Brook, measuring its drop in height from Kings Road, all the way to its entry into the Thames at River Lane in Petersham. The heights, they recorded, confirmed the direction of its flow all the way to the Thames.

Mid 1930s aerial view from Kings Road, looking north ©SHC

1924 aerial photograph looking north towards a very agricultural Ham. © Historic England

The Latchmere Brook, just outside Ham Gate, has benefitted from the considerate attention of the Ham & Petersham Association

Sources:
Duncan Hawkins – A product of its environment: revising Roman Kingston
London Archaeologist Spring 2007
SHC K58/14/36 - Section of Latchmere Brook from Kingston Barracks to outfall Petersham Meadows

Picture Credits
NLS: Reproduced with the permission of the National Library of Scotland
SHC: Reproduced by permission of Surrey History Centre
GE © Gordon Elsden

A House in the Country (Worthy Dicks and his family)

It was a bright Spring morning in the year 1923 when Worthy James Dicks left his house at 28 Hudson Road in Kingston (near Elm Road) and began a walk that would reshape the lives of all the members of his family. Worthy was a happy, jovial man of good Wiltshire Quaker stock, immediately recognisable by his ready smile and walrus moustache.

Worthy had a grocery shop on the front of their house which his wife, Ellen managed. When not using his horse and cart to replenish the stock for the shop, Worthy sold shellfish, prawns and winkles around the streets and pubs of North Kingston. At events at Hampton Court and Epsom Downs he set up marquees from which his daughters served refreshments. But now his circumstances had changed.

In the last year he had inherited his father's pig farm near Seend in Wiltshire. Having sold the farm, he had acquired the means of supporting his large family. Yet, what he desired was a house in the country where they could all live together, a situation that his present small Victorian era house, fronted by the grocery shop, was unable to provide.

His eldest daughter Eleanor, called Nell, had married Sidney Howard from Elm Grove. Sidney and two of his brothers, Samuel and Jack, had all fought during the war. Sidney had been seriously wounded by shrapnel and hospitalised for eighteen months. He would need the aid of a stick to help him walk, for the remainder of his life. Samuel, his elder brother who had served with the East Surreys, had been killed at Arras in Northern France, but his body had never been found.

Two of Worthy's younger daughters, Edith and Win, had recently, with great occasion and joy, married two brothers Ernie and Ollie Hayward. They had met the brothers shortly before the two young men had gone off to fight in France. Mistakenly, they had ended up writing to the other brother over the long period of the war. On their return, some years later, they discovered their mistake but having developed some intimacy and confidence through their letters, they married the brother they had been writing to. They celebrated a double wedding on Monday 16th October 1922.

Photograph taken in Hudson Road (near Elm Road). From back left: Sidney Howard Looking down. His wife Nell (Mother of Eva, Joyce and Grace) to the right of him. Grandad Worthy Dicks with the large moustache. Charlie Hayward, Granny Ellen Dicks and to her left, Doll (laughing). Front Row: Ernie & Edith, Win and Ollie.

Taking a Stroll

Worthy Dicks walked the length of Elm Road and at its junction with Park Road, turned left along Park Road until it dissolved into a muddy track. He followed this track past the sports grounds of Kingston Grammar and Hodgsons Brewery on his left until he came to a gate that deterred his further progress into a large field holding some cows. Unknowingly, he had followed the course of the Latchmere Brook, out of Kingston into the Parish of Ham. To his immediate left were fields running down to the Latchmere Brook. To his right at the end of another field ran the imposing wall of Richmond Park. Ahead, in the field to his right was a large lake with a small orchard lying between it and the Park wall. Slightly ahead to his left was a smaller lake, a gravel pit reclaimed by nature.

After due enquiry, he purchased the land at auction from Park Farm Estates (farm land previously owned by the 2nd Earl of Liverpool, the Prime Minister between 1812 and 1827). On the park side of the track he built three houses. In January 1926, Edith and Ernie with their daughter Eileen aged 3, along with Win and Ollie moved together into a house that they named Haycroft (now 234 Park Road).

Nell, her husband Sidney and their two daughters Joyce also aged 3 and Eva, aged 14 months, moved into the adjoining house which they called Thornham (236 Park Road). It was named after the small farm in Wiltshire where they had spent their honeymoon.

A year or so later, Worthy with his wife Ellen and their younger children William and Dorothy (Doll) moved into the detached house on the end with a small plot of land connected to it (now 238 Park Road). Worthy named this house Littleworth. The land of each of the three houses ran all the way back to the wall of Richmond Park. Worthy also rented the large field at the end, that was owned by Ham Sand & Ballast Company. He kept a small herd of cows in the field to provide the family with milk. Having come from a family that produced good Wiltshire Ham, it was natural that he also kept pigs on the land that ran adjacent to his house. Furthermore, a country setting wouldn't be right without numerous chickens and a cockerel to sound the morning alarm every day at first light. This call was complemented by the clarion bugle calls which, without exception, announced reveille and retreat at the East Surrey Barracks in Kings Road.

Here at the house named Littleworth, on a lane that the grandchildren nicknamed Nanny Goat Lane, he and his wife Ellen lived for the remainder of their lives. The three girls, Joyce, Eileen and Eva, at the time of the move, were so young that their earliest memories came from growing up in this pastoral environment.

The Dicks Family in Lower Park Road

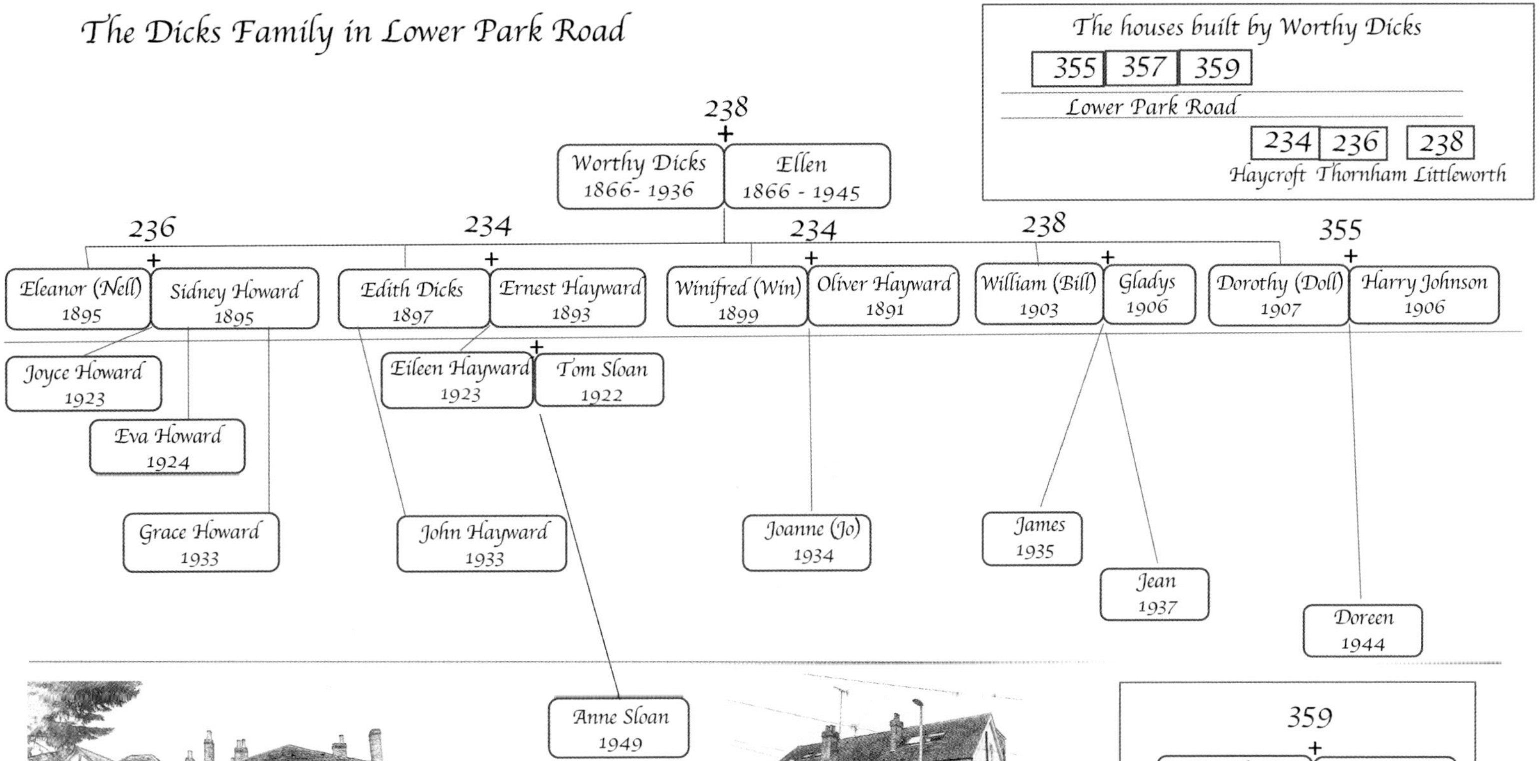

238 236 234
Littleworth Thornham Haycroft

355 357 359

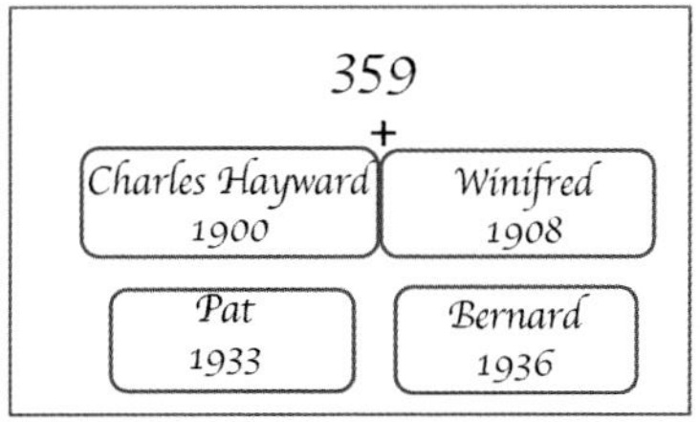

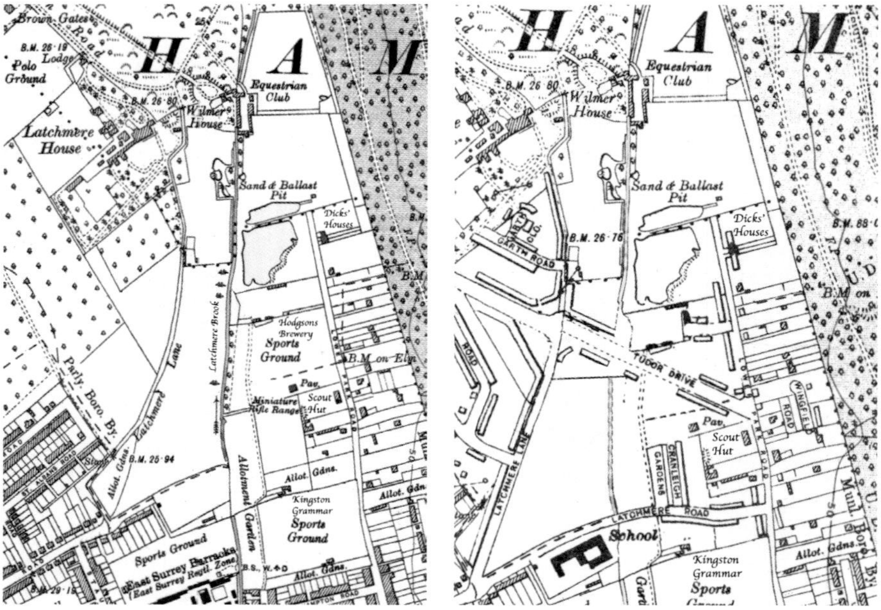

Two maps showing the location of the three Dicks houses at the end of Lower Park Road.

The first, pre-Tudor Estate (1934), shows the orchard of Ham Farm and Hodgsons Brewery sports /cricket field & pavilion. The Latchmere Brook is clearly visible.

The second (1944) shows the planned Tudor Drive cutting through the sports field and the change to Latchmere Lane. The Orchard has already been torn up. Latchmere School has been built.

A Simple Life

The houses when initially built had no gas or electricity. In the back garden just outside the back door was a water pump that drew water up from a well. However, they also had running water and the luxury of flush toilets that emptied into a cess pit. Each of the houses had a kitchen range that burnt logs and coal.

It was very dark at night, especially when there was no moon. Downstairs was lit by paraffin lamps but when they went to bed, they took candles with them, the dancing flames struggling to light their way. They became very used to darkness and it was a bit of a shock when streetlights were established along Park Road in 1936. A year later they were connected to the gas mains and had gas lights with their delicate mantles established halfway up the walls of the downstairs rooms; the gentle whoosh of the burning gas breaking the silence.

They also had a big paraffin heater to warm the water for the bath. Downstairs a big copper, heated with logs and coals, boiled water for washing their clothes. The clothes were transferred to a sink and then passed through a mangle before being placed on the washing line to billow back and forth in the breeze. One day while Granny (Ellen) was putting up her washing on a line, a lady arrived from Park Gate House to complain that the washing was ruining their view. Granny Ellen gave her short shrift and the lady departed leaving a flurry of dust in the wake of her motor car. In the end, the owners of the house planted a row of fast-growing poplars to shield them from the view of the washing.

A Country Setting

Eva has a very strong memory of the wonderful butterflies and flowers in the large field: buttercups, daisies, dandelions, primroses and her favourite, the towering pink rosebay willow herb. She clearly recalls her jovial grandad with his rosy cheeks and big moustache, reassuringly supporting her on the back of a cow as he slowly led them back across the field at the edge of the Latchmere Brook to the shed where the cows were milked every evening.

Eva also remembers the large number of pigs that her grandad kept on the land near to his house (nearly a hundred according to John): *Grandad was so pleased when his prize boar won a competition and a rosette at Kingston Cattle Market. He also kept geese, chickens and a few ferrets. He fed the ferrets down a rabbit hole in the field, then caught the rabbits in a sack as they popped out. Nearly every week we enjoyed rabbit pie or rabbit stew along with a good supply of eggs and the occasional dish of chicken and pork.*

Nell grew vegetables in her garden and when the girls were young, she gave them each a small plot to grow their own flowers. Eva was delighted when her first pack of Virginia stock seeds grew into pretty lilac coloured flowers with a delightful smell.

Eva also remembers, when only five years old, her grandad giving her the cream from the top of the milk churn. Her mum put the cream in a small bottle and Eva carried that bottle around with her all day long, giving it an occasional vigorous shake. By teatime she had made her own butter, enough to cover one or maybe two slices of bread. She was so pleased with herself for making her own butter.

The children soon became familiar with the various songs of the cuckoos, blackbirds, thrushes, robins and wood pigeons that frequented their gardens and flew over the wall from Richmond Park: *Grandad used to shoot pigeons and Granny would make him a pigeon pie every week. Granny said that the pigeons gave him indigestion, but he loved them all the same.*

Old Joe

Eva recalls the story of their cat Old Joe: *Over a period of weeks, Grandad became increasingly concerned because an animal was getting into the chicken coops and randomly killing his chickens. One day he came to see my mum to express his concern that our cat "Old Joe" was the cause of the problem.*

A few weeks later Grandad discovered a chicken that had been killed in the coop. Unusually angry, he dashed round to our house to accuse Old Joe of the murder. He accompanied my mum into the back garden and there was Old Joe, cleaning blood off his fur.. with a dead weasel on the ground in front of him.

That was the end of the random slaughter of the chickens and Old Joe's reputation went up considerably with Eva and her sisters.

The Lakes

The two lakes in the end field had originally been gravel pits but nature had been left to work its magic as the pits gradually filled with water. The large lake was up to twenty feet deep in places and all the children were warned to stay away unless adults were present. Bill and Ollie made a diving board and during the hotter days of the summer they swam across the lake with the girls on their backs. When Eva was about eight, her uncle Bill took her into the Lake but let her go. She couldn't swim and panicked. Uncle Bill swiftly grabbed hold of her but her Mum, Nell, gave him a chill warning, *Don't ever do that again Bill.*

The large lake with Uncle Harry Johnson, (Doll's husband). Richmond Park is in the background with the park wall.

Nature had turned the landscape around the smaller lake to the right in front of their houses into a local beauty spot. The lake bordered by reeds and shrouded by trees was the home to dragonflies, frogs, toads, newts and many birds. One day an artist stopped at the end of the lane and sitting himself down with his easel spent the rest of the day painting the smaller lake. His careful, attentive work that day, has given us, many years later, an impression of the natural splendour of the lake.

At the end of the big field and on the other side of the Latchmere Brook was an equestrian club, based near Wilmer House. As soon as they heard the polo bell ring, the three girls ran across the field to watch the charging horses, from their side of the brook. When accompanied by an adult they used the cut through next to the equestrian centre at Wilmer House to get to Ham Common.

The smaller picturesque lake

St Paul's School

Before she went to school, Eva was desperate to learn to read and write, and took advantage of the books that her older sister and cousin were reading. These included *Just William* books by Richmal Crompton. In 1929 she accompanied Joyce and Eileen to St Paul's Infants & Juniors School in Borough Road. They walked a mile to school then came back at lunchtime (lunch break was from 12pm until 2pm) and so each day they were walking four miles to and from school. By the time Eva arrived at St Paul's School at the age of five she could already read and write and she became one of their star pupils. At this time, every class had between 35 to 40 children.

Eva was left-handed and it was the policy of schools, at the time, to correct the children to write with their right hand. Because Eva was left-handed, she was unable to attend the sewing class and so she had to knit instead, which for her was a great shame.

A Muddy Track full of Lakes

The lane back to Kingston from their house was no more than a muddy track. When they first went to school, the girls, on rainy days, left home wearing their wellie boots. They walked along the raised bank above the path. On reaching the beginning of the tarmac road they changed into their school shoes and left their boots in the branches of an old oak tree, standing sentinel nearby. The boots were always there when they returned. When Joyce and Eileen later made their way together to St Luke's School in Elm Road, they entertained themselves by naming all of the big puddles in the lane after English lakes. Each morning they greeted the puddles by their more celebrated names. At times, after it had been raining, numerous streams appeared on the slope above Park Road, the water charging impatiently down the hillside. It was this water that was caught at the bottom of the slope by the Latchmere Brook. Although they could not see the Latchmere Brook across the fields they could see its route marked out by the alder and willow trees along its bank.

Photo taken in 1929 in the front garden of Haycroft. Eva, aged 4 on the back of Eileen's trike. Joyce to the left. Their special horse chestnut tree is in the background

The Chestnut Tree

On the other side of the lane, outside of their house, was a large horse chestnut tree with its characteristic twisted trunk. In the Spring it produced magnificent cones of creamy white blossom and in the autumn when its conkers fell, the girls would thread them with string to make necklaces. They were very possessive about their horse chestnut tree and were quick to inform any children who wandered down the lane that the tree and therefore the conkers belonged to them. Eva was very upset, some years later when the tree was cut down. To this day, she has a leaf from that tree kept safely between the pages of a journal.

The Park Wall

The high wall separating Richmond Park from their garden was a temporary restriction to their entry into the park. The two elder girls, Joyce and Eileen were really excited when Uncle Bill put the ladder up enabling them to climb up onto the wall. Eva wasn't so sure. Once they were on the top and attempting a few brave steps along the wall, Bill pulled the ladder up and lowered it to the other side to enable them to enter the park. Eva, however, was terrified by her perilous situation on top of the wall. Not able to conquer this fear she, in future, chose to run all the way round via Kingston Gate to meet them on the other side. Seeing the opportunity that her predicament presented, the older girls suggested that Eva buy ice-creams for them as she was running round. The ice-cream man inside Kingston Gate had a bicycle with a fridge on the back: *Stop me buy one.*

Hodgson's Brewery's sports field and pavilion was located where the end of Tudor Drive now meets Park Road. On the other side of the sports ground, where the Tudor Estate now stands was a huge orchard with apple, pear and plum trees. A little further along towards Kingston was Kingston Grammar School's sports field. The Bentalls store held their summer sports day at Hodgsons' field. Eva recalls winning a race at the age of three and being delighted with herself. With an older sister and an older cousin, it was rare for her to win anything.

Clothing

Eva recalls that one summer, when she was about five years old (1930), a party took place in the grounds of Park Gate House. Irresistibly drawn by the music from the large band, she ran across Grandad's field to stand and stare at the gathering of the smartly attired men and the beautifully dressed women.

Clothing for Eva and her sisters was very functional. For the majority of her childhood, Eva received the hand-me-downs from her older sister Joyce and her cousin Eileen and the occasional purchase from a jumble sale. Her mother had a friend who was a tailoress and on special occasions she made the girls dresses which were also invariably handed down. It wasn't until she went out to work that Eva could purchase clothes of her own.

From their front bedroom windows, they could watch the firework display at Canbury Gardens at the end of the annual summer regatta. Every year, in the field that was owned by Uncles Ernie and Ollie in front of their house, they spent a month or so building a large bonfire that was lit in the darkness on the evening of 5th of November.

Christmas

Christmas was a time of great excitement for the girls and Eva recounts:

Oh, my goodness, yes! We used each of the three houses in turn to host Christmas for the family. We made our own paper chains and if we were lucky had party balloons. After tea we played lots of games; musical chairs, blind man's buff.... Later in the evening the adults liked to play cards. In fact, the Haywards were very fond of playing cards and we could often hear them though the walls of our house.

Father Christmas came to visit them and Eva was struck by his passing resemblance to her father's brother, Uncle Jack.

Ernie & Ollie's Joint Venture

Uncle Ernie and Uncle Ollie had purchased the land opposite, the size of two football pitches, and turned this into an area for rearing pigs and a large plot for growing vegetables and fruit for consumption by the family. They had a number of fruit trees: apple, plum, cherry and pear. They also had blackcurrant bushes that produced blackcurrants the size of grapes, thanks to the pig manure that was liberally scattered around them. Because of the farm, the family always had plenty of good food.

Ernie and Ollie were both extremely practical, and built their own pigsties and a hen coop. They also made the boilers to cook the food waste that was collected in metal bins from the local restaurants, schools and collection points in local neighbourhoods. Ernie even repaired their shoes with pieces of leather that he shaped and fixed on a shoe last. They built a small sawmill on the farm and obtained a licence to fell trees in Oxshott woods which they cut into pea and bean sticks and logs, for sale locally. They also used to cut and shape the sticks for the jumps on the local racecourses, of which there were many.

Ernie also kept several hives of bees on the land, providing honey that the family very much enjoyed. He made a glass hive that he used to take to show the students at Kingston College.

Aunt Doll

Aunt Doll ran a café in Canbury Park Road near the junction with Elm Road and opposite the Hawkers Factory. They made good simple food at a reasonable price and the cafe was very popular with the workers in the factory. Doll was often given free tickets for the shows at the Empire Theatre or the Granada Cinema and would routinely treat the elder girls to a show after dinner in her cafe. When Edith and Win were younger, they helped their father (Worthy) serve refreshments in a marquee at Epsom Downs or Hampton Court. Aunt Doll was really upset when they both got married and left her alone to serve refreshments. However, when Auntie Doll later got married to Harry Johnson, her dad built a house for them just opposite. Charlie Hayward, the younger brother of Ernie and Ollie took another of the houses and the third was sold to a local grocer, a Mr Jordan (355 to 359 Park Road).

Perhaps because the age gap was only 16 years, Eileen was very close to her aunt Doll and her uncle Harry and spent a lot of time with them. Harry had a working garage at the end of his garden with a deep pit to allow him to work on the underneath of the cars that he was repairing. He often gave Eileen 6d for washing his car, a fortune in those days. A few years later Doll and Harry adopted a little girl called Doreen.

Yet at home, Eileen was spoilt with the attention of two mums and two dads. After surviving the horror of the war, the two brothers Ernie and Ollie were inseparable. If Eileen's dad gave her money at Christmas, her uncle Ollie would take her shopping. In the house Edith took charge of the cooking and Win the cleaning.

A Change in Ambience

Eva's younger sister Grace and Eileen's younger brother John (by some ten years) were both born in 1933. Pat, the daughter of Uncle Charlie and Aunt Winnie was born the same year in one of the three new family houses over the road. Josephine (Jo), daughter of Aunt Win and Uncle Ollie was born a year later also in Haycroft. Jim and Jean, the children of Bill and his wife Gladys, were born in 1935 and 1937, respectively at Littleworth. Bernard, the son of Charlie Hayward was born in 1936. A flurry of seven babies within a period of five years.

From what had been a halcyon environment for the elder girls, the houses now resounded with shrieking babies. The younger cousins remained very noisy children and a little too wild for the liking of the calmer and definitely more sensible older girls. After so many years, being the only child in the house, Eileen was only too happy to go out for some peace and quiet. She took a sudden interest in helping her Dad pricking out seedlings and preparing the seed beds when she needed to get away from the howling in the house.

In the midst of this in 1934, at the age of eleven, Eileen and Joyce transferred to St Luke's Secondary School in Elm Road.

Granny Ellen Dicks

In the autumn of 1936 Grandad Dicks had a stroke. He never fully recovered and died while recuperating at home. Yet in the latter years of his life, Worthy Dicks and his wife Ellen had the good fortune to introduce all of his children and grandchildren to the bucolic life that he had enjoyed as a child, with a house in the country but, most importantly of all, with a large supportive family all around them. Bill now inherited the house and pig farm and here, with his wife Gladys, they raised their family.

An Introduction to Cricket

In the summer of 1933, when she was nine, Eva was taken with Eileen, Joyce and the two babies, John and Pat, in prams, to watch a game of cricket at the nearby sports field of Hodgsons' Brewery. Her Dad, Sidney, who still had to walk with the aid of a stick had been asked to make up numbers. Although he couldn't run, he was delighted to take part as he loved cricket. Although the other children were soon bored, Eva was enthralled by the game. Much to her disgust she had to go off to the Park with the other children. Her father, to his great delight, was called to the field and by goodness, did he enjoy the celebrations of their win. Many bottles of beer were drunk that long summer evening in the pavilion. Years later after the sports fields and pavilion had given way to the extended Tudor Drive, some of the residents of the upper end of Tudor Drive were bemused by the large quantities of beer bottles that they discovered buried in their back gardens.

Eva shared her father's passion for cricket. A solid grounding in maths and a sharp mind provided her with the ability and the confidence to keep score for the local team. This gave her a really good understanding of the game. When she was later working in London she would go to the Oval, after finishing work, to watch any matches that were on. She clearly remembers getting up very early in the morning with her father to sit in the living room of Thornham and listen to the radio broadcast of the Ashes matches being played in Australia. This was the only time that her mother ever witnessed her getting up early. Years later she scored for the 2nd team of Dorking Cricket Club and for many years since, she has been one of the Vice Presidents of the Club.

Shortly after the war an Australian service team with two International players Keith Miller and Lindsay Hassett played in a match at the Hawker sports ground near to the river. For local cricket supporters, including Eva and her father, this was paradise.

Final year at Tiffin Girls' in 1941. Joyce Bushell, Joyce Farrow & Eva on the Sports field where Fern Hill School is now located

1936 Eva and Tiffin Girls' School

In 1936, Eva passed the 11+ and went to the Tiffin Girls' School in Penrhyn Road. She was the first in her family to go to a grammar school. Her mother was very proud, but her dad didn't seem to care that much. At that time, Tiffin was called a secondary school, an endowed school. To go there you either had to pass the 11+ or pay an annual fee, which meant that quite a lot of the girls came from relatively wealthy families. Eva's uniform consisted of a white blouse and a black gym slip with no pleats, bought from Hides in Kingston which was quite expensive. Ellen, her mum, managed to get a grant towards the uniform costs and Eva also had free school dinners, though this did tend to make her feel a little uncomfortable among the wealthier children.

Eva was quite overawed on her first day as she joined a class of thirty girls who came from Kingston, Surbiton, Tolworth, Molesey and Ditton. At the end of her first day, still feeling a little overwhelmed, she boarded the trolley bus back to Kings Road. When she got off at her stop, another girl in her class, Joyce Farrow, also got off. From that day on they became close friends and remained friends, along with Joyce Bushell, until Joyce Farrow died in 2017, some 81 years later!

A year later the school moved to a brand-new building on Richmond Road. It had a quadrangle in the centre, a gymnasium, tennis courts and a playing field. (The Kingston Academy now uses this same building). The girls played netball and hockey in winter and tennis and rounders in summer. Eva really enjoyed the broad range of sports which greatly helped to develop her self-confidence.

Eva's biology teacher, Miss Kirkwood was fairly old, though most of the teachers appeared fairly old to the girls. Miss Kirkwood happened to mention the seeds of the rosebay willow herb during one of the lessons. Eva collected a bunch of these flowers from her Grandad's field and took them in for Miss Kirkwood. When she presented them, Miss Kirkwood, matter of factly, said, *thank you very much* and then placed them down on her desk and that was that!

Eva loved music and drove her cousin John mad with her continuous singing. She also enjoyed history and geography but struggled with maths. Fortunately, at the age of sixteen, she passed her matriculation exam in five subjects and this enabled her later to take up a Government training course which qualified her to work as an engineering draughtswoman at a company in Grosvenor Gardens near Victoria Station.

Looking back, Eva reflects that Tiffin Girls' School was a really good school that gave her an all-round education and a solid foundation for the rest of her life. It was a really good time in her life. Mind you, she did a lot more homework than her sisters and cousins.

Beginning work

When Eileen left school in 1938 at the age of fifteen, she went to work at Bentalls, sewing and making alterations. They had to wear a black uniform that she was not very fond of. She also worked at the 50 bob tailors making alterations. Her first weekly wage was 8s 4d (just over 40p today).

The 2nd World War

Eileen and Joyce were seventeen and Eva was nearly fifteen when the war started in September 1939. The younger cousins that included John, Pat, Jo, Jim, Bernard and Jean ranged from 6 years to 2 years old. Very soon the strident calls of the air raid sirens became imprinted in their minds.

Eva's family had an Anderson air raid shelter built in the back garden of Thornham. Initially, her father insisted they all go down every time the sirens sounded. Ernie and Ollie made a bomb shelter for the family on their land across the road. It was more robust than an Anderson shelter and a lot more comfortable. Some steps led them down into the shelter which was unusually cosy because of the heating that had been installed. Eileen, however, disliked hearing the crunch of the snails' shells underfoot, as they ran to get there! John recalls many evenings spent inside the shelter during the Blitz with his mum reading to him and Jo, both snugly tucked up in their bunk beds. Two favourite books were *Christies Old Organ* and *The Wishing Chair* by Enid Blyton.

There were air raid shelters all around Latchmere School. The school backed on to the East Surrey Barracks and quite often, John and his mates would chat to the soldiers through the wire. They could also hear the soldiers firing their weapons on their range.

During the bombing raids they could clearly see the enemy bombers flying over Kingston on their way to London. *If things got a bit hot for the bombers, they would drop their bombs and scoot off.* John clearly remembers watching a dog fight in the sky from his back garden. Unfortunately, a German fighter escorting the German bombers on this occasion shot down a British fighter.

RAF Reconnaissance photograph taken in 1944 showing the Latchmere Brook and the bomb craters. © Historic England

One day a German plane flew over and dropped a cluster of three bombs: one near Park Gate House, one in the middle of Latchmere Brook and one on the common. His dad was repairing the roof of one of his pigsties at the time and was knocked off the roof with the force of the blast. The bomb made a deep hole in the Latchmere Brook and also blew out all the windows in their house. Incredibly, John's dad was unscathed but Grandma Hayward, who was staying with them at the time, died of shock.

Another bomb dropped near Park Gate House and blew out a number of the poplar trees. Eva came back from work and saw a gap in the trees that had for years screened the families' washing from the big house at Ham Gate.

The third bomb dropped in Ham Common and made a huge crater. John and his mates made the most of this *Wall of death challenge*. They had to cycle like fury around the upper part of the crater but as soon as they lost speed they fell into the bottom. This got very messy, especially after it had been raining and the bottom was full of mud. The one who stayed up longest was the winner.

Richmond Park suddenly became very busy with a lot of activity. There were three army camps in the Park. Eva and her friend Joyce would often walk together through the Park. They also cycled together to Hampton where Joyce had a family friend with a tennis court in their garden. Joyce later went and joined the Women's Royal Naval Service, known as the Wrens.

Ernie became an ARP Warden and patrolled the streets through the night to make sure that lights were out. On occasions he spent the night helping people whose houses had been bombed.

As more and more men joined up, the Post Office sought women to help fill the vacant positions. Uncle Gib (Brother of Ernest, Oliver & Charlie) and uncle Charlie already worked for the Post Office, and they helped Eileen to prepare for the entrance exam. She revised all the counties in England, but in the exam, she got Ireland! However, she still passed. Eileen was then employed, working on the counter of many different Post Offices in the area. She cycled to all of them.

Eva's sister, Joyce, in 1942 at the age of nineteen joined the Women's Auxiliary Air Force whose members were known as WAAFs. After her basic training she became an operator of barrage balloons in Regents Park. They had accommodation and messing huts in the Park and she came home at weekends. This was a far cry from the party balloons that she had so enjoyed at their Christmas celebrations.

The Cattle Market

In the late 1930s and early 1940s, a cattle market was held on Fairfield every Monday. John's dad (Ernie) loaded the pigs in a rickety old truck and drove them to the market. On occasions he would also buy pigs. It was great fun for the children to see all of the animals and the various auctions taking place.

What a mix of raucous noise, indelicate smells and general commotion, especially when the animals tried to break free from the pens!

During the war Ernie and Uncle Bill were issued with licences as to when they could sell their pigs. They were only allowed to kill one pig a year for their own consumption and inspectors would routinely visit the farm to check their stock. Nevertheless, Ernie and Uncle Bill were smart enough to ensure that a surplus number of pigs would disappear from their respective farms prior to each of the visits.

Latchmere Brook

The Latchmere Brook ran between the farmland owned by Ernie and Ollie and a farm bordering Latchmere Lane known as Wilcox's farm. As Spring unfolded each year, John and his cousin Jo, went in search along the bank of the brook for frogspawn. They took it home and stored it in an old tin bath at the bottom of the garden to watch the tadpoles gradually develop into tiny frogs. There were willow and alder trees on either side of the brook which was fed by smaller streams flowing down from Richmond Park. John remembers the bats flitting back and forth over the farm at dusk. Jo, his cousin was scared stiff of them.

The Latchmere Brook running through the landscape. © Historic England

There was a fallen tree that crossed the Latchmere Brook and provided them with a convenient path over to Wilcox's farm. The brook was up to 10 feet wide and quite deep though it never appeared to flow. There were areas of the brook that were particularly deep, especially where the large bomb had fallen. They had a lot of fun running across the fallen tree but on one occasion, when he was probably showing off, John fell into the brook. He went completely under, but it was the shock of the cold water that fuelled his panic as he flapped his way to the bank. John had never had the benefit of swimming lessons, so it was very much a case of trial and error.

They had even more fun trespassing on the farm of Farmer Wilcox especially when he chased them off. A close friend, Reg Powell, quite stoutly built with fair hair, who lived near the corner of Park Road and Kings Road, used to accompany John and his cousin Jo on their excursions into enemy territory. One day Jo fell into a well on the farm. Reg, who was quite strong, reached down and pulled her out by her long hair. John remembers Jo shrieking quite a lot. They then had to make up a story as to why she was soaking wet.

Reg later helped John learn to swim in the Thames at Canbury Gardens. They would swim with the current for a distance, turn around then try and swim back. At times the current was very strong, and they struggled to make progress.

End of the Lakes

During the war, the decision was made to start filling in the lakes with debris from the bombed streets of London. An endless stream of lorries came down their lane to offload debris into the pit. John's Dad and Uncle Ollie worked on behalf of the owners of the land to collect tolls from the lorry drivers who were dumping rubble there. They had a truck on a short railway line to take the rubble from the lorries to fill in the lake. When not being used, the children rode up and down the line in the truck. One night a lorry driver arrived at the site after it had closed. He attempted to unload it himself, just outside the gate. They found him the next morning buried under his rubble.

After the war, prefabs were built on the filled land. Unfortunately, because the land hadn't been given sufficient time to settle, they began to sink. In the 1950s and early 1960s the prefabs were demolished and replaced with more permanent housing. The land at the end of Park Road where the lakes had been was assigned for use as council owned allotments. Kingston Horticultural Society have since based themselves there, on this land that was originally in Ham.

Towards the end of the war, when he was 11 years old, John began working at the weekend with the local milkman, earning half a crown on Saturdays and 1s 6d for a shorter shift on Sunday. With his savings he purchased a Hercules Super Kestrel push bike. He was so proud of this bike and had it for years. With his mates Tommy Russell and Reg, they occasionally cycled all the way to Brighton, had a swim then cycled back a different way. Tommy was a small chap but a good swimmer and diver. Ernie Robinson was dark haired and well built.

The gang all used to play football together. *We chucked our jumpers down to make goals and had a match with anyone who turned up.*

John and his mates, including Reg Powell and Owen Walter, used to love charging around the farm and riding on the backs of the pigs. They also collected dog ends from the area. From these they extracted the remaining tobacco and made their own roll up cigarettes which they secretly smoked round the back of the pigsties. *We weren't that old but thought that we were really grown up.*

The boys all collected shrapnel and after each raid they enthusiastically went charging up the road in search of the precious metal fragments. Between them, they amassed quite a collection.

John's father, Ernie, on returning from northern France after the 1st World War, had brought back a revolver that he had taken from a German soldier. He had been careful to blank the weapon so that it couldn't be fired. He also had a shotgun with cartridges which he used to shoot the rats that visited the pig farm. John and his friends used to load the empty cartridges and play battles with each other. One day he shot at his friend Raymond de Jardin. John was knocked to the ground with the recoil of a live round. In a state of shock, he looked up wondering what had happened to Raymond. Fortunately, he had missed: *We both laughed our heads off.*

They spent a lot of time playing in Richmond Park. After all, their house backed onto the park and they looked on it as an extension of their garden. Quite often, John's mum prepared them some sandwiches and they disappeared in the park for the whole day.

They didn't need a ladder but instead cut grooves into the wall. The park keeper once caught John climbing over the wall and brought him back to his house to establish that he did, in fact, live there.

Towards the end of the war they watched the doodlebugs flying into London. They could see the beams of the searchlights in Richmond Park searching the sky and hear the thump of the big guns that were camouflaged on the high ground.

Sweets, along with everything else were rationed during the war. John's mum (Edith) often sent him to wait in the queue at the butchers on the corner of Park Road and Kings Road.

One day in January 1945 a V2 rocket landed near this junction and destroyed Reg's house. When the house was flattened, everyone was out except for their Jack Russell called Jip. Two days later when they cleared the rubble, they found Jip and he was incredibly still alive, though a little dazed. Reg and his family were later rehoused just opposite to John's house on Lower Park Road. Eva had been at home at the time that the rocket exploded. She was really frightened by the colossal bang: *a truly dreadful noise*. Many people were killed and injured. A lot of homes were destroyed, and many others were rendered uninhabitable. Fortunately, it was a Wednesday and so the post office that was nearby, was closed. Otherwise many more people would have been killed. The post office, however, was obliterated.

Eileen's Story

When Eileen was working in the Post Office at Tolworth, she became friendly with Daphne Roberts, whose Dad also worked there. They didn't like going to dances in Kingston because they were frequented by too many Yanks (who were stationed in Bushy Park).

One day in November 1943 they were invited to go to a dance at a British army convalescent depot (102) on the high flat ground of Richmond Park near Kingston Gate. The depot consisted of a guard post next to the road and a row of accommodation billets on the other side of a concrete square that was used for muster parade and drill. They were pointed in the direction of the Naafi. There were about 30 – 40 men based there at that time.

The Naafi committee had arranged a popular local singer, Donald Peers, to accompany the band. (His signature song was "In a Shady Nook by a Babbling Brook")

The ladies gathered on one side of the hall, and they were asked to choose a partner. Eileen saw a chap wearing tartan trews and a dress jacket. She shyly approached him and asked him for a dance. He willingly accepted and she learnt that his name was Tom, from Troon, serving with the 9th Battalion of the Kings Own Scottish Borderers. Having not yet seen conflict, he was convalescing from a fractured ankle that he received playing football. Tom and Eileen began seeing each other and at Christmas, with Tom being on his own, Eileen invited him to join the family at their house, Haycroft.

On Christmas Day there was a terrible pea souper fog which stopped all of the public transport. Aunt Else, Dad's sister, and cousin Peggy walked all the way from Richmond

Tom in the 9th Battalion of the Kings own Scottish Borderers

Eileen & her younger brother, John

(we used to visit them when we went skating, we also sometimes skated on the Thames when it was frozen!). When Tom arrived at the house, Eileen's Dad (Ernie) went out the other door! He initially couldn't cope with his daughter having a boyfriend! *But he soon came round.*

A wonderful table had been set with at least sixteen adults sitting down for Christmas dinner at the main table. With the animals that they kept on the farm, they had ample meat for all of them.

In the New Year, as Tom's ankle became stronger, he had to complete forced marches down the Kingston bypass and run around the inside of the park. It was apparently very important that he regained his fitness. At the end of January 1944 Tom was shipped up to Colinton Barracks in Scotland for an intensive six-week fitness programme and put through the mill. He was then posted down to barracks at Micheldever. From here he was able to meet up several times with Eileen in Kingston. On one occasion, when he arrived very late at Haycroft the Haywards were all playing cards. Tom explained that the train had been delayed because of an overheated wheel. Uncle Harry (Johnson) looked up and declared, *I've heard many excuses but that takes some beating.*

Tom and Eileen often went to the Regal Cinema and on one occasion were sitting there when the air raid sirens went off. At the time there were quite a few rocket bombs landing in or near Kingston, creating considerable devastation.

Then Tom suddenly stopped visiting and writing. Eileen was extremely upset, believing that she had been ditched.......

Tom's Story

At the beginning of June 1944, Tom was transferred from the camp at Micheldever to a closed camp near Havant where he joined his new company in the 9th Battalion of the Kings own Scottish Borderers. The men were confined to camp without any means of communicating with the outside world. Red Caps (Military Police) were on the gates checking everyone and everything going in and out. A few days later, they attended a secret briefing for an imminent operation, the invasion of France at a place code named Sword Beach (Lion-sur-mer). Field Marshall Montgomery had chosen Tom's Regiment to spearhead the invasion and nicknamed them *Monty's Ironsides.*

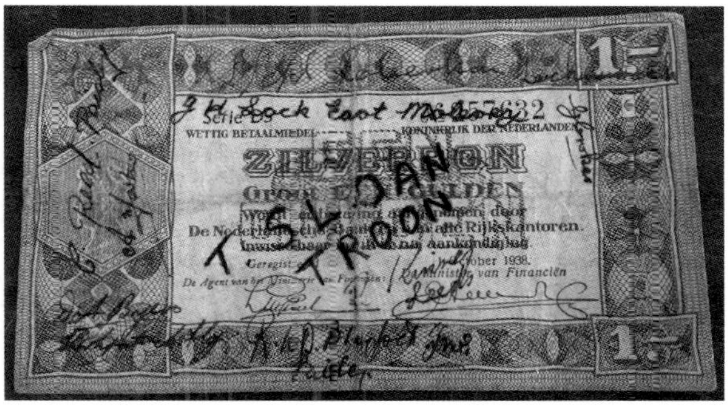

Tom and his squad mates all signed each other's issued French and Dutch bank notes. Only Tom survived the landing and advance into Germany.

Tom and the other members of his company were shown a map of the road that they needed to reach and secure behind the beach. They were also issued with French and Dutch bank notes. He and the fellow members of his section signed each other's notes as a record of the invasion. They were intended to depart on the 4th but the invasion was cancelled owing to bad weather. Instead they occupied a number of requisitioned houses along the Southsea sea front.

Tom's company boarded their boat on the evening of the 5th to cross the channel to France. It was a slow rough crossing and many of the soldiers were seasick. In the half light of dawn on the 6th they could make out the French coastline. The Invasion was on!

The battleships all around them started up a tremendous battering of the shoreline firing salvo after salvo that rocked the huge ships. Still some distance from the beach, the sailors manning their landing craft, brought it to a halt.

Final approach to Sword Beach on 6th May 1944

A long, deep and difficult wade ashore

Taking cover on Sword Beach IWM

Amidst the rolling swell the sailors lowered gang planks with support ropes either side of the craft. Tom was very apprehensive, principally because he couldn't swim, and he had no idea as to the depth of the water. With his hand grenades firmly secured to his belt his spare ammunition belts around his neck and his rifle held above his head in his right hand he quickly made his way down the gang plank and into the cold bracing sea. In their left hands they were all holding folded up bicycles. Fortunately, the sea came only as far as his waist though the incoming waves rose uncomfortably high.

Tom, surrounded by the other members of his platoon, waded slowly ashore. The coastline was being relentlessly shelled by the Navy but the German artillery was returning fire to the beach, causing many dreadful casualties. Tom was accompanied by another soldier, the two of them slowly wading through the water. Tom looked back to see the chap slowly drop to his knees, then collapse forwards, with his head missing. *It was horrendous,* recalls Tom.

(*Whilst the crackle of gunfire and rumble of explosions filled the ears of those landing on French soil that day, those on Sword Beach heard another noise, one that would lift their spirits in their most fearful hour. It was the sound of bagpipes. Private Bill Millin stepped off his landing craft and into the icy waters of the English Channel. The man next to him was shot in the face and killed instantly, his body dropping into the sea and sinking below. Dressed in his father's World War I kilt and armed only with a ceremonial dagger, Millin began wading through the waist-deep water towards the shore. As he did, he started playing Hielan' Laddie on his bagpipes, the deadliest performance of his life.* Courtesy of Sky History)

Arriving at the beach, Tom immediately jettisoned his folded bicycle and struggled up the beach. He was intently focused on getting to the road that ran parallel to and behind the beach. This was their target location for regrouping, though nothing had gone quite as planned.

Amidst the incoming mortars, machine gun rounds and sniper fire, Tom raced on to the road at the top of the beach. But as soon as he got to the road a Messerschmitt fighter descended and strafed the road with high calibre machine gun rounds that ripped great chunks out of the road. The men scrambled for cover either side of the road. Those members of the platoon that had survived the beach landing now had the opportunity to reform within their company. The Division was to pay a very high price, incurring 15,000 casualties including 2,586 killed in action during their forthcoming advance into Germany.

That first night, despite being a rookie, the sergeant chose Tom to go out on a reconnaissance patrol in enemy held territory. He didn't get much sleep that night or any other night until the end of the war. Some of the men who had broken down during that first day were quietly withdrawn from the advance, not to be seen again. Other men who had gained credit as marksmen could not stop their hands shaking. No one knew how they would react until they were involved in their first battle.

The advance was slow and frustrating. The food was *atrocious* and they would not change their clothing until November. The shelling was abominable. *You never knew which one was coming for you.* Tom believes that he kept himself sane and alive by taking communion with the chaplain before each advance. At the end of each day's advance they would dig themselves fresh scrapes in the ground and use the earth to cover themselves, partly to keep warm. On occasions, at night the Germans would begin shelling their positions and, *the place would light up.*

November found the company trying to cross the well-defended river Maas. With the onset of winter and dreadful weather they were stuck on the west bank, being continually shelled, day and night, by German artillery. By now Tom was an accomplished grave digger though he never lost his compassion for his fellow soldiers who had lost their lives. He would carefully wrap their still bodies within a blanket before burying them. Tom buried a lot of British soldiers.

While slowly advancing through Holland, they experienced one particularly cold patch. One night, while dug in, endeavouring to keep warm in a shallow scrape surrounded by deep snow, they came under sustained fire from an enemy mortar unit. The *moaning minnies* named after the loud screeching sound of their shells, shredded their nerves. This was the night that the oldest man in the company reached the end of his tether: *The following morning, he quietly stood up before us. Holding a hand grenade to his chest he pulled the pin out. We buried what remained of him, in the cold hard earth.*

On another occasion Tom was sitting quietly writing a letter to Eileen with a green fountain pen that she had given him during one of their meetings. It was a treasured possession that he had kept close to him throughout the advance. *With the warning of an imminent artillery barrage we all jumped for cover. A shell landed very close and partially buried me in the trench. Despite spending much time frantically looking for it, I couldn't find the pen.*

It was a great relief for Tom when he was made the driver of one of the company supply lorries, in charge of a five-ton GMC left hand drive truck. Tom recalls, *I clearly remember the afternoon of New Year's Day in 1945, when I was returning with stores for the men and crossing a wide-open field. On the far side of the field was a row of tall trees. Suddenly a formation of Messerschmitt fighters appeared flying low over the treetops and coming straight towards me. I genuinely feared that I was about to die. When they flew past me without opening fire, I felt a surge of relief*

He later discovered that they were targeting the allied airfields and had destroyed many planes with numerous casualties.

His company finally got over the River Maas and slowly advanced on Cologne: *Cologne was a right old mess.* He remembers clearly being on a street in Bremerhaven on the day that the war in Europe came to an end. Unfortunately, amidst the celebrations, one of his mates drank from what he believed to be a bottle containing alcohol and died from poisoning.

His company was then sent back to Belgium and here they prepared to fly to Kentucky in the US to take part in the invasion of Japan. He was sent home on leave to Scotland and Eileen came up to join him. They were together in Troon when they heard that the Atom bomb had been dropped.

The men were immediately recalled to their units and they were shipped to Belgium before a long journey down to the south of France. From a French port they boarded a ship to Egypt. *Kitted out with a Yankee vehicle*, he drove into Palestine where they were based ten miles from Tel Aviv. They later returned to Egypt and were based near the entrance to the Suez Canal. This was a great posting as he was tasked with teaching other soldiers to drive. He also had the opportunity to learn to swim in the warm, salt-rich water. Number 46 was the number of his unit for being demobbed. In December 1946, five years after enlisting, he finally travelled home from Palestine to be demobbed at Aldershot.

In Aldershot he received his demob suit and a pass to travel home. He immediately made his way to a post office in Tolworth and joined the queue. When Eileen looked up to greet the next customer, there he was! The next day they met with Canon Beard, the vicar of St Andrew's Church in Ham to arrange their wedding.

On 31st May 1947, a delightfully warm spring day, Canon Beard married Tom and Eileen at St Andrew's church. Tom recalls, *Canon Beard was a wonderful man.*

After their marriage, Tom returned to Troon with Eileen to find work. Eileen's father Ernie and her uncle Ollie, after tending their pigs and land first thing in the morning, were now both working during the day for Frederick Payne, the undertaker. Ernie was his chauffeur. With little work in Troon, Ernie managed to get a job for Tom in the undertakers shop in Kingston. He was asked whether he minded dealing with dead bodies. He replied, *After all I've been through in the War, it wouldn't be a problem.*

This was the start of a long and worthwhile career. Tom, who was a skilled organist, played the organ at St Paul's Church in Queen's Road for twelve years with a further seven years at St Peter's Church in Norbiton.

After the war in 1947 Ernie and Ollie's farm was requisitioned for £1,500 as the housing shortage was now more important than the food shortage and the land was badly needed for cheap housing. The Government built houses and prefabs all along Park Road. Many of these were built by Italian and German prisoners of war. John recalls, *there was no animosity between us and them and we all picked up a few words of German and Italian.* Eva and her sisters would also chat to them and occasionally her Mum would make them a cup of tea.

However, Ernie had lost his precious farm and the source of all their pork, vegetables, fruit and honey. It had been his dream to build a house on his land for Eileen and Tom after their marriage. Unfortunately, he was not allowed, despite promises to the contrary at the time of requisition.

Uncle Bill's (Dicks) pig farm survived because his house was built on the same plot. However, he was unable to continue renting the large field at the end of the road. Unfortunately for Bill, the people who then moved into the prefabs complained about the smell of the pig farm and Bill was forced to close the farm down. Bill bought a farm in Kent before emigrating with his family (auntie Nin (Gladys), Jim and Jean) to Australia in 1950, in search of his house in the country.

A few years later, because the land had not been allowed to settle many of the prefabs began to sink.

In 1948 Eileen and Tom went on holiday with her parents Edith and Ernie and her brother

John. They travelled via boat from the Tower of London to Margate. While there, Ernie went out for a walk and saw a television in the window of a shop. He was so taken that he bought it and brought it back on the boat and train. Thereafter the whole family crammed into the lounge of Haycroft to watch the Cup Final!

In 1951, Eileen's dad Ernie, bought Eileen and Tom, with their two-year-old daughter Anne, a house at 5 Deacon Road, a road that runs parallel with Canbury Park Road in North Kingston, for £1,500.

In 1957 John married Doris and they built a house in the back garden of Haycroft (234 Park Road), that later became 25 Wilmer Close, once the new road was developed. They lived in this house until 2000 when they moved to Christchurch in Dorset where they have been ever since, a fifteen-minute walk from Christchurch Harbour.

In 1960, Eva moved with her husband Ken Armstrong to Deepdene in Dorking. It was her father who introduced Ken into the Civil Service where he spent his working career. She is still living in Dorking following the cricket, whenever she can.

Looking back:

Eva *"I had a wonderful childhood in the countryside, and it was very sad to see it all go"*

John *"We felt that we were in the country at the end of a remote dusty track, surrounded by fields and Richmond Park. It was fabulous! You made your own entertainment; you used your imagination."*

Anne's Story

Having survived the brutal and at times harrowing allied advance across France and Germany, Tom was now relieved to settle down with Eileen and quietly support a family. Their first child, Anne, was born in 1949.

An early memory for Anne is visiting her grandparents (Ern & Edith Hayward) at Haycroft, 234 Park Road, and being entertained by *Watch with Mother* on their television. This was a special treat because many of the other children in the area had no opportunity to watch a television.

Entertainment

They regularly listened to the radio, *Two-Way Family Favourites* and on Saturday evenings, the *Billy Cotton Band Show*. On Saturday mornings Anne liked to listen to *Children's Favourites* introduced by Derek McCulloch known as Uncle Mac. (His opening words in his grandfatherly tone were, "*Hello children, everywhere!*" followed by the string orchestra signature tune of *Puffing Billy*).

In the 1950s and 1960s Anne's parents, Eileen and Tom and her Gran Edith, all enjoyed going to *Old Tyme* Dancing at the 1st Kingston Hill Scout Hut near the junction of Park Road and Tudor Drive. Mr & Mrs Sparks were two of the demonstrators (the others were Arthur & Queenie). They also gave lessons in their garage/studio in Barnfield Avenue.

On Tuesday evenings, while Anne was still living at Deacon Road, she used to go to a children's meeting called Happy Hour run by Uncle John Hayward and his wife Doris who also ran the Crusader youth group. Uncle John spent a lot of time looking after disadvantaged children, picking them up from their homes at Kingsnympton flats and dropping them off home afterwards. Uncle John ran games and quizzes with sweets as rewards. His teachers at Latchmere wouldn't have recognised him!

In 1962 the family moved from Deacon Road to 11 Cardinal Avenue, close to Latchmere Recreation Ground.

Ham Common & Richmond Park

Anne loved cycling in the dips and bumps in Ham Common. Some of these were bomb craters. When it snowed, they would make their way to Richmond Park and sledge down the hill just inside Ham Gate then right across the frozen pond. In her childhood the pond often froze during the winter and remained frozen for a long time.

Food

Anne's mum went shopping every day to buy food as and when needed. At the butchers, in Canbury Park Road, she often chose a piece of braising steak then requested for it to be put through the mincer. It was quite mesmerising to watch the long worms emerging out of the other side. They also bought bones to make a stew from the marrow inside the bone. After they moved to Cardinal Avenue, they bought their meat from the butchers shop on the corner of Kings Road opposite to St Agatha's School. The quality of the meat was very good and reputedly Princess Alexandra of Thatched Lodge obtained her meat there. For other items, Anne's mum shopped daily at a small grocer's shop run by Mrs Tickner on the corner of Elm Road, near to Hudson Road.

Chicken was a special treat. Liver and onions was a popular dish. Gammon with butterbeans was served every Wednesday. Anne grew up hating Wednesdays.

On Sundays they had a joint, either beef with Yorkshire puddings or lamb with mint sauce. They grew their own mint in the garden. On Monday, using up the leftovers from the Sunday roast they would have cold meat with salad. Eileen also had her own mincer and would make lamb croquettes in breadcrumbs.

They always had a good breakfast to start the day. This would be egg on toast or porridge, though they never had any cereals. Mum thought that they were a *rubbish American import, not real food*. During the week they had their main meal at lunchtime and Anne came home from school to join the rest of the family. For dessert they had milk pudding or rice pudding or milk vermicelli. Or even spotted dick, which was a favourite. Tea in the evening was cheese or scrambled egg on toast, dropped scones or toasted crumpets. Anne loved to toast the crumpets herself with a toasting fork, carefully turning the crumpets over the embers of the fire.

At the weekend she enjoyed elevenses to keep her going, maybe bread and dripping, made from the drained off fat from the joint. She used to sit on the doorstep eating this: *Wonderful!*

Their fruit mainly consisted of apples and bananas. The milkman sold orange juice which was really delicious and occasionally Anne used her pocket money to buy a carton of juice.

The Corona man visited occasionally. If you bought a drink from him, you got 3d back on the empty bottle: *That was a treat, not regular.*

Clothing

Eileen made all of Anne's dresses. Anne recalls, *she was incredible with a sewing machine and even made matching dresses for my dolls.*

Christmas

Christmas was a joyful time: *If I was really lucky, I found the sixpenny bit that was hidden in my serving of the Christmas pudding.*

All our Christmases were spent at 234 Park Road. Haycroft had the most amazing dining room table that sat up to 18 members of the family. We inserted a handle in one end of the table and wound it open. Christmas was a time when we played lots of games such as Squeak Piggy Squeak and Blind Man's Bluff. Only Grandad Ern and Auntie Win smoked so we weren't plagued with smoke. Grandad and Auntie Win used to sit by the fire and blow the smoke up the chimney.

Holidays

Every year they had the luxury of going on holiday with their Grandparents Ern & Edith Hayward. For many years they stayed at a guest house in Clacton on Sea. The owner Mr Godden was very friendly and on rainy days allowed them to stay in the guest house and play games. Grandad Ern loved spending time in the garden and would also go along to Mr Godden's allotment to help out. Even though they were on holiday, they would find Grandad Ern and Mr Godden, each morning, peeling potatoes in the garden. Grandad always wore his suit on holiday, even on the beach.

Tom and Eileen remained at 11 Cardinal Avenue for 57 years until Wednesday 26th June 2019 when they moved to Northumberland to be close to Anne, so that she could keep an eye on them. Their departure brought to an end the story of the family of Worthy and Ellen Dicks, a family that had lived in the vicinity of the Latchmere Brook for a total of 117 continuous years.

Quite a story!

Above: 2005 Reunion of the cousins. Back row: ***John Hayward****, Beverley & Jim Dicks (son of Bill),* ***Jo (nee Hayward)****, Grace (nee Howard) & Alan, Front row:* ***Eva*** *(nee Howard),* ***Eileen Sloan*** *(nee Hayward), John's wife Doris*

Above right and right: Tom appointed as a Chevalier in the Ordre national de la Légion d'honneur, awarded in recognition of his brave and resilient contribution to the liberation of France during the Second World War. The Légion d'honneur was established in 1802 by Napoleon Bonaparte. It is France's highest distinction.

Sources:
Family history carefully researched by Mike Shaw

Picture Credits
All pictures courtesy of the Howard/Hayward/Sloan families unless otherwise indicated
NLS: Reproduced with the permission of the National Library of Scotland
IWM: Reproduced with the permission of the Imperial War Museum

The East Surreys – Kingston's Regiment

The East Surrey Regiment emerged in 1881 from the amalgamation of the 31st and 70th Regiments of foot and local Kingston militia units. To accommodate the Regiment, the Kingston Barracks, as it was commonly known, was completed in 1875 on 16 acres of land that had formerly been part of Park Farm, a farm belonging to the 2nd Earl of Liverpool, Robert Jenkinson. The Lord of Liverpool had served as the British Prime Minister from 1812 to 1827 overseeing the War of 1812 with the United States and the final defeat of Napoleon at Waterloo. The location of the Barracks was identified by the Kings Road running along its southern boundary and the Latchmere Brook defining its eastern boundary

The Keep of the East Surrey Regimental Barracks in Kings Road

On 1st July 1881 the East Surrey Regiment was formed from the 31st and 70th Regiments of Foot. They became, respectively, the 1st and 2nd Battalions However, the Regimental badge of the East Surreys was a combination of the badges which were worn by the 1st & 3rd Royal Surrey Militias.

1913 Map showing The Latchmere Brook running up the east boundary of The Barracks. NLS

Mid 1930's - aerial view showing The Barracks from the south. ©SHC

Thousands of men were trained at the Barracks before going overseas on various campaigns and fighting for their country in the two World Wars. During the 1st World War alone, more than 84,000 men were trained there. At a cost of 7,000 killed and many more seriously injured, they displayed exceptional bravery winning 62 battle honours and seven Victoria Crosses. R C Sheriff, a former Kingston Grammar pupil, served as a Captain in the 9th Battalion of the East Surreys and was awarded a Military Cross. His experiences on the Western Front were captured in his award-winning play *Journeys End*, that was more recently made into a 2017 movie.

The Latchmere Brook marker stone outside the wall of the Barracks. St Agatha's Church was built along the East side of the Brook. GE

The Regiment's early history finds them stationed around the British Empire, garrisoned in India, Ireland, the Sudan and South Africa. On the east side of the Latchmere Brook, next to the Barracks, St Agatha's church was built to support the local Catholic Community and many of the Irish wives of soldiers in the East Surreys who had returned to the Depot after their tour in Ireland.

After the 1st World War, the two retained Battalions (the 1st and 2nd) undertook tours of Ireland, Palestine, Gibraltar, Egypt, Shanghai, Hong Kong, India and the Sudan. In 1938, while based in the Sudan, soldiers of the 1st Battalion, The East Surrey Regiment were used in period uniforms for scenes in the movie *The Four Feathers* based on the 1902 novel by A E W Mason. Ironically R C Sheriff was one of the script writers of the movie.

The 2nd World War

On 18th May 1939, local Kingston lad, Frank Gilby, aged nineteen, followed his elder brother and many other local young men into the East Surrey Regiment. He was part of the British Expeditionary Force that was sent over to France to support the French army against the German advance. During the subsequent withdrawal from Dunkirk he was seriously injured. He was lucky enough to be evacuated on a hospital ship but then spent a long period in convalescence. He was medically discharged in June 1942.

The evacuation from Dunkirk. IWM

His daughter, Christine was born in December 1944 at Elm Road in Kingston. Christine recalls that when she was young, any thunderstorm alarmed her father. He would come up and sit on their beds to make sure that she and her sister were not frightened, though she suspects that he really needed their company. He never talked about Dunkirk. It was all too painful for him. Frank died at the age of 57.

Christine went to Latchmere School between 1949 and 1955. Ironically Latchmere School used to hold its sports day in the field that was part of the East Surrey Barracks.

1948 aerial view showing the East Surrey Barracks from the East. The Keep facing onto Kings Road is on the right. The drill square is in the middle and the depot sports field to the left centre of picture. Left of the sports field is Latchmere School. The open space, top centre is Dinton sports field that was previously used by Kingston Grammar School. © Historic England

George Birdsall, Regimental Sergeant Major of the Kingston Depot of the East Surreys

One man who served with the 1st Battalion of the East Surreys from the end of the First World War to the mid 1950's was George Birdsall. A highly capable soldier, he climbed through the ranks to become the revered RSM of the Kingston Depot. He takes up the story of the East Surreys in the next chapter.

Brigadier G. Roupell VC, Colonel of the East Surrey Regiment, carrying out an inspection before the last passing out parade at Kingston Barracks on 1st May 1959. He gave one of his dress swords to newly commissioned George Birdsall on the outbreak of the 2nd World War. ©SHC

The Keep in 2019 GE

Sources:
The Final Years 1938 – 1959
The story of the East Surrey Regiment

Picture Credits
NLS: Reproduced with the permission of the National Library of Scotland
SHC: Reproduced by permission of Surrey History Centre
GE: © Gordon Elsden
IWM: Imperial War Museum

Regimental Sergeant Major George Birdsall of the 1st Battalion of the East Surrey Regiment based at Kingston Upon Thames

George Birdsall – A Distinguished Soldier of the East Surreys

This is the story of George Birdsall, who married into a local family and became the revered Regimental Sergeant Major of the East Surreys at the Regimental Depot in Kingston. Later, after being commissioned as an officer at the beginning of the 2nd World War, he fought with the Regiment in North Africa and Italy. According to a close friend in the Regiment, George experienced "a hard war".

George Birdsall was born on 14th December 1901 in Deptford, one of twelve children. His father was a leatherman from a long family tradition of tanners. George's elder brother, William, was killed in France during the 1st World War.

Despite this, George was feeling rather cramped at home and needed to get out, so at the age of 17 ½ years he pretended that he was 18 and joined the army (you needed to be 18 to join without consent). Within eight months, in March 1920, he sailed for India with the Machine Gun Corps, the first of three postings to the Far East.

In 1921 in the rank of Lance Corporal, he was transferred to the 1st Battalion of the East Surrey Regiment who had their depot in Kingston Upon Thames. Later that year he embarked for Egypt to join the 1st Battalion. The Battalion travelled from Egypt to Khartoum in the Sudan in April 1923 then some six months later they embarked for Hong Kong. They remained in Hong Kong for nearly three years before transferring to India in November 1926.

From November 1926 to October 1937, the Battalion served continuously at three stations; Lahore, Fyzabad and Rawalpindi. During this period, they honed their mountain warfare skills with training exercises alongside various Gurkha Regiments in the Muree and Simla Hills.

Annual inspection by Maj Gen C Luard, 9th September 1926, Hong-Kong

Trooping the Colour on Hong Kong Island in 1926

George took every opportunity that the Army offered to further his education, and this helped to accelerate his promotion through the ranks. In October 1927, in the rank of Sergeant, stationed at Kuldana, 7000ft up in the Murree Hills, he was awarded the General Certificate of Education 1st Class.

Images of the Murree Hills Cantonment, 35 miles from Rawalpindi

1929: The Sergeants of the 1st Battalion, East Surreys in Victoria barracks, Rawalpindi. George is 2nd row 4th from right ©SHC

1929: The Sergeants' mess in the Rawalpindi Garrison ©SHC

George (left) in the Sergeants' mess at Rawalpindi

In March 1931, George returned to the Regimental depot at Kingston Upon Thames, on leave. This was George's first home posting for nine and a half years. He was now a Class 2 Warrant Officer, a Company Sergeant Major, moving ever closer to the top spot!

Social life tended to revolve around the activities of the respective messes. The Sergeants mess arranged a dance in their mess at Kingston Barracks and it was here that George met Ellen Kent, known as Dolly, daughter of Henry and Louisa Kent, living at 176 Elm Road.

On Boxing day in 1932, George married Dolly Kent at St Paul's Church, Kingston Hill. He was now an honorary member of the Kent family and introduced into a wider social network and a lot more pubs, especially the Wych Elm in Elm Road and the Willoughby Arms!

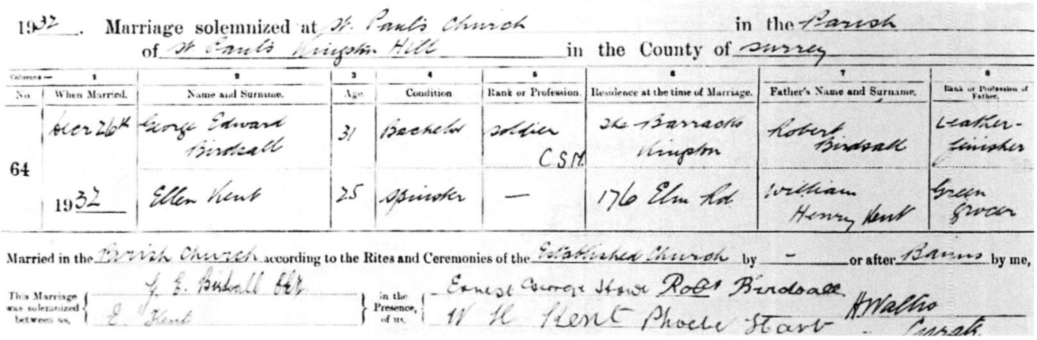

1932. Marriage solemnized at St. Pauls Church in the Parish of St Pauls Kingston Hill in the County of Surrey

No.	When Married.	Name and Surname.	Age.	Condition.	Rank or Profession.	Residence at the time of Marriage.	Father's Name and Surname.	Rank or Profession of Father.
64	Dec 26th 1932	George Edward Birdsall	31	Bachelor	soldier CSM	The Barracks Kingston	Robert Birdsall	Leather-finisher
		Ellen Kent	25	Spinster	—	176 Elm Rd	William Henry Kent	Green Grocer

Married in the Parish Church according to the Rites and Ceremonies of the Established Church by — or after Banns by me,

This Marriage was solemnized between us, G. E. Birdsall CSM, E. Kent

in the Presence of us, Ernest George Howe, Robt Birdsall, W H Kent, Phoebe Hart

H Walters Curate

Marriage Certificate of George Birdsall and Ellen (Dolly) Kent

Dolly and George had six children (George, Valerie, Bill, Queenie, Stephen & Peter). George always considered that he would have had more if it hadn't been for the wasted years of the war.

In March 1934, George sailed for India to rejoin the 1st Battalion of the East Surreys at Lahore. This time he was a married man accompanied by a wife and young son, George Edward Jnr.

This must, on occasions, have been quite daunting for Ellen with all the ritual and discipline of army life and the high standing of her husband within the Regiment. In December 1934 the Battalion transferred from Lahore to Fyzabad. In July 1935 their second child, Valerie, was born. George had since been promoted to Class 1 Warrant officer a Quartermaster Sergeant Major (QSM)

George and Dolly on their wedding day. 26th December 1932

1st Bn The East Surrey Regiment on parade in Lahore

September 1935 in the Sergeants mess in Fyzabad. Farewell dinner for Lt Colonel H St G Schomberg CBE DSO, the commanding office of the 1st Bn The East Surrey Regiment. George is standing at the back, third from right. ©SHC

On the back of the original photo was written;

The last snap of George & the gang prior to leaving Fyzabad at 3.25pm on 14th May 1936

L to R: George Jnr on George maj knee, Mrs Birdsall + Val, William Histed. Behind Freddy Livermore & Tim

In November 1935, Lieutenant-Colonel G.R.P. Roupell VC, became Commanding Officer of the 1st Battalion. Roupell, a veteran of the East Surreys had earned his Victoria Cross for conspicuous gallantry at the defence of Hill 60 in Belgium in April 1915. He held George in high regard and later gave him his old dress sword. George was quietly proud of his ownership of this sword.

The following year the family left Bombay on board the 'Viceroy of India' destined for England. The ship arrived at Gravesend on the 1st June 1936. The total time on overseas service had been 12 years 9 months out of George's total army service of 17 years.

On arrival back at Kingston, George was appointed the Regimental Sergeant Major for the Regimental Depot of the East Surreys at Kingston. He had now achieved the exalted rank of the most senior non-commissioned officer in the Regiment. At the age of 35, he was also the youngest RSM in the British Army, principally because he was, in reality, six months younger than officially recorded.

While serving as RSM, George and his family lived in a house in Chestnut Road, Kingston, close to the river. His children knew when he was on parade because they could hear his voice. As RSM of the East Surreys, George also spent time at Sandhurst, drilling the young officers.

The drill ground at the Barracks in Kingston. George Birdsall, the Regimental Sergeant Major was undisputed master of this domain. ©SHC

1939 – Farewell visit of Major General Sir John Longley. RSM G E Birdsall is sitting next to him with Major R A Boxshall on the other side. They are accompanied by the Corporals of the Battalion. ©SHC

George remained very much a man's man, comfortable with the rough antics of the Sergeants Mess. His teeth allegedly were badly damaged as a result of his mess trick of chewing glass.

In 1938 Dolly's parents, Henry and Louisa Kent, moved into 30 Lawrence Road in Ham and George rented a house in Broughton Avenue, just around the corner to enable his wife to be close to them. George junior attended St Andrew's Junior School next to Ham Common.

When war was declared in September 1939 the 1st Battalion was sent to Colchester to be brought up to full strength with the introduction of 250 reservists. They underwent intensive training to become fully competent in the handling of the Bren Light Machine Gun and the Lee Enfield Rifle. George was instrumental in the training programmes and the logistical readiness of the Regiment in preparation for battle.

On 2nd October 1939, the Battalion embarked from Southampton as part of the British Expeditionary Force. George was kept behind to organise the ongoing training and battle readiness for all the new recruits.

Shortly before Christmas, George visited 30 Lawrence Road and was surprised to meet his brother in law, Tyke (Charles) Kent. Realising that Tyke was absent without leave (AWOL), George arranged to return early the following morning to accompany Tyke back to Pirbright depot. The following morning, they took the bus to Cobham but needed to get another bus to Pirbright. They went in a local pub for a couple of pints but ended up missing the bus, so they stayed till closing time. George accompanied his brother in law back to the depot first thing the following morning.

Following the chaotic evacuation from Dunkirk at the beginning of June 1940, George learned that the 1st Battalion of the East Surreys had suffered heavy losses with 36 men killed, 152 wounded and 81 missing. As RSM, his primary task was to oversee the rebuilding and re-equipping of the battalion.

George's considerable experience was now more important than ever, and in September 1940, he was commissioned as an officer.

The Battalion spent the next two years as part of the home defence in anticipation of a German invasion. George was sent to Scotland to supervise their ongoing training while his wife and children had to endure the German bombing campaign over London. Dolly and the children moved in with her parents (Henry and Louisa Kent) and her younger siblings, Harry, Jimmy and Queenie, at 30 Lawrence Road.

George Jnr recalls that they had an Anderson shelter in the garden of 30 Lawrence Road and a Morrison shelter, a steel table, downstairs. After each bombing raid the fireplaces were heavy with soot, which had been shaken out of the chimneys. Shrapnel damaged the roof tiles, smashed the windows and a large piece of shrapnel was firmly embedded in one of the interior bedroom walls. Many of the houses along Lawrence Road were hit by incendiary bombs. George Jnr attended the Russell School in Petersham until the school was bombed. He recalls how he felt on hearing the news, *the best day of my life.*

During his childhood, George Jnr attended eleven schools.

Every time Grandma Louisa saw George Jnr slouching, she would shout, *pull your shoulders back.*

The Battle Axe Division

The Surrey Star worn by members of the 1st Bn The East Surrey Regiment on the upper arm

In June 1942 the 1st Battalion of the East Surreys was reassigned, to be part of the newly formed 78th Infantry Division. Known as the battle-axe Division, they would go on to fight with great distinction and much loss, in Tunisia, Sicily and Italy.

In October 1942, after two years of training and preparation in England and Scotland, George Birdsall along with 34 officers and 758 other ranks of the 1st Battalion of the East Surreys, made their way to Glasgow where they boarded HMS Karanja, part of a large convoy of ships that had gathered in the Clyde. At dawn on 27th October, the convoy of 49 ships accompanied by their protective screen of warships left the Clyde bound for North Africa. Operation Torch, the first Anglo-American operation of the war, had begun.

During the night of 7th November 1942, they landed on beaches near Algiers. Formed up ashore, they embarked on a five-hundred-mile rapid advance from Algiers to Tunis along poor roads made worse by the winter rains. They were harassed all the way by the Luftwaffe, which enjoyed air superiority. On 27th November they engaged with enemy forces in strength at Tebourba.

By early December the East Surreys had been badly mauled and forced to withdraw from Tunis to Medfez. Fifty seven percent of the Regiment were killed in one savage week of fighting with devastating losses of 11 officers and 438 men. George, once more, played a key part in the rebuilding and replenishing of a shattered Battalion.

On 25th July 1943 the Battalion, which had been brought back to fighting strength, landed near Syracuse on the south east coast of Sicily. They were part of the 78th Division which advanced steadily though Catenanuova before making a bridgehead across the River Dittaino.

On the night of 1st August, they launched an attack against a key outpost of the German defences near Centuripe. After heavy fighting against the Hermann Göring Division and the 3rd Parachute Regiment throughout the day and night of 2nd August, the town was finally secured on 3rd August. The German Army despite steadfast resistance was now in retreat and by 8th August the 78th Division had advanced onto the north-west slopes of Etna. Randazzo fell on 13th August and the 78th Division was taken into reserve to prepare for the invasion of Italy.

Infantry fighting through Catania in Sicily IWM

In September 1943 George Birdsall gained a battlefield promotion to the rank of Captain.

At the end of this month, the 78th Division was shipped to Taranto located on the heel of Italy. They now joined the allied campaign up the Adriatic coast where the German Army had established a series of strongly fortified defensive lines known as the Volturno, the Barbara and the Gustav lines along the Biferno, Trigno and Sangro rivers.

The division fought a notable action at the Battle of Termoli on the Volturno Line and was one of Montgomery's lead divisions for the attacks on the two subsequent defensive lines. The division was then rested for a week at Campobasso.

1st Battalion, The East Surrey Regiment, move up for the attack on the Gustav line on the Sangro River

In December 1943, the East Surreys were transferred to a remote section of the front, high in the Apennine Mountains to guard the Allied Army's left wing. Amidst a bleak and barren landscape, the soldiers were confronted with freezing temperatures and deep snow. Their discomfort was compounded by their remoteness from any towns which might offer temporary relief, a relief desperately missed over the Christmas period.

The New Year was to bring little reprieve. In February 1944 the 78th Division was moved up to the Cassino Sector to support a third offensive by the Allies on the Cassino Line. The attack failed. At the end of March, the East Surreys were moved into the mountains behind Cassino to relieve a Gurkha Battalion of the 4th Indian division that had suffered many casualties. Below are extracts from The Bowl by Major R C Taylor:

Battalion Headquarters was located in an area known as "The Bowl", safe from observation by the Germans in the monastery, and therefore ideal for supplying the forward rifle companies. It was a small natural amphitheatre, a rocky re-entrant in the steep hill with olive trees scattered around, and a small level area about the size of a tennis court.

The rifle companies of the 1st Battalion were way up above the bowl on exposed rocky ridges known as Snakes Head and Phantom Ridge. Their positions were once again cold and bleak and overlooked by well entrenched German positions, making any movement in daylight, impossible. The ground was hard and rocky so that only shallow trenches could be dug with piles of loose stone providing negligible protection. The carrying parties from the rifle companies could only move under the cover of darkness to descend the steep slopes to "The Bowl" to replenish their supplies of food, water and ammunition

Everything had to be brought up a steep narrow track, a distance of about five miles, carried by mules or porters. Sometimes the mules, or porters, never reached The Bowl as the nightly shelling tended to scatter them far and wide, so at times even drinking water was severely rationed. By dawn the supply train had to be well away, and The Bowl would be quiet except for the occasional shelling, until night came around once again with its hectic activity. With the supplies would come our Quartermaster, George Birdsall or his RQMS, 'Nobby' Clark, and back with them would go the sick and the wounded.

The following is a transcript of the citation for the Battlefield MBE which George Birdsall was awarded on 24th August 1944:

Captain G.E.BIRDSALL is now in his third campaign as Quartermaster to this unit. Thanks to his devotion to duty, tact and energy, the Battalion has never lacked either supplies or equipment. The arduous nature of the campaigns has often caused for considerable improvisation of methods of getting supplies to the front line, and the fact that they have always got through, even in face of enemy fire, reflects the greatest credit on this officer. In addition, it has been necessary three times completely to re-equip the Battalion during the period under review, and this was successfully done in the minimum of time. There can be no question that by his excellent administrative work this officer has made a fine contribution to the fighting efficiency of this Battalion.

Supplies being brought up by mule train IWM

The Allies finally broke through but there was to be no reprieve for the East Surreys as they took part in the advance up the Liri Valley continuing to fight northwards from Rome towards Arezzo. After heavy fighting at another German defensive line, the Trasimene Line, the division was, in July 1944, finally removed from the front for a period of rest and recuperation in Egypt.

Early in October 1944, the 1st Battalion of the East Surreys returned with the 78th Division to Italy and travelled on a circuitous route from Taranto that took them through Assisi, Perugia and Arezzo to San Apollinare in the Tuscan Apennine mountains, north of Florence.

Narrow tracks full of shell holes, wound up through the barren mountainous landscape. With the onset of heavy rain, the track was churned into mud. The 1st Battalion's objective was to secure Monte La Pieve and the massive razor-backed ridge of Monte Spaduro, which blocked the advance to the Lombardy plain.

On the night of 23rd October, the 1st Battalion began their assault on well entrenched enemy positions on Monte Spaduro. Their approach was up three and a half miles of steep muddy tracks. Following an intense artillery barrage, "A" Company, commanded by Major Saunders and "D" Company led the assault with "C" Company bringing up the rear.

By one o'clock in the morning the two lead companies were pinned down by enemy machine gun fire and snipers concealed in the cover of deep gullies on the mountainside.

Fighting in the ruins of Monte Cassino IWM

After a brief rest the battalion renewed their assault, endeavouring to flush the enemy out with mortar fire. A further attempt to advance resulted in a soldier being shot in the head by a sniper. Endeavouring to break the deadlock, Major Saunders, with two soldiers in support, worked his way through cover to the gully and charged the suspected position. Four German soldiers with two Spandau light machine-guns surrendered. For his decisive action and bravery Major Saunders was awarded the Military Cross. Many years later he became the Chairman of the Hong Kong and Shanghai Banking Corporation, based in Hong Kong.

George and the Battalion were now rewarded with another miserable winter holding their position in the high mountains confronted regularly with bitterly cold winds and driving rain.

In the spring of 1945, the 78th Division rejoined the Eighth Army. One of the army's objectives was to break through the German defences on the rivers Senio and Santerno and then drive through the Argenta Gap, a strip of land between Lake Comacchio and flooded marshland south of the river Reno. Here they would form a pincer with U.S. Fifth Army attacking through the central Apennines to surround and destroy the German armies south of the River Po in Northern Italy.

The allies enjoyed the luxury of air superiority. Throughout 10th April, some 1,200 allied aircraft bombed and strafed a ten square mile area on the Santerno River, to clear a path for the planned 8th Army crossing. From their taxi ranks high in the sky, planes literally peeled off, in turn, to strike anything that represented the German army.

On 14th April, Captain Birdsall accompanied his battalion as they joined up with the 2nd Battalion, Lancashire Fusiliers: *Every yard of ground was heavily contested as the Surreys fought their way across the flat orchard country. Snipers, Spandau machine guns and anti-tank guns hidden in hedges, ditches and farmhouses were putting up a bitter defensive fight.*

They crossed the river Reno and then had to negotiate extensive minefields before reaching the outskirts of Argenta. They encountered strong enemy fire as they approached Fossa Marina, a canal running north-eastwards from Argenta across the entire width of the Gap.

On the evening of 16th April after dark, the Surreys moved forward and despite taking numerous casualties, secured a base from which the Lancashire Fusiliers endeavoured to cross the Fossa Marina to establish a bridgehead on the opposite bank. At midnight, after a bitter struggle, a foothold had been secured across the canal. Despite determined counterattacks the positions were held throughout the night until they were reinforced the following morning.

It wasn't only the front-line troops who were suffering from the unrelenting pace of the Surreys rapid advance in hostile territory. For seventy-two continuous hours the Commanding Officer, Lieutenant Colonel Hunter had gone without sleep. On the verge of collapse, he was ordered to the rear for some rest.

For Captain Birdsall, the planning to support his men in their blitzkrieg through Italy was relentless. He had to ensure that water, food and ammunition reached the frontline troops. He also had to ensure that the wounded were all accounted for and properly treated. Not forgetting the grim task of identifying the soldiers who had been killed and recording the location of their burial. The dead were usually buried right where they fell, invariably by their squad mates. Many of these men were soldiers that George had put through their paces on the drill square at Kingston Barracks. It all now seemed, a very distant memory.

On the 22nd the Surreys were ordered to cross the Po di Volano, a major tributary of the Po River. Overnight they established bridgeheads on the opposite bank to secure the crossing of the Battalion in rafts and boats the following morning, at first light. They suffered the loss of three men killed and ten wounded. This was their last engagement of the war.

Captain George Birdsall and the 1st Battalion were at Corlo when Field Marshal Montgomery accepted the surrender of all German armies in Italy on the 4th May 1945. George had been with the Battalion, at war, for six years during which time they had fought their way from Algiers to Tunisia, secured the Island of Sicily and defeated the German army in Italy. The final victory in Italy by the allied army was outstanding. They had achieved what many had considered impossible. In less than four weeks they had broken the German defensive line, fought their way through the Argenta Gap, through and over the numerous canals and rivers of the Po Valley, then pressed onwards to force the surrender of the formidable German army. The combined casualties for both sides amounted to 700,000.

Captain Birdsall was acknowledged as a remarkably efficient quartermaster who had achieved miracles in keeping supplies and comforts flowing in extremely difficult circumstances from the landing of the Battalion at Algiers until the end of the war in Northern Italy. As well as his campaign medals and MBE, Captain Birdsall was also awarded the Meritorious Service Medal (MSM). This was presented to a select few soldiers for devotion to duty in a theatre of war.

Yet, despite the victory and the end of the war, George Birdsall wouldn't get to return home and meet up with his family for another year.

In 1949 George was promoted to Major (Quartermaster) and a year later their youngest son, Peter, was born at their army house in Chestnut Road. A few years later he and Dolly and their family moved into 30 Lawrence Road so that Dolly could look after her ailing father, Henry.

Major Birdsall retired from the army in January 1955, after thirty-five and a half years' service. He could have stayed in the army for another two years but quite frankly, he had simply had enough.

A dining out function was held in the Officers Mess at The Barracks at Kingston to celebrate his distinguished service and give him a memorable send off!

Kingston 4784.

Subject:- Dining Out of Major Birdsall.

Colonel T.Mac.D.Baker CBE,TD,DL,
Lieut Col. D.G. Dickson. MC,TD,
Lieut Col. T.A. Buchanan. DSO,MC,TD,
All Officers on Posted Strength.

9/
16 Dec 54

1. The dining-out of Major Birdsall and dining-in of Lieutenant Rousell will take place in the Depot Officers Mess at 1930 for 8 p.m. on Thursday 6 Jan 55. Major Birdsall is shortly retiring from the Regular Army after thirty five years service.

2. Will officers who wish to attend please inform the P.M.C. or the Adjutant by 1 Jan 55.

[illegible]
Capt for Major.
P.M.C. 6th Bn The East Surrey Regiment

The Barracks,
Kingston-upon-Thames.

Copy to:- Major G.E. Birdsall. MBE.)
Lieut C.G. Rousell.) You have been warned!

Following his experiences during the War, George was a lot more relaxed with his younger children. After the shocking waste of life that he had witnessed, he had come to realise how precious life truly was. It was important that his children enjoyed themselves while they had the opportunity.

When George Junior was called up for National Service, his father gave him sound advice: *don't ever volunteer for anything*.

Peter recalls that his father did not sleep well, troubled by his memories from the war and he suffered a lot of nightmares. Coincidentally, just over the back fence from George's House in Lawrence Road, Arthur Muddiman was living in Randle Road. He was another survivor of Monte Cassino and was similarly experiencing frequent nightmares.

Every day, late in the afternoon, dressed in his suit and regimental tie, George could be seen walking briskly up Dukes Avenue and along Ham Parade. Here, he would stop at Threshers wine shop and buy a bottle of sherry. It helped him sleep!

When Peter was sixteen, he borrowed a motorcycle but was arrested for a traffic misdemeanour and summonsed to court. His father accompanied him, dressed immaculately, as ever, in his suit and regimental tie. After Peter had stood up, the court clerk instructed, *will the defendant's father stand up*. George remained sitting. Peter looked down anxiously. The clerk again repeated, Will the defendant's father stand up. Back straight with his arms braced, knuckles upwards, on his knees, George remained sitting. Peter by now was very anxious. The Court Clerk relented, *Will the defendant's father please stand up*. With this small measure of politeness, George promptly stood up.

Dolly lived until October 1978. George died a few months later on 22nd February 1979, aged 77. He was buried alongside Dolly at Kingston Cemetery in his suit and regimental tie. Their gravestone bore the crest of the East Surrey Regiment.

A bugler, representing the East Surreys, in full ceremonial uniform, played the last post over their grave.

MBE Military Division, The 1939-1945 Star, The African Star 1st Army Bar, The Italy Star.
The 1939-1945 Defence Medal, The 1939-1945 King George VI Medal, The King George V 1935 Jubilee Medal, The George VI 1937 Coronation Medal, The George VI Long Service & Good Conduct Medal (Regular Army), The George VI Meritorious Service Medal (MSM)

Sources:

Documents collected by Peter Birdsall. www.queensroyalsurreys.org.uk
Evans Bryn - With the East Surreys in Tunisia, Sicily and Italy 1942-1945
Taylor RC (Major) - The Bowl
The Daily Telegraph - Obituary for Sir John Saunders July 2002

Picture Credits

All pictures are courtesy of George and Peter Birdsall, sons of Major George Birdsall, unless otherwise indicated
©SHC: Reproduced by permission of Surrey History Centre
IWM: Imperial War Museum

1952 aerial photograph of Kingston Market Place © Historic England

Kingston Market Place
Courtesy of Owen Walter

Market Traders of Kingston – The Kent Family

Without realising it, Charlie Kent has played out the majority of his life within a short distance of the hidden Latchmere Brook. It lay underground at the bottom of his grandparent's garden in Elm Road. As a child he inadvertently tumbled into the brook near Latchmere Lane and was completely soaked. In his later years, with his wife Alma, he lived only a short distance from the Brook, in Cardinal Avenue on the Tudor Estate.

This is the story of Charlie Kent and his family.

Early Days

In 1911 William Henry Hutchens Kent (Henry) and his wife Louisa were living with their four children Henry (Harry), Charlie (Tyke), Edward (Jimmy) and Ellen (Dolly) at 174 Elm Road in Kingston. The house had a shop front where they sold fresh cod and herrings and also rabbit. Louisa was able to pauch (gut and skin) up to 200 rabbits a day. The family, through generations, had been rather partial to roast rabbit with onions and strips of bacon. "*Lovely*" recalls Charlie.

William had gained his name Hutchens from his Uncle Harry Hutchens (brother of William's mother) who in the 1880s was feted as being the fastest man in the world over 200 yards.

Louisa Kent with her children. Top right: Charlie, then clockwise Jimmy, Tommy, Ellen & Harry

In March 1915 at the age of 35, Henry answered the nation's call to arms and enlisted in the army at Aldershot. At this time, his wife Louisa was living at 13 Wood Street with the children and another baby Tommy. Within two weeks Henry was serving in the Labour Corps in Rouen in France where he would remain until December 1917. He wasn't the most obedient of soldiers in the ranks, punished on at least four occasions for being absent from roll call and being drunk. He was finally discharged, intact, in June 1918.

William Henry Kent

On his return to civilian life he converted a shop in Elm Road to a greengrocer's, selling fruit and vegetables. There were four shops, side by side in this part of Elm Road. Henry's greengrocer's, a corn chandler, a bakery and a fishmonger. At this time Elm Road had more than twenty small shops.

The fruit and veg were sold from the shop on tick (credit) and every Sunday, Louisa visited the regular customers in the vicinity of the shop to collect the money. Shortly after, Henry established the first Kent fruit and veg stall in Kingston market where his four sons learned their trade. This would have been 100 years ago.

Each evening, after closing the shops and the stalls, Henry very much liked to go for a drink. His favoured pubs were the Willoughby Arms in Willoughby Road and the Wych Elm. On many occasions, when he had drunk too much, his mates loaded him in the back of his cart and the horse would find its own way home to his house in Elm Road, with its stable in the back yard.

On Boxing Day in 1927, Charlie (Tyke) Kent married Louisa Smith at St Paul's Church on Kingston Hill. They lived at 5 Cross Road, Kingston and it was here that Charles Ferguson was born in 1928 and a few years later, his sister Doris. Charlie's earliest memories are sitting in the family's grocer's shop in Park Road and, unknowingly, beginning to learn the trade!

Louisa also took a horse and cart laden with fruit and veg on a round in Ham. Occasionally, she would take a very excited young Charlie with her. They travelled up Dukes Avenue, along Dysart Avenue, round the back of the fields, between the football and cricket grounds then along Lock Road. They didn't trade in Ham Street because there was already a grocery shop in the street. Charlie clearly remembers greeting the milk cart and baker's cart, both also horse drawn. His greeting for the bakery delivery man was always more enthusiastic because he stood a good chance of being given a jam tart. The ice company had a cart carrying large blocks of ice: the cart required two horses to pull it. In two houses, one in Dukes Avenue and one in Lock Road, Louisa and Charlie were often invited in for a cup of tea.

1944: Cricket & football pitches, Butler's Farm and the The Dukes footpath in Ham.
© Historic England

School Years

From the age of five Charlie went to St Paul's School in Borough Road. He walked by himself from his home in Cross Road to school. They then moved to Craven Road. In the 1930s they moved nine times. Charlie recalls that during the great depression of the 1930s, *life was very hard.*

Charlie also spent some 18 months at St Andrew's School in Ham Street after his father opened a greengrocer's shop further along the street. Charlie played football for the school at right half and helped them win the cup in 1938/39. Charlie got to know many of the kids in Ham, including Chas Redknapp, Harry Rapps, Ernie Church, Dennis Stevens and Barbara Stroud.

When his father was called up during the 2nd World War, the family moved back to St George's Road in Kingston. During this period Charlie went to St Paul's and then St Luke's Secondary School.

From the age of 10, preparing for life on a market stall, Charlie's mental maths was excellent. He could add up a list of items, calculating their price from their weight in his head, all the while talking to his customer. He never had any need to write anything down. Many years later, this ability also made him a favourite for keeping the score when playing darts. "*Come on Charlie, keep the score, you can do it good*" urged his mates. All the market traders had this skill, a skill that they passed down, from father to son.

Memories of the Local Area

On November 30th 1936, at the age of 8 years, Charlie was standing outside the shop in Elm Road watching the sky in the east glow red. Apparently, Crystal Palace was burning down in one of the greatest fires seen in London. Four years later, London would be ablaze for months!

Charlie remembers trolley buses running round a circuit down Park Road from Kingston, turning left into Kings Road, past the Barracks, then left into Richmond Road. "*I used it regular*".

The roads were free of traffic and this enabled the children to play marbles along the length of Elm Road all the way from Canbury Park Road to Park Road.

Ham Farm Orchard

Ham Farm had a large orchard that extended across most of the land that now forms the southern part of the Tudor Estate. There were many varieties of fruit trees. These included Coxes, Laxton Superb & James Greave apple trees, Conference, William & Hazel pears and Victoria plums. In Spring, the extensive orchard was awash with blossom which drifted down with the breeze and made a white carpet on the ground.

Despite the fact that his dad had a grocer's shop and a stall in the market, Charlie often went scrumping in the Ham Farm orchard. The fruit always tasted sweeter! He never got caught. Many years later he would buy a house in Cardinal Avenue, that was built on the land of that lost orchard.

Where Latchmere School is now located, there was a large wooden hangar that served as a dance hall at the back of the East Surrey Barracks. Behind it was a large plot of stinging nettles. Charlie remembers the large barrels of beer outside the dance hall. He also clearly remembers the stinging nettles, because he fell into them. On the northern side of the Barracks was a firing range and Charlie and his mates occasionally went to watch the soldiers firing their rifles.

Charlie had, for company, a dog called Basil, a special Heinz 57 breed, and a small Welsh cob called Billy. Charlie often rode Billy around the streets of Ham to meet up with his mates. Basil followed happily behind, until distracted by something far more interesting, and off he would dash.

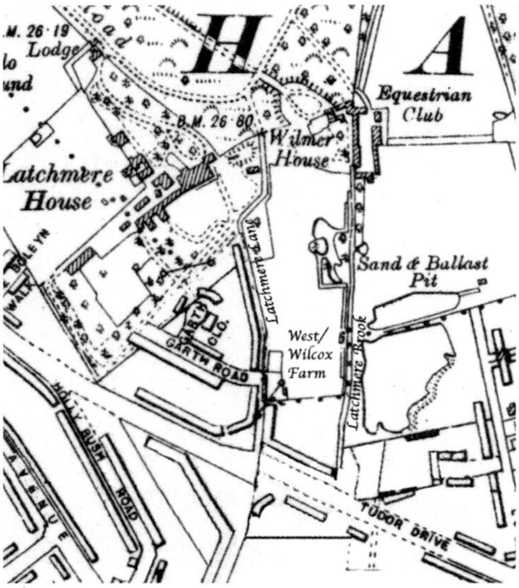

West Farm later called Wilcox's Farm on the east side of Latchmere Lane. NLS

West's Farm

East of Latchmere Lane and to the North of Tudor Drive was West's Farm (later known as Wilcox's Farm). This comprised a stable block backing onto Latchmere Lane and a farmhouse with about 6 bedrooms. The farm kept pigs and chickens.

The Latchmere Brook, several feet wide, ran past its eastern perimeter. Charlie on one occasion successfully jumped across the brook. Yet, landing on the other side he lost his balance and despite a frantic waving of his arms, tumbled back into the stream. Unfortunately, at the time, the rain had washed a lot of pig sewage from the pig farm into the brook and he came out stinking.

A polo pitch was located behind the farm. Charlie picked up a horseshoe from this field and it now hangs on the wall next to the front of his house in Cardinal Avenue.

Park Road Pig Farm

There was another pig farm in Park Road that backed onto the wall of Richmond Park. This was owned by Bill Dicks (son of Worthy Dicks), a short man, thick set and very strong. He had about 30-40 pigs and several chickens that used to scratch around. When Charlie was about 10 years old, he began working for Bill, up to 5 hours a time, cleaning out the sties, laying down straw, boiling up the food waste and feeding the pigs. For this he would receive half a crown. Charlie loved working there and was so excited when he accompanied Bill to the market in Fairfield to sell and buy pigs.

Bill later sold his small farm and emigrated to Australia. Many years later, Charlie was delighted when Bill came to see him on a brief visit to England to catch up with his family.

1947 aerial photograph showing Butler's Farm and The Dukes, a footpath before Dukes Road extended to Lawrence Road.
© Historic England

Lawrence Road & Butler's Farm

In 1938, aged ten, Charlie began work part time (Saturdays, after school and holidays) on a stall in Kingston Market.

Often, after work, Charlie accompanied his grandad Henry on the bus to Ham Common. They stopped in the Hand & Flower where his grandad enjoyed a couple of pints while Charlie had a glass of lemonade. They then walked down the passageway (Warner's Lane) then along Dukes Avenue until it turned into Dysart Avenue. Here they picked up the ancient footpath lined with a hedge, called *The Dukes*, that ran through the fields to the end of Craig Road. On the left of this path just before Craig Road was Butler's Farm, a small farm that housed pigs, chickens, a couple of horses and two fierce Alsatian dogs that were secured by a length of chain. Leaving this path Charlie and his grandad cut through the fields, to the left of the farm, to reach the rear garden of 30 Lawrence Road, a house that had been purchased as a new build, by his grandad Henry.

George Birdsall Jnr, (Charlie's cousin) recalls that Butler's Farm was located where Randle Road is now situated. He clearly remembers about a dozen cows being kept there.

The Dukes was bordered on one side by the rear garden fences of the large houses on Ham Common and a hedge, adjacent to Butler's Farm and open fields, on the other side. It was no more than a track and not wide enough for a horse and a cart George also recalls that Vera Lynn stayed at Lawrence Hall Hotel on Ham Common (now the site of the Cassell Hospital).

Charlie often walked to 30 Lawrence Road on Wednesday evening and stayed for two nights. At this time, the house in Lawrence Road, in contrast to Charlie's own home, enjoyed the luxury of electricity and hot water. Coal fires were located in two downstairs rooms and two bedrooms, though they were rarely used.

Granny Louisa and grandad Henry died while living at 30 Lawrence Road and were both buried in the graveyard of St Andrew's Church, before the graveyard was full up.

The Kents in Ham

Charles (Tyke) Kent had moved with his family into Ham Street just before the war to take on a greengrocer's shop with a flat above. This shop was located next to the butcher's, run by Frank Birch, six houses up from the Crooked Billet (a pub identical in design to the Cardinal in Tudor Drive). A fish and chip shop in Back Lane was run by Harry Kent. Charlie's favourite shop in Ham was Dunkley's sweet shop in Ham Street opposite the Crooked Billet.

In Ham, popular pastimes were bird nesting (the collecting of eggs from nests) in the fields and sandpits. Sand martins nested in the sand pits. They were warned that a number of children had drowned in the deep lakes that had formed around the sand pits.

In 1939, Henry and Louisa were living at 30 Lawrence Road with their sons Jimmy and Tommy who were both working in the fruit and veg trade. Tommy later moved into a house, a few doors along. Charlie's cousin, John Kent lived until 2016 across the road on the corner with Langham Gardens, in a large house with a swimming pool. His uncle Harry lived in a semi-detached house in Broughton Avenue, until a large bomb landed on its doorstep and blew the house down.

Henry's daughter, Dolly married George Birdsall who became the Regimental Sergeant Major of the East Surrey Regiment. He was a very smartly dressed man. They later moved into 30 Lawrence Road to look after grandad Henry Kent. Members of the Kent/Birdsall family have lived in this house in Lawrence Road since it was built in 1935.

The Barrow and Stall

All the brothers did their bit on either setting up the stalls in Kingston Market or taking the horse and cart to the London markets. It was given that they all took on a fair share of the work.

Their horse was kept in a stable next door to their house in 2 Elm Road with a lock-up used for the cart and the hand-pulled barrow and stall. The three stalls in Kingston Market had to be assembled every morning and broken down every night. The stall was taken by hand-pulled barrow, a journey that took no more than 15 to 20 minutes. Every morning they would set up at about 5am and open the stall at 7:30am. During the week they closed the stall at 6pm. They then had to break the stall down, place it on the barrow and pull the barrow back to the lock-up in Elm Road. There were no lights at the market, so they used paraffin lamps during the winter.

On Sunday they worked in the morning until midday getting all the empty boxes ready to take back to the main London market and get a refund. The council meanwhile cleared the market stall area and hosed it down. In the afternoon, Charlie's dad wanted him and his sister out of the house so they went along to the Sunday school at the Baptist Church in Queen Elizabeth Road from the age of seven to about ten. Here Charlie accepted the prayers and hymns but really enjoyed the games that they played.

This was hard living and despite coming across all sorts at the market, Charlie reflects: "*I kept myself honest*".

An Early Morning Trek into London

Three to five days a week, depending on how quickly the vegetables and fruit were selling off the stalls, they got up at 3:30am to collect new produce from the London markets. Charlie was really excited during his first trip at the age of ten. That excitement was soon to wear off as they encountered the cold of winter.

Their house had no heating, no hot water and no lighting. During the winter it was cold when they went to bed and cold when they woke up. They took a jug of water to bed with them so that they could fill a bowl and have a cold wash before dressing. When it was really cold the water would freeze in the jug. He didn't always wash!

Charlie had meagre clothing that he had got second hand. A shirt, a cardigan and a coat with shorts (even in winter) and white plimsolls on his feet. He had no gloves for his hands. He was rarely warm during the winter. They tied potato sacking around their feet and on the feet of the horses to stop them sliding on the ice in winter.

Charlie took five minutes to harness the horse to the cart. During the dark mornings, they lit two lanterns one on each side of the cart. They placed candles inside a square box with a door with red glass on the outside to provide a red light.

The Journey into Covent Garden

From leaving Elm Road, the horse pulled them down York Road, left into Dagmar Road, left into Park Road, right into Alexandra Road, across Queens Road to Crescent Road and up the steep hill to the A308. They turned left up Kingston Hill, past Wimbledon Common to Tibbet's Corner and left to descend the hill to Putney Bridge. They continued along the Chelsea embankment, past Waterloo Bridge to arrive at Covent Garden and then find a spot to park the cart in Tavistock Street. This took on average about 2 ½ hours, getting them to the market before 6am. Their horse was called Bob, 17 hands tall. Charlie recalls: "*the horse knew exactly where to go*".

The roads were clear of motor traffic, and they mainly encountered horse and carts. In the 1940s there was only one car parked in Elm Road, a Ford Prefect that belonged to Mr T A Pow, the headmaster of St Luke's School.

There was only one seat on the cart for Charlie's dad who held the reins. With no gloves, Charlie who was standing on the foot board, kept one hand in his pocket while holding onto the raves (rails of a cart) with his other hand to prevent himself from falling off the cart. His hands were freezing, and he shivered with the cold for the entire trip into London. When it was raining, they got soaked and were wet for the rest of the day. As some sort of protection, they formed a hood in a potato sack and fitted it over their heads and backs to keep off the worst of the rain. Charlie recalls, "*you got there, you were froze. It was hard*". They were glad to get back after those trips.

On icy mornings, they had to reverse the horse and cart up the steep slope of Crescent Road. Fortunately, on the way to market up Kingston Hill and past Wimbledon Common, the cart was empty. Returning when the cart was laden, they descended the hill but had a foot brake on the cart to slow it down.

On arriving at Covent Garden, they immediately went into one of the many inviting cafes that were packed full, noisy and warm. For half a crown they could get a cup of steaming hot tea and a delicious steak and kidney pudding with boiled potatoes and cabbage. A number of pubs were open to cater for the night porters who were finishing their shifts. Charlie recalls a chap playing an accordion outside one of the pubs.

If they were running late, they had to wait a little longer for their breakfast and would stop on their return journey at a van on Wimbledon Common. Charlie can visualise to this day the welcome cup of tea and the tasty tikki snack pies (beef & gravy).

During the war, there were no lemons, oranges or bananas available. They placed orders for fruit consisting of various types of home-grown apples, pears and plums. They also purchased potatoes, carrots, cabbages, sprouts, parsnips, leeks and other home-grown vegetables.

Brentford Market

This was Charlie's favourite, a good old-fashioned market.

After selecting and paying for the produce they had selected, they needed to wait for the porters to take it on a barrow to their cart which could be some distance away. At the age of 14 to 15, Charlie was given 3d to get the bus back to Kingston and help out on the stall. Instead he pocketed the money and ran back to the stall via Kew Bridge, past Kew Gardens, through Richmond, over the incline to Petersham, past Ham Common and along the Richmond Road. It used to take him just under the hour. After all, his great Uncle Harry Hutchens was, in his time, the fastest runner in the world!

Harry Hutchens, the fastest man in the World.

Stray Dogs

At this time, it was common to encounter packs of up to a dozen stray dogs roaming the street. These could unsettle the horse and the horse would bolt in panic, pulling the cart behind him. If you weren't on the cart you could only run after it until the horse came to a halt or fell over. Meanwhile the produce would invariably be strewn all over the road. This was a big worry for all of the traders.

Food

Meals were very simple but a favourite pudding of Charlie's was bread pudding made with bread, lard and raisins.

Every Sunday lunchtime the muffin man made a tour of the local pubs with a hat on his head supporting a large tray carrying muffins. He would ring a bell as he arrived shouting out "*Muffins*". Other traders visited the pubs selling winkles, prawns, whelks and jellied eels. "*Lovely, eat em regular*": reflects Charlie.

The War

As well as Tyke's greengrocer's shop in Ham Street, the brothers also occupied three fruit & veg stalls in Kingston and a greengrocer's shop in Elm Road.

Most people had Anderson air raid shelters installed in their back gardens. These tended to be very damp with a lot of condensation, and through the night they got soaked with the water dripping from the ceiling.

One day, before his dad was called up, Charlie and his dad were travelling over Putney Bridge on the cart and saw bombs dropping on flats on Chelsea embankment. A block went up in flames. Charlie dashed inside and knocked on the doors to get people out. He entered one flat and found an elderly man lying in bed. He helped him up and got him outside to safety. Because the building was beginning to collapse, they had to move their horse and cart and continue on their way to Covent Garden.

One afternoon as he was watching the bombs raining down on London from the German bombers, he saw a strange yet beautiful light in the sky. On questioning this, his dad told him that it was the sun reflecting off of the dropping bombs.

After his dad, Tyke, was called up into the Army Service Corps, the family had to move from their house and shop in Ham Street to a house in St George's Road near the corner with York Road in Kingston. Altogether, three of the brothers went off to war leaving the women and the elder children to keep the family grocery business running as best they could.

There were air raid shelters under the market, which are still there today. The market children used to sing with their mums so they couldn't hear the bombs exploding. The market was never hit but their shop in Elm Road was destroyed by a direct hit. On one occasion while they were down the shelter, someone pinched their till from the stand.

At this time, Charlie was at St Luke's School in Elm Road. They didn't learn much at school because the kids were so tired with the night-time raids. Many of them fell asleep on the desks.

Suki (Susan) Pepperell, 35 years old ran a wet fish shop in Elm Road, just along from the Kents. She was married to Bill Pepperell and they had a son called Billy. They lived above the shop. She was a really nice lady but because the damp in the Anderson shelter caused her too much discomfort, they installed a Morrison shelter, a metal cage, inside her home. Her house was bombed and collapsed around her trapping her in the cage. Much to everyone's horror, she burnt to death before she could be saved.

Charlie recalls: *Many years later my family were attending another funeral and sitting near to Billy Pepperell. Billy coughed a number of times. My dad (Tyke) leaned forward and quietly said to him "It's not worth you going home*". Somehow, they all managed to retain their sense of humour.

Rations were 8 ozs. of meat a week with a bit of cheese. They ate a lot of vegetable stew and rabbit, a meat that was more readily available. Following in the tradition of his granny, roast rabbit was a favourite when served with onions and strips of bacon. Charlie Lin sold horse meat off his stall in the market place.

One night in 1942, the family were together in their air raid shelter in the back garden of their house in St Georges Road, in the midst of a heavy bombing raid. At about 9pm a large bomb came down, "*like a hurricane*", and landed in the middle of the road directly outside their house. The huge explosion destroyed the houses on both sides of the road and filled the air with choking dust. They could hardly breathe. Charlie's house collapsed on top of their Anderson shelter, trapping them inside. The fire brigade had to come and dig them out. As soon as he was freed, Charlie tried to dash back into the remains of the house to find his precious bird egg collection. He remembers the fireman angrily shouting at his mum "*get hold of him*".

After a night on the floor in the school hall they moved to 15 Lowther Road to live with his aunt. He spent many more nights in the air raid shelter especially after an unexploded bomb went straight through the roof and window of his bedroom, while he was in it.

Every morning after a raid, Charlie eagerly went out to look for shrapnel, to add to his collection. It was less delicate than his lost egg collection.

Charlie arrived at the site of the V2 rocket that exploded at the junction of Kings Road and Park Road, a few minutes after it went off. It had been an enormous explosion. The air was thick with dust as houses were continuing to collapse, with bricks tumbling down. He saw a woman hanging out of a window screaming. She was badly crippled by the blast. Many people had been killed and loads of houses had been destroyed.

Charlie remembers, one late afternoon while on the stall in the market, looking up at the sky as a wave of RAF bombers were heading off on a bombing raid in tight formation. An old WW1 veteran shouted out, *go on my boys*, and they all cheered.

In 1942 at the age of 14, Charlie left school and went to work full time (6 days a week) on the stall with his mum, Louisa. On Saturday, the stall remained open until 10pm to accommodate the people coming out of the pubs. He was earning 7s 6d a week. Of the brothers, only Uncle Harry was working the stalls and he needed all the help he could get to keep them going until the other men came back from the war. They had no idea how long the war would last and were simply surviving from day to day. Charlie's father did not return home until 1946. By then, many houses in the area were empty.

National Service

In 1946, just as his Dad came back from his military service, Charlie was called up for national service. He was 18 years old, 5 foot 7 inches tall and weighed only 8 stone and 6 pounds. For some reason his service was extended for a year so he did three years instead of two, but he didn't mind.

Charlie loved the army. After years travelling up to London and back on the horse and cart in all weathers and working the stall, the army was *a piece of cake*. For the first time in his life he wore good warm clothing (denims and good boots). He ate three meals a day and had a warm bed. Six weeks basic training at Canterbury Barracks included drill, 5-mile route marches and rifle training. His instructors were Sgt Major Oliver and Corporal Brown. They were good blokes and most importantly they were fair. Charlie understood that you needed to have discipline in the army. He was then sent to the Shorncliffe Barracks to be trained for the Army Catering Corps. At Chilwell barracks he and his fellow cooks prepared meals for 2000 men. He earned £1 a week, enough to cover the cost of tuppence sandwiches in the Naafi and a pint in a local pub that he made last for the whole evening.

Coronation baths in Penrhyn Road

Having completed his national service, Charlie returned to work on the market stall. From handling the sacks of potatoes, he got very dusty. Every morning after setting up the stall Charlie popped off to the Coronation baths in Penrhyn Road to enjoy the showers and the baths. Many of the local coalmen also used the showers to clean off the coal dust which covered them. It's difficult to appreciate how many coalmen there were. Everyone was using coal and it had to be delivered. Cromwell Road was the main depot and there was a local coal yard in Elm Road from where coal was distributed to all of the individual houses.

In 1948, his dad Tyke, bought an ex-army truck. Although the journey to Covent Garden was shortened to half an hour, they invariably spent a lot of time repairing punctures and fixing the vehicle. They couldn't afford new tyres. Nevertheless, this was luxury in comparison with the horse and cart.

Charlie believed that he was "*too skint to die*". He had been born in a recession that seemed to continue through all of his life.

Marriage

One evening after work, Charlie stopped off at the Old Crown Pub at the edge of the marketplace. A couple that he knew were showing off their wedding photographs. Charlie looked through them and saw an attractive girl.

Who's that there? he enquired.

My sister was the answer.

Is she married? continued Charlie.

On learning that she wasn't married or fixed up:

I'd like to ask her for a date.

The Old Crown near the Marketplace, receiving a delivery of Hodgsons beer. Today there is a flower stall in the same position.

Alma, the sister, was working at the Odeon at the time. She accepted the invitation and in February 1957 they married. Alma joined Charlie on the stall in Kingston Market and they worked together until 2008, when Charlie was 80 and Alma 77 years old: "*We enjoyed our life and enjoyed the chat and banter with our regular customers. We had a good old laugh*".

Entertainment

Routinely after finishing work on the stall at 6pm, Charlie met up with other market traders in one of many Kingston pubs. In later years, Alma would go home because after spending all day with Charlie on the stall, she needed a break!

Over the years, Charlie tried every pub in Kingston, but his favourites were the Three Fishes in Richmond Road, opposite the Regal Cinema (ABC) just before the railway station, the Wych Elm in Elm Road, the Willoughby Arms in Willoughby Road and the Borough Arms in Park Road.

During the war the Three Fishes was a favourite of the American GI's. "*There was a bloke in there playing the piano. There were quite a lot of fights in the Three Fishes as the English lads and other Canadian soldiers wanted to fight the Yanks*". However, Charlie got on very well with the Americans and they used to give him King Edward cigars, even though he was only 15 years old. During the latter part of the war, the Americans, who were based in Bushy Park, had a big impact on the town and trade was extremely good because of them. Charlie remembers the night when a GI, walking along the parapet of Kingston bridge, fell into the river. They often had open nights at the camp in Bushy Park and Charlie on one occasion was invited along with other local residents to join the soldiers and enjoy free beer.

Kingston had its own brewery, Hodgsons', at the back of St James Road. They had large dray horses that pulled the carts holding the barrels of beer that would be delivered to local pubs. Charlie knew some of the guys in the brewery. One of them, Len Chapman, often invited him in "*Here Charlie, try a pint of this*". It was a mild beer, a lovely beer and a pint of ordinary cost 8d. Charlie and his mates played darts and drank half pint measures. If you lost a game, you paid for the next half. Charlie was good at darts and very good at keeping score.

Police Force

Police officers walked a beat pushing their bicycles and called in at police boxes located around the area. Charlie was friendly with Tom Gudge, a plain clothes police officer, who lived in Latchmere Lane. At the time, burglars were breaking into the gas meters to get the money out. They could get as much as 30 shillings from each meter.

Charlie reflects that in the old days, the youngsters had more respect for their teachers, their elders and police officers. "*You had to show respect, that was a must*".

Meeting the Queen

In 1992, the Queen and Prince Phillip visited Kingston Market. They were introduced by the Mayor of Kingston to two of the stalwarts in the market, Charlie and Alma.

Cardinal Avenue

Charlie and Alma moved into 25 Cardinal Avenue in 1986 and lived there together until 2020, when Alma died.

Charlie and Alma meeting the Queen at their stall in Kingston Market

Looking Back

A final comment from Charlie on his life as a market trader:

"Snow, fog, rain, whatever, had to go."

"Grannie Louise always said If you don't work, you don't eat!"

"It was hard work, but I really enjoyed it"

Charlie sitting quietly alone outside his home in Cardinal Avenue in 2020. On the wall behind him is the horseshoe that he picked up from the polo field, next to the Latchmere Brook, when he was a child. At that time an abundant orchard was located where he is now sitting.

Sources:
Family history carefully researched by Mike Shaw

Picture Credits
All pictures are courtesy of the Kent family unless otherwise indicated

NLS: Reproduced with the permission of the National Library of Scotland

The Grocer in Park Road
– Ernie Porter

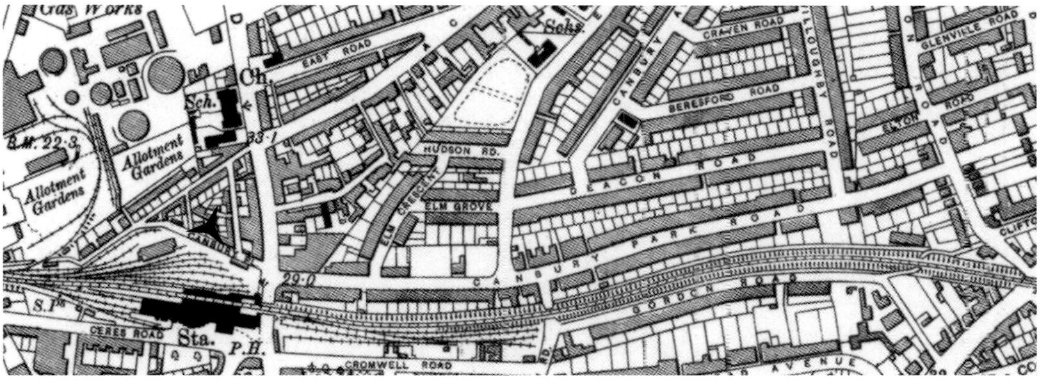

1933 OS Map showing the streets, north of the Railway line in Kingston. Canbury Place was on the opposite side of Richmond Road to Canbury Park Road. NLS

I was born in February 1928 at 7 Canbury Place in Kingston, the youngest of nine children (five girls and four boys). A couple of the children were old enough to be my parents but the children in those days looked after one another.

My father (Alfred) was a horse dealer who knew the trade inside out. During the 1st World War he bought and sold horses for the army. He used to buy horses from all over: here, there and everywhere. He hired out horses to the local bakers and milkmen. Because petrol was rationed during the war everyone used a horse and cart. He always had two or three working horses and the rest were hired out.

When my brothers and sisters were old enough, they were each provided with their own horse and cart. With the carts, loaded up with fruit and vegetables, they travelled through the streets of Kingston, Norbiton and Ham, selling the produce. One of my sisters worked a night shift at Hawkers in Canbury Park Road then did a round with the horse and cart during the day.

My mother sold fruit and vegetables from a shop on the front of our house in Canbury Place, to locals and people getting off the trains that stopped at Kingston Station. Placed in a bushel box that served as a cradle on the footboard of the cart, I accompanied my father on his round.

My father rented a yard with a stable in Cowleaze Road for the working horses. I remember that part of the recreation ground down by Latchmere Lane was fields and here my father used to turn out his horses. Just north of the recreation ground was a large orchard, which I occasionally lost myself in when I was a youngster.

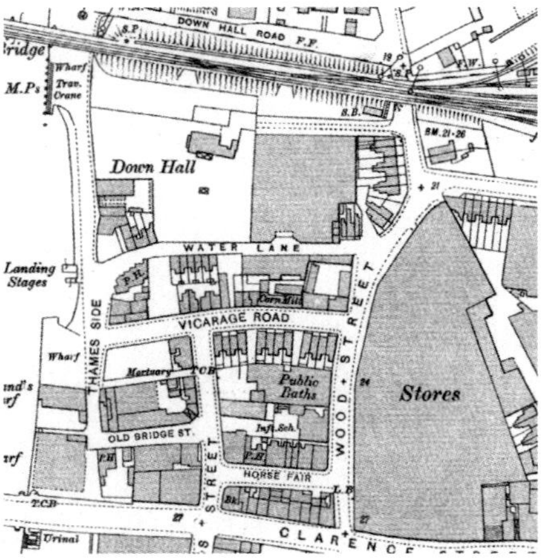

1934 Map showing the Public Baths in Wood Street opposite Bentalls (Stores). NLS

Our House

The small, two up two down house in Canbury Place had electricity and gas for the cooker. There was no heating. We had a tin bath which was placed in front of the fire. One day a week the girls had a bath, the next day the boys had a bath. Being the youngest, I was the last to go in the bath. As we got older, we went to the baths that were located in Wood Street opposite Bentalls.

Working with Horses

I had two or three ponies or small horses when I was young, and I used to ride these around the streets and on Ham Common. I learnt to ride very well, without a saddle.

When I was about eight my father called me over, "Come on, I'm going to have a look at a couple of horses" and in the horse and trap we set off for Woking. Here my dad bought a couple of horses from some gypsies. While he finalised his deal, he told me to ride them back. I jumped on the back of one and led the other. You had to learn to ride bareback. I had seen an elder brother leading a string of 6 horses. At the top of the lane I didn't know which way to go so I made a choice and hoped for the best. My father soon caught me up in his horse and trap and secured the trailing horse to the back of the trap: I was very much relieved!

"My father was very shrewd and both he and my mum worked very hard"

"What my father told you was worth knowing"

"You learnt right from wrong and you worked hard."

"You did as you were told and that was it"

On Sunday mornings we worked very hard cleaning the harnesses and the horses and sorting out all of the empties to be returned to the market. The old man was very particular and made sure that we got on and did our job.

Christmas

At Christmas we also sold Christmas trees. We sold anything that we could earn 2 or 3 bob for, as long as it was right.

Every Christmas when I was young, my mother and father took me into Kingston shortly before Christmas day to look in the shop windows and see what I wanted. Then on Christmas day I always got a great present. We had some lovely festive Christmases with all the family together and our other relatives from Battersea joining us.

School

I didn't go to the Borough Road School until the age of 7. I then went to the Richmond Road School. The teachers were very strict. I was quite lonely there because I worked every evening and at weekends and didn't have any spare time to make friends. With the horses and stable there was always something to do. I didn't like school. It wasn't my life. I was used to being out in the open air.

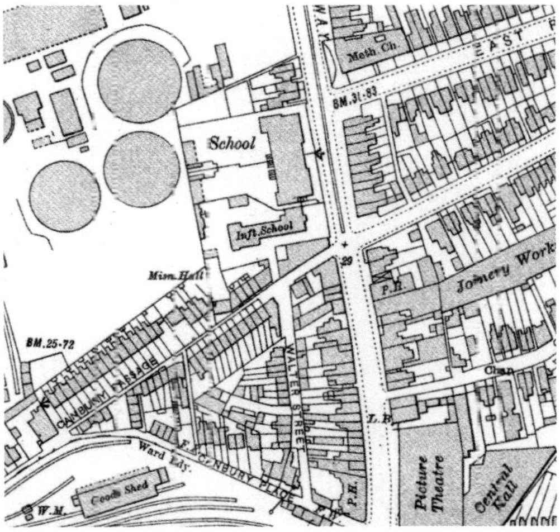

Above: 1934 map showing the school NLS

Top left: Richmond Road School opened in 1907 GE

Left: 1924 aerial view of Richmond Road School. The boys were nicknamed the gas works kids © Historic England

The War

I remember looking up and seeing the German bombers in the sky. The house in Canbury Place was hit by a bomb and so we had to move to Canbury Park Road. Not having access to an air raid shelter we hid in the cellar of the house. That was fine until the water pipes fractured and the cellar filled with water. They were hard times, but we got through it.

I remember one bad night at Canbury Park Road. Bombs fell on three sides of our house, one in Cromwell Road, one by the Canbury Arms and a third by the Regal cinema. We became so used to it that we didn't take any notice. I was more worried about the poor horses in the stables.

Brentford Market

Our house at Canbury Park Road had a stable at the rear of the house. My brothers had now all gone off to fight in the war, leaving me alone with my older sisters. Three times a week I travelled alone to Brentford Market to buy produce. "I had to do what I had to do". My grandfather was one of the first customers at Brentford Market shortly after it started up. My father also sold horse harnesses and brushes in a cafe in the market. Anything to do with a horse, he sold it.

I used to get up before 5am. I quickly got dressed and went and fitted a nose bag full of oats on Polly (Poll for short) who stood 15 hands tall. I then came back in for a cup of tea before securing all of the harnesses connecting Poll to the cart. In winter three paraffin fuelled lanterns were fitted, a red lantern at the back and two white lamps at the side. They used to last a long time. I then drove the horse and cart down Richmond Road, through Richmond, past Kew Gardens and over Kew Bridge to Brentford Market. There were no cars parked on the road. On arrival, I sought out my favourite suppliers and gave them their orders and paid them.

While the porters were loading my cart, I went into Mr Walterton's café for a hot breakfast of egg and sausages with toast and tea with two sugars, which cost 1s 6d. Occasionally, I had a piece of boiled haddock on the bone. This took about 30 minutes. The café was invariably packed but welcomingly warm in winter. It had a table in the middle and a raised bench running down the side. If you were stuck at one end, everyone had to move to let you out, but they didn't mind. On seeing me each morning Mr Walterton cheerily welcomed me: "Come on young Porter, have your breakfast"

When fully laden there was no room on the seat, so I sat myself on the foot board at the side of the cart for the return journey.

On the way back, I stopped at Matthews the bakers on the Kew Road, just before Richmond, to buy a 6d bag of doughnuts. I used the clock at Richmond Station as a marker. I needed to be there by 8:30 to give me time to be in school by 9am. If I was running a bit late, I encouraged Poll, although laden, to pick up her pace. On passing the poppy factory she sped up and then broke into a canter to enable her to get the cart over the small hill just before the Dysart Arms.

I had to get through a full school day before returning home for dinner. I then harnessed Poll to the cart once more and by 4pm I was back on a round, selling produce from the cart. My first stop was on the corner of Park Road and Elton Road. I then went on to the Council houses in Ham. My last call was after 9pm at the First and Last Café on Ham Parade where I normally ordered a roll with two sausages inside and a cup of tea with two sugars. Occasionally, the few friends that I did have, met me in there for a chat and a laugh. It was a brief opportunity in the long day to simply relax. I didn't stay too long, however, because I felt sorry for Poll outside. Everyone knew me on my round. "Hello Ernie", they would call out.

It broke my heart when my father sold Poll (to the knacker's yard) but as he said, "horse was horse".

Covent Garden

If we needed something special, I made the longer trip to Covent Garden. There was a stall in the basement of the church that sold the finest steak and kidney pies, full of gravy – delicious!

Clothing

Even in winter I never had a pair of gloves. I simply tucked the reins under my legs and withdrew my hands into the sleeves of my coat. It didn't make much odds, I just got on with it. Poll knew what to do and the route to and from the market.

Yet my father always ensured that I had plenty to eat and wore good clothes. He took me to a tailor in Waterloo Road to have a suit, consisting of coat and trousers, made for me for 50s. The trousers were so thick that you could stand them up on their own, but they lasted a long time and they were warm.

Food

My mother was a good cook and I had a cooked meal every night before doing the round. Steak and kidney, haddock on the bone. My father through his contacts could get hold of chicken, duck and rabbit and we never starved.

Scarcity

During the war we bought potatoes, carrots and cabbage. If it could be bought the right way, we would sell it the right way. Oranges were very scarce and strictly allocated. Local apples were Coxes. I remember apples from Canada that came in big barrels. You knocked the top off the barrel. As a youngster I liked to climb inside the empty barrels but one day I badly gashed my back on a nail.

I was occupied all of the time. My father didn't like to see me sitting around. At the end of the day I had to feed all of the horses and put the straw down for their bed.

I remember one weekend when I was sitting on the boards.

"What's the matter?", he said.

I replied, "Everything's done, horses done, and I've swept all of the yard".

He thought about this for a moment then quickly said, "Go and give that yard another run over"

One Sunday afternoon as I was planning to go to the cinema with my mates I went to get cleaned up. My dad called me down:

"What are you doing?"

"I'm having a wash"

"What for?"

"I'm going to the pictures with the boys".

"No, you're not. You get out there and clean those harnesses. That's better than going to the pictures"

"My father stood no nonsense. No ifs or buts with him"

"When the old man used to call me, he only called me once"

"He was hard but he was good. He knew right"

End of the War

When I was 16 in 1944, my dad bought a motor, an Armstrong Siddeley with a drop-down side. This was the beginning of the end for the horses and carts.

All my brothers came back from the war and immediately went out back to work as if nothing had happened. Two of my sisters had husbands in the army. At the end of the war, they emigrated to South Africa. One of them worked for the Post Office and supervised Post Offices throughout Rhodesia.

Ernie doing national service

National Service

This wasted two years of my life. It wasn't my scene.

The Park Road Shop

In 1953, at the age of 25 years, I rented my own house and shop at 41 Park Road for £2 10s a week. After marrying Eileen, I bought the house and shop. Eileen worked in the Park Road shop while I worked the streets. There was no set agreement of areas to work but everyone knew each other, and we all got on.

We managed to get hold of oranges and sold them, three for a penny. The best oranges were Spanish Navel oranges, full of flavour and juice. Jaffa oranges were all right. I sold carrier bags for a penny and kept them on a rail around the top of the shop.

I later managed the shop and employed a lad to do the round. I have been working in the shop in Park Road ever since.

My Cart bound for the USA

I bought a cart, known as a London Trolley, from my cousin and had my name E. Porter painted on the front rail. Many years later a friend told me that he had seen the cart in a hotel foyer in a city in America. It was just as when I had owned it.

Looking back

"Right from a kid I would get up before 5 in the morning"

"I have no regrets at the way I was fetched up"

"I was used to the long days and the cold weather and I've been soaked through a fair few times, but I never needed a pair of gloves"

"We took life as it came, and I just got on with the job"

Ernie's cart at Epsom Racecourse

Picture Credits

All photos courtesy of Ernie Porter unless otherwise indicated

NLS: Reproduced with the permission of the National Library of Scotland

GE © Gordon Elsden

Mad about Sport – Eric Lavender

Eric Lavender was born in April 1934 and lived the early years of his life in Salisbury Road in New Malden.

Bomb damage in New Malden

On 16th August 1940, Eric and his mum accompanied his dad to his RAF base at Melksham. While they were away, a bomb landed in the garden and destroyed the back of the house. It was fortunate that they were out because the bomb landed directly on their Anderson shelter: *"I took this personally and had the strong feeling that Hitler had tried to kill me. This frightened me especially when I heard Hitler giving one of his raving rally speeches on the radio".*

They had to move to his grandparents' home at 164 Canbury Park Road. This was uncomfortably close to the Hawker factory which was also located in Canbury Park Road and was building Hurricane fighters. They stayed there for the remainder of the war.

It seemed that they had raids every day at the beginning of the war and they were continually in and out of the shelters. The Anderson shelter in Canbury Park Road had four steps down: *this was difficult for my grandma who had bad legs. I would help support her as she went down backwards into the shelter. The shelter was damp, cold and dark and very uncomfortable. In the end we gave up going down into the shelter and took our chances. Every time we heard the siren there was a sense of fear and excitement and after the relief of a distant explosion the searching question, "where had it landed?".*

After each bombing raid, Eric and his mates went in search of shrapnel. Sometimes the disfigured metal was still warm. Eric prided himself on a cracking collection until someone threw it all away. That appeared to be a common complaint amongst all the lads of the time. Who was the mystery shrapnel snatcher?

A few years later, the doodlebugs were launched at London and these spread fear and destruction before them. An air raid siren gave them warning of another V1 flying bomb that was approaching along the railway line: *We were just going down into the shelter when we heard the motor splutter. We all froze and held our breathe, mindful that it would now begin a rapid descent before creating a massive explosion. But strangely the rocket turned and glided away from us to land at the edge of the hospital where it destroyed a building. It just goes to show how unpredictable they were.*

A massive V2 rocket, that gave no warning of it's arrival, landed nearby and obliterated three houses in Deacon Road as well as damaging many others including the house of a friend of Eric's, George Draper.

A group of Italian prisoners of war were held in a building in Elm Road, where the primary school is now located. An anti-aircraft gun was located on the Elm Road Recreation ground alongside a searchlight. Eric also recalls seeing a barrage balloon anchored here.

On VE day they had a street party. The boys in the neighbourhood collected a lot of rubbish which they piled up to make a huge bonfire. Unfortunately, the fire was so intense that it burnt a hole in the road.

The House in Canbury Park Road

They had electricity and a gas cooker. In the absence of a fridge, a larder served as a cool room and their bottles of milk were placed in a bucket of water. Also, in the scullery (kitchen) was a large copper. This was filled with water that was boiled and amidst a cloud of steam the washing was done. Washing was always done on Mondays.

In front of the street door was a step painted in cardinal red paint. This step was routinely polished. *Come to think of it, my grandma was always polishing something. Similarly, my Dad's mother had a large black range in the kitchen, and this was always gleaming.*

Food

There were lots of things that we simply didn't have during the war. But we got used to it. We always had plenty of vegetables, but meat was limited. On Sundays a chap with a horse and cart came down Canbury Park Road selling shrimps and winkles. Puddings were great. A favourite was spotted dick pudding and custard. It was fantastic with a thick white outer skin, pure lard!

Bananas didn't become available until Fyffes established a warehouse beside Kingston railway station. Apples and pears were in abundance and they could collect these themselves from the numerous fruit trees in the gardens of houses beside the railway line: *We were accomplished scrumpers, equipped with poles with a long nail hammered through the end that could snag the juiciest of apples!*

A little further up the street was a small shop called Triggs which sold biscuits. But you could also buy broken biscuits and fill a bag with them. His grandma sent him off, warning him, *don't get any rubbish.*

Occasionally they had fish and chips from the local fish and chip shop in Canbury Park Road. Near to where they lived was also a General Store, a dairy, a greengrocer's and a butcher's.

Gary's fish bar in the Richmond Road was one of the best fish and chip shops around. Next door was a cake shop where they could buy a slab of bread pudding on the way home from Richmond Road School.

The Local Area

The Canbury Arms on the corner of Canbury Park Road and Elm Road.

Eric's grandad had chickens in the backyard which laid eggs. He also had a goose. It often walked with him to the Canbury Arms and waited patiently for him outside while he had a few pints, before walking back with him. Eric sadly recalls that the goose ultimately ended up on their dining table!

Eric remembers being taken into the Canbury Arms. He enjoyed a lemonade but didn't enjoy so much a hard tack biscuit that was rock hard. He remembers a blind chap who played the accordion in the pub.

Every two to three days, Grandma sent Eric along to the pub with a china jug with a cloth cover to keep the flies off. Each time she clearly reminded Eric to make sure that they did not put too big a head on the ale. After the jug had been filled and the cloth cover placed carefully on top, Eric walked cautiously back home not daring to spill a drop!

Another of his jobs was to take a bucket into the street and collect the droppings from the delivery horses.

Prince Phillip in Canbury Park Road.
Courtesy of Owen Walter

A little further along Canbury Park Road was Fred Lavender's Fruit & Veg shop (no relation). Fred was a big jolly bloke who had a cattle farm near Box Hill and also kept cattle in Bushy Park. Eric became an errand boy working on Saturday mornings from 8am to 12:30pm. One of his key jobs was to boil up beetroots, which gave off a very earthy smell. He had a bike with a large tray on the front. Fred prepacked orders and kept them in the back of a truck at the end of Canbury Park Road. Eric collected the orders from the truck and delivered them locally. Some deliveries were the other side of Kingston towards Surbiton. This was a great job especially at Christmas when he and the other delivery boy received generous tips. They pooled the tips they received and shared them equally.

Playing outside

Canbury Park Road had very few cars parked outside the houses, so the boys had the run of the street for their football matches. They also played cricket on the road using a lamp post as a wicket.

In Richmond Park they made fern camps. Ticks weren't a problem in those days. They were free to roam around the park without being disturbed. In fact, they roamed everywhere with little restriction. There was a great sense of freedom.

There was also a strong community spirit. In Canbury Park Road all the front doors were open, and everyone looked out for each other. They kept their house key under a flowerpot.

Eric and his friend George Draper often went swimming in the stretch of the river alongside Canbury Gardens. Leaving Canbury Park Road they crossed Richmond Road then cut through past the Three Fishes Pub. As soon as they arrived at Canbury Gardens, George began his Tarzan (Johnny Weissmuller) impersonation. What he lacked in physique he more than made up for with enthusiasm. As they began crossing the gardens, he progressively stripped off his clothes. Then arriving at the riverbank, unhindered by surplus clothing, he let out a great Tarzan ululating yell before launching himself into the chilly water.

Comics

Every Saturday, Eric eagerly visited the local paper shop to buy a copy of the Beano or Dandy. These were very popular. When he was a little older, he progressed to the Hotspur.

Mental Maths

Prior to the war, Eric's father had a large milk round in Tolworth and occasionally Eric accompanied him on the milk float. Halfway round they exchanged the empties with full bottles then resumed the deliveries. On the float, his father carried a thick black book with the details of all the customers and the deliveries that had been made and a final column showing what they owed. When he came to tot up, Eric watched him simply run his finger down the column adding up all the figures in his head.

Uncle Ernie

Uncle Ernie Deadman was as strong as an ox. He lived in Bonner Hill Road and kept a pig farm nearby in a massive field. Eric used to love going up there to see all the pigs. His uncle collected bins of swill from the American army camp in Bushy Park. Eric was amazed at what the Americans wasted! His uncle picked up the metal bins, full of swill, without any effort. He then chopped it all up, boiled it and then fed it to the pigs. Eric's family enjoyed the pork that came their way.

Fairfield Cattle Market Courtesy of Owen Walter

Eric's grandad managed the weighbridge at the Fairfield Market. The cattle market on the Fairfield was fascinating. There was a massive cattle shed and all sorts of livestock including sheep, cattle, pigs, chicken and geese. Eric loved to watch the auctions of all the different animals. It was great fun to visit. It was thriving, bustling and alive.

Kingston

Eric remembers coal merchants along the length of Cromwell Road. Coalmen assembled here to load the coal onto their horse-pulled carts wearing their distinctive leather smocks which fitted over their head and back. There were different grades of coal being sold and plenty of slack (dust) that made the place really grimy. Yet it was always bustling with activity.

On some days when you walked into Kingston the smell was awful. There was a tannery down by the river which stank and a foundry down a small lane that ran past the Empire theatre.

School

Eric went to Richmond Road Primary School and remained there until he was eleven. It was pretty strict and if you stepped out of line you got a clip around the ear.

The bombing proved very disruptive to their education. *We couldn't get much done when we had been awake half the night.*

On passing the 11+, Eric went to Tiffin Boys' School. When he first arrived at the school it was all very daunting. The masters all wore mortar boards. The headmaster was J.J. Harper, a former Brigadier, and he was very strict. George Spriggs, the maths teacher wore rubber soled shoes and you could not hear him creeping up behind you. He carried a heavy book which he dropped on your head if you weren't paying attention.

One day, Eric was caught entering the school not wearing his cap. He was therefore given six of the best with a slipper for being inappropriately dressed. The indignity of it all was that the punishment was given by a prefect who was only 16 or 17 years old.

The pupils sat at single desks with an ink well in the top corner. Initially, they had a nib on a wooden shaft but later on they took in their own fountain pens along with set squares and rulers.

Eric didn't much enjoy maths and Latin. Apart from these two subjects, he came to enjoy school, especially the sport. He excelled at cricket and was also quite good at rugby. Given a choice between cross country and rowing, he chose rowing because he thought it would be easier as he would be sitting down. That was a mistake!

Respect

Eric was brought up to open doors for women and stand on the outside of the pavement. As a child the rule was generally that children should be *seen but not heard*. You often saw a police officer patrolling on his bike. He chatted to you and you freely chatted back. If you were misbehaving, he simply told you off. "*I wish they were as visible now*"

Entertainment

Radio programmes were much looked forward to. In the upstairs bedroom of the house, which served as their living room, there was a whacking great Ferguson radio which was large on cabinet and small on radio. This was the main source of their news and information. They tuned in more or less every night as the amusing radio programmes helped lift morale.

On this radio they listened to ITMA starring Tommy Handley.

Recording ITMA, 1945: Conductor Charlie Shadwell (right) laughs at Tommy Handley and Dorothy Summers during the recording of an episode of It's That Man Again. ©IWM

It's That Man Again (commonly known as ITMA) was a BBC radio comedy programme which ran from 1939 to 1949 during which Tommy Handley found himself in various comical situations. The programme is remembered for a number of catchphrases.

"Don't forget the diver"– spoken by Horace Percival upon entrance and exit as a diver. This became a very popular catchphrase in Britain during the Second World War.

"After you, Claude – no, after you Cecil" – Moving men spoken by Jack Train and Horace Percival. This phrase was used by a number of RAF pilots as they queued for attack.

"Can I Do You Now, Sir?" and "TTFN (Ta ta for now)" – Spoken by Dorothy Summers' character, Mrs Mopp.

In Town Tonight was an early chat show programme broadcast on Saturday evening from 1933 to 1960. *Its theme tune was the Knightsbridge March by Eric Coates. It was introduced by an announcer crying "Stop" to interrupt the sound of busy central London, before going on to say;*

Edmundo Ros wiki

"Once more we stop the mighty roar of London's traffic and, from the great crowds, we bring you some of the interesting people who have come by land, sea and air to be In Town Tonight". At the end of the programme the voice would say "Carry on, London".

Friday Night is Music Night with Edmundo Ros

Friday Night is Music Night is the world's longest running live orchestral music radio programme. During the 1940s and 1950s, Edmundo Ros and his orchestra played Latin-pop songs, that set British feet tapping every Friday evening.

Dick Barton Special Agent, whose distinctive introductory tune, Eric clearly remembers, so many years later.

Dick Barton – Special Agent was a radio thriller serial that was broadcast in the BBC Light Programme between 7th October 1946 and 30th March 1951. The serial followed the adventures of ex-Commando Captain Richard Barton MC who, with his mates Jock Anderson and Snowy White, solved all sorts of crimes, escaped from dangerous situations, and saved the nation from disaster time and again. It was aired in fifteen-minute episodes at 6.45 pm each weekday evening.

Later in the 1950s after they had returned from national service, Eric and a group of mates often met up to tune into the Goon Show.

Hawkers

On leaving school, Eric succeeded in getting a job at the Hawker factory in Canbury Park Road. He worked here for two years until he was called up for national service.

National Service

When Eric was 18 years old, he signed on for 3 years in the RAF and was therefore considered a regular serviceman rather than a national serviceman. He did his eight weeks basic training but got the impression that his rather short drill sergeant, Sergeant Jones, disliked tall people because he called Eric some very offensive names:

Nevertheless, we were all knocked into shape and at the end of the eight weeks were as smart as ever we could be. We went in absolutely useless and came out as a unit. We were good but we had to go through the mill to get there. It was Sergeant Jones who gleefully told Eric his posting: *I am pleased to tell you Lofty. You have been posted to the Middle East.*

Accordingly, his group were shipped out to Malta but fortunately for him, Eric remained in Malta while the other chaps headed off into remote bases in the desert. Malta turned out to be a dream posting. He became a musician in the RAF Band and of an evening played in a small band. They worked in the morning and spent the afternoon on the beach, improving their swimming technique!

They were on parade for Queen Elizabeth when she visited Malta. They also put on a big show for Haile Selassie, the Emperor of Ethiopia:

There were 120 of us in a massed band led by the Royal Marines. I was a drummer in the front rank and despite the nerves it was a fantastic experience, that I will never forget. Whenever I see Trooping the Colour or any other military pageant, it takes me back.

I also played cricket for the Middle East Command team. There we were in the Middle East playing at the Officers club with its well-tended grass pitch.

Queen Elizabeth Inspects the Armed Forces in Malta in 1954 Pathé news

Although a golden rule in the forces was never to volunteer, Eric willingly volunteered to make up the crew on Lancasters that were used on search and rescue from their base in Malta. The big planes took off from the landing strip, made a circuit of the island then touched down briefly on the landing strip before taking off again to do another circuit.

Back to Hawkers

After my dream military service in Malta, returning to a working routine of 8am to 6pm at Hawkers in Canbury Park Road nearly killed me.

Golf and the Sudbrook

In the 60's Eric became a member of Richmond Golf Club in Sudbrook Park, Petersham. He remembers the stream (the Sudbrook) running through it and the pond. It was here, over the pond, that he got a hole in one.

No better way to finish!

Richmond Golf Course - Courtesy of Richmond Golf Club

Making the Best of It – The Clements Family

All Saints Church, Kingston

Christmas Day in 1898 saw an additional celebration for the Clements family, the marriage of Edward George Clements, a coal merchant by profession, to Louisa Woodhaus at All Saints Church in the Market Place of Kingston Upon Thames. Their son, Harry Clements was born in 1912. From the very start, he had to compete for space, attention and food with four brothers and two sisters in a small two up, two down Victorian cottage in Norbiton.

Having made it through childhood, Harry married Kathleen Dawes at St Paul's Church in Queen's Road on Monday 22nd April 1935. Harry was at the time working as a groundsman at the Coombe Hill Golf Club. Kathleen's father was also a groundsman at the Golf Club.

St Paul's Church, Queen's Road

Shortly after war was declared, Harry and two of his brothers, George & Albert, made their way to the Kingston recruiting office of the East Surrey Regiment. After his basic training, Harry managed to secure a reasonably comfortable posting in the catering corps, or so he thought.

Harry went away for the duration of the war, leaving behind Kathleen and their daughter Yvonne, aged four, in a flat in Park Road. Not long after the blitz began, a bomb seriously damaged their flat and they had to move out. They were to endure much bombing through the course of the war. Yvonne remembers standing on the balcony of their flat in Florence Road as darkness fell, and seeing a red glow over London. London was well and truly burning. She remembers the large barrage balloons that were positioned above Hawkers and Kingston gas works and powerful spotlights sweeping the sky in search of enemy bombers.

Bomb damage typical of that found throughout Kingston and New Malden

It was already dark when Yvonne and her mum heard the wail of air raid sirens outside their flat on the evening of Boxing Day in 1942. It had already been quite an exciting evening as Yvonne's Auntie Tilly had just given birth to her cousin, David, in the same room. On hearing the sirens, they had quickly wrapped the baby in a blanket and placed him inside a drawer before tucking him under the bed. Yvonne recalls that she was sitting on a table at the time when the bomb exploded outside their cottage. The force of the blast shattered all of their windows and threw Yvonne, like a rag doll, across the room. She was quite shocked but was luckily unscathed, though a little dusty. Fortunately, along with Auntie Tilly and the baby, her mum was also unharmed and able to comfort and reassure her.

Despite the devastation caused by the bombing and having been bombed out of two homes, Yvonne was never consumed with any lingering fear. She was simply comfortable in the knowledge that her mum and her family were always around, and they would somehow sort it all out. Even when her mum was working at the Hawker factory in Canbury Park Road, there was always someone to look after Yvonne. All the neighbours knew each other and there were plenty of aunts and uncles around. There was never a locked door in any of the houses.

Yvonne attended St Paul's School in Borough Road, a nice little school with a village feel about it. She remembers that a number of the Barnardo's Boys (orphans) who were living in a big house opposite the hospital in Galsworthy Road, also attended St Paul's. By all accounts, they were very well looked after and were dressed with better clothes than the majority of the urchins who lived in the area and who depended on hand-me-down clothes: *Mind you my mum was a dab hand with a needle and could rejuvenate clothing that she picked up at local jumble sales.*

St Paul's School in Borough Road

After D Day, Harry's unit was supporting the front-line troops as they advanced through northern France. Being so close to the front they came within range of the German artillery that never seemed to cease pounding their lines. Just outside Caen, a shell landed amidst their position but failed to explode. Within minutes another shell exploded among them and killed most of the men in the unit. Harry was very seriously wounded and would not have lived if it had not been for the skill of a battlefield surgeon. Having suffered severe injury to his rib cage and chest, he was brought back to England on a hospital ship. He was fortunate that he missed the first allocated ship, as it was sunk.

VE Street Party in Richmond Park Road. Families also came from Shortlands Road, Cross Road and Elm Road. Yvonne is bottom front looking back at the camera

Harry and his family were very pragmatic about his recovery. There was no time for sympathy. "*You silly sod, get on with it*" reflected this attitude. Nevertheless, during his convalescence, Harry was greatly supported by both his family and the British Legion.

After the war, work was scarce and Harry with his disability was considered unemployable. He therefore had to make his own arrangements. Fortunately, the people of Norbiton and Kingston Market were a tight knit community and helped each other out. Lacking sufficient means to buy his own horse and cart, Harry rented a barrow to sell fruit and veg in the Apple Market in Kingston. He purchased produce that was slightly on the turn from the stall holders and sold it to people who were grateful for fruit and veg at a lower price. In this way, a gap in the market was filled and no produce was wasted. Yvonne recalls that her dad worked for long hours in all weathers, to house, feed and clothe his family.

Harry Junior was born in 1946 at their home in Portchester Road in Norbiton, near the hospital. Soon after, the family moved into a prefab home in Lower Park Road. It was a delightful bungalow with a small front garden and a large back garden. It was warm in winter, well ventilated in summer and actually had a bathroom with a separate indoor toilet. This was luxury indeed! No need to take the tin bath down from the nail in the wall.

Though only five years old, Harry clearly recalls a Hurricane flying over the prefab in Park Road. The canopy was pulled back and the plane was so low that Harry could clearly make out the pilot looking down in his direction. Was that a wave from the pilot?

Unfortunately, they did not stay there for long (because of subsidence) and moved first to Manorgate Road then back to Harry's grandparent's house in Cross Road though they were evicted from there by the landlord. However, with the assistance of the British Legion, who did a lot of good work helping war veterans, they managed to raise enough money to pay the deposit for a house at 64 Shortlands Road.

Aerial photo showing the rear of St Luke's School and the rear boundary wall that would have marked the route of the culverted Latchmere Brook. © Historic England

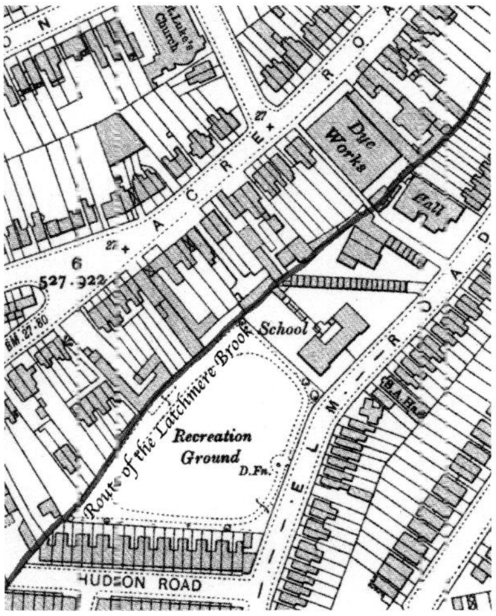

1934 map showing the course of the culverted Latchmere Brook defining the north boundary of St Luke's School. NLS

At the age of 11 in 1947 Yvonne went to St Luke's Secondary Modern School in Elm Road. The girls were schooled on the first floor and the boys on the ground floor. Their playgrounds at the back of the school were separated by a high fence.

The first school that Harry went to was Latchmere. He was in one of the huts on the west side of the school next to the road. He remembers long afternoons, looking out of the open door across the road to the recreation ground, willing the time to pass until he could go home.

When his family moved to Manorgate Road, Harry transferred to St Paul's Primary School in Borough Road.

When Harry was about 5-6 years old, Lenny Hitchcock their next-door neighbour, built him a small barrow, which he called a *Barney Barra*. From that moment on Harry didn't go anywhere without his barrow, especially as he could help his mum by carrying the shopping on the barrow. Collins, the local Rag & Bone family, had a yard on the south side of the Wych Elm pub in Elm Road and they paid for old clothing and newspapers, measured by weight. Harry collected newspapers from the neighbouring streets on his barrow and earned a few coppers from Collins.

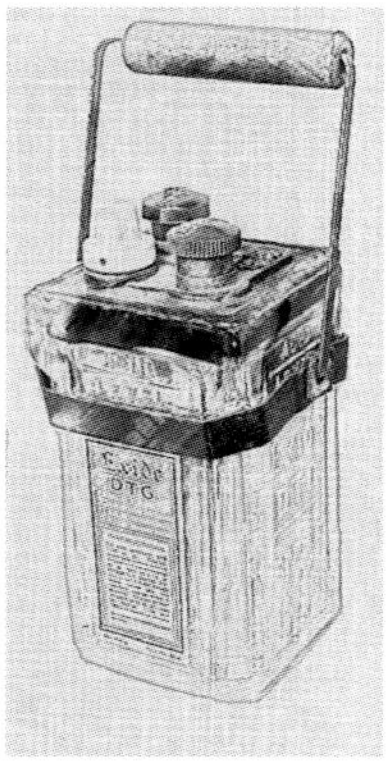

Accumulators that needed charging for the wireless sets.

At this time all wireless sets, which were an essential source of family entertainment, contained a two volt accumulator to heat up the valves. They also contained acid and had to be carried carefully. Harry earned some extra cash by collecting the accumulators of elderly neighbours on his barrow and taking them to KT Magnetos in Elm Road for recharging. For a kid wishing to earn a few bob, a good *barra* was indispensable!

At the age of eleven, Harry went to St Luke's Secondary School in Elm Road that continued to keep boys and girls separated, with the boys still grounded on the bottom floor. It wasn't a large school and had only one class for each of the four years. The school was located next to a large recreation ground. It was big enough to accommodate two football pitches, and the school football team used to train and play matches here against other local schools.

Mr Whitehouse was the headmaster and he maintained his air of authority with a handy cane. Nevertheless, the school provided a positive and sporting environment for the boys. Harry played in the football team and the cricket team. He remembers the heavy leather footballs which became really dense once they were wet. Many a time he couldn't lift the ball sufficiently when taking a corner kick and the boys headed the ball at their peril. As a member of the school swimming team, Harry went swimming once a week at the Number Two pool at the Coronation Baths. They often competed against other schools in the Number One pool where the 50-yard lanes were separated by cork floats on a rope.

Mr Gadd, the P.E. Teacher from Australia, although quite young, was very fit and wouldn't stand any mucking around. Harry remembers the enthusiastic tennis matches between Mr Gadd and Mr Phillips, the English teacher, and the solid whack of the ball which clearly indicated the commitment of the two players. Mr Fizzy was the French teacher, a veteran from the 1st World War with a little moustache and an injured leg. He was always smartly dressed. Mr Berg taught science and Mr Abbot, the music teacher, suffered from a curvature of the spine. Mrs Farrington was the only female teacher and she taught maths. Harry recalls that she was very fair and approachable and made a nice change from the sterner male teachers.

At the back of the school was an open square that had two large green posts which appeared to support the rear of the building. If you misbehaved or weren't paying attention you were sent out to stand beside one of the green posts. There you stood in trepidation, hoping that the headmaster didn't see you. If he did, you had to relate your misdemeanour then wait while he decided upon your punishment. This could range from picking up litter, writing lines or getting two strokes of the cane on your hand. Caning took place routinely in the headmaster's office. *Bergy also had a cane in his classroom that he would exercise whenever he saw fit. Fred Fizzy had a proper cane with a handle. It was a real whippy thing that brought tears to your eyes.* Mr Whitehouse also carried out regular bicycle inspections to ban those which weren't road safe. Invariably, many of the bikes had been constructed with parts found at a local dump.

In Harry's final year, Mr Whitehouse took a group of them aside to give them extra tuition to prepare for their City & Guilds examinations. He hoped that it would give them something extra and a better start in life. He wasn't a bad chap after all!

St Luke's Secondary Modern School in Elm Road

1924 aerial view showing St Luke's School on Elm Road with St Luke's Church behind. Many of the children in the area checked the clock below the spire to make sure that they got home in time for tea! ©Historic England

1960/61 St Luke's School Football team. Harry Clements (Junior) back row far left. Half of the boys in the team were orphans who lived at the Dr Barnardo's home in Galsworthy Road, opposite the hospital

A solitary remnant of St Luke's School that can be seen today in Elm Road. GE

There was a lot to do as a kid in this area. When not at school you could play cricket or roller skate along the car free streets or explore Richmond Park from dawn to dusk.

A great favourite on warmer days, when aged 11 to 12 years, was to go swimming in the Thames from Canbury Gardens. They hastily changed in the bushes before launching into the Thames near the coffee shop (where Boaters in now located). They then swam out to a nearby island and from there swam across the Thames to a boat house on the Teddington shore. Having paused to regain their breath they swam back, sometimes against the pull of a forceful downstream current. This definitely improved their stamina!

Harry remembers his mum, Kathleen, taking him and his younger sister Angela, rowing on the Thames in a skiff that they hired from Turk's boathouse on Lower Ham Road. What his mum lacked in technique, she made up for in enthusiasm. Yet, she never did quite get the hang of it. On their way back, against the current, she managed to crash the boat through a number of fishing lines, much to the vocal displeasure of the fishermen.

The water outlet that discharged warm water from Kingston Power Station into the river provided a popular place to catch bleak as well as the larger perch that used to prey on the bleak.

Harry's first rod was a simple affair, bought at Woolworths in Kingston. It was made from a piece of doweling with curtain hanger type fittings screwed in to make eyes for the line. Instead of buying hooks and line, Harry trawled a magnet along the tow path to pick up any metal hooks that had been lost by fishermen. Hopefully a decent length of line would still be attached to the hooks. Harry then tied all the separate pieces of line together to make his own fishing line. His mum helped out by making a paste from old bread that would harden around the hook. If there was any spare, a piece of cheese was attractive to roach.

Harry recalls that on many evenings, a regular group of old boys came down on the train from Balham to fish for eels in the river. They bought bleak for a couple of pennies from the boys. Then making themselves comfortable by the river's edge they fished through the night, casting far into the middle of the river, using the bleak as bait to catch eels. These were then taken back on the train to Balham for the next night's dinner.

1948 Aerial view of Kingston Power Station to the north of the railway bridge © Historic England

While fishing, the boys could watch the tugs shepherding the coal barges up the river to the power station. Normally there would be four or five barges connected together in a line but on occasions Harry watched them two abreast with the tugs working really hard, keeping them moving upstream against the current. Once moored to the river bank alongside the power station, a huge very noisy conveyor belt connected to a five storey tower by the river, lifted the coal and coke high over Canbury Gardens and dumped it into the yard of the power station, forming a multitude of black pyramids, the tips of which could be seen over the high wall.

The barges, which had been fully laden with their gunnels barely above the river, once liberated from their cargo, rose some five to six feet above the water. This then made a very tempting jumping platform for Harry and his mates to launch themselves into the river. However, before they caused themselves a mischief, Harry was warned off by his uncle who worked at the power station. **Danger - Deep Water - Strong Currents.**

The Fyffes banana warehouse was located down the side of Kingston railway station in Ceres Road. The bananas were imported in long boxes from the Caribbean and other exotic locations. His Uncle, Bill, lived in a flat that overlooked the warehouse and often as Harry left, his uncle would warn him to watch out for the spiders. Apparently, it was quite common for large spiders to be found still alive in the boxes among the bananas. That caused quite a stir among the workers.

A 1948 aerial photograph showing the Railway line west of Kingston Station. The original Latchmere Brook ran along the northern edge of this railway line to the Thames. The Fyffes warehouse is in the middle of the picture. © Historic England

Princes was a wet fish shop in Elm Road. Popular fish at the time were cod, skate, haddock and rock salmon. Rock salmon was a fancy name for the poor man's cod which was actually dogfish. It had a soft spine that the children used to enjoy gnawing on.

Bentalls was not somewhere where Harry and his family would normally shop but it was nice to walk through to see how the other half lived.

There was always a big procession at Christmas from outside Hawkers along Richmond Road to Bentalls. The route was lined with children and their parents, who amidst much excitement and celebration, watched the slow procession of colourfully decorated floats with Christmas and winter scenes and a float with Father Christmas and his helper, Jimmy Jingles with bells on his hat and his shoes.

You could go and meet Father Christmas for a shilling at Bentalls. Outside, the brightly lit Christmas themed window displays were a feast for the eyes. Every year, Father Christmas was settled in a different landscape within the large store. One year they had a space theme with one of the lifts disguised as a rocket. With the upward motion, the children genuinely felt that they were flying into space.

On every other Saturday afternoon from September to May, you could hear roars from the Kingstonian Football Ground, as the K's closed in on goal. "Come on you K's" shortly followed by "bloody rubbish K's". Kids could get in after half time for nothing. The ground had a covered stand on the south side and was open to the elements on the other three sides with the vast expanse of the well-tended grass pitch in the middle. Kitted out in red and white scarves and bobble hats, many of the old regulars added to the shouts and roars with their wooden football rattles. It was a good place to broaden your knowledge of the English language. Furthermore, someone really should get that referee a decent pair of spectacles!

The Kingstonian's football ground in Richmond Road. The Shell garage is still there. © G. Wilkes

K's fans celebrate a 3-1 win against Wimbledon on 8th February 1964. The fans are on the steep bank separating the first team pitch and the reserves pitch. When things weren't going well on the first pitch the fans could watch the reserve team instead. Courtesy of Philip Windeatt. Phil is the young boy far left on top of the hill, with arms outstretched.

With Harry senior selling fruit and veg, there was always plenty of fruit in the house. In fact, young Harry got fed up with it and gave much of it to his mates at school. At the time they ate a lot of meat. His mum bought her meat from Colman's the butchers in Park Road. On occasions with a sizeable order of chops, the butcher threw in a few kidneys and some sausages.

Quite often on Sunday evening, Harry enjoyed a seafood tea. There was a chap on a tricycle who toured the local streets selling brown shrimps, whelks and winkles and with a slice of bread and butter they were delicious. It was also a lot of fun picking the winkles out of their shells with a pin.

Rationing throughout the war, and for quite sometime after, ensured that the population had a reasonable amount of food and a relatively balanced diet. This combined with a lot of exercise taken in the great outdoors kept many youngsters very fit. Yet, for fear that they were under-nourished they were also given dried milk, orange juice and cod liver oil.

Harry didn't enjoy the spoonful of cod liver oil. To try and get rid of the taste and the grimace on his face, he was then given diluted orange juice or rosehip syrup. However, he really enjoyed the large spoonful of Virol, a brown, sweet and very sticky malt extract (a by-product of the brewing industry) that was provided by the clinic and packed full of nutrients and vitamins A, B and D.

Having made a reasonable recovery, Harry Snr continued to work in the Apple Market to earn a few extra pounds to supplement his disability pension. He dreamed that one day young Harry would own a truck which would enable them to drive to the London markets to buy their fruit and vegetables and thereby make a decent return on them rather than having to buy their produce from the stalls in Kingston. It never happened Harry, supported by his mum, had other plans and he was prepared to graft hard to achieve them.

On leaving school at the age of 15, with his City & Guilds qualifications, Harry got a job at an engineering workshop near Leatherhead. Every day, he cycled to work and back from his home in Shortlands Road. On one night a week, after a quickly eaten dinner, he then cycled through Richmond Park to attend evening classes at Richmond Technical College.

As soon as he was old enough, Harry purchased a motor bike. He and his mates parked their bikes outside coffee bars in Kingston and Richmond. Once inside they listened to the music on the juke box and generally chewed the fat. They had a favourite coffee bar at Box Hill. Using this as a base, they took turns burning up and down the A24, giving the bikes a bit of welly.

Harry senior (right) with his drinking mate, Albert Fry in the Canbury Arms in the late 1940s. Note the shove ha'penny board behind.

One early morning in May 1976, Harry senior set off to walk to the Apple Market, as usual. He collapsed by the railings of the recreation ground in Elm Road. He died that evening, shortly after tea. He was 64 years old. Yet he had considered himself fortunate to have survived the terrible injuries that he had incurred during the war.

Yvonne reflects that her dad had been a grafter to the end, a man who had knuckled down, got on with life and endeavoured, with the loyal support of his wife, Kathleen, to simply make the best of the circumstances that they found themselves in. He had also lived and died, a proud Kingstonian.

Yvonne recalls that it wasn't just a life of grey skies and hard graft:

"There was a pint with the Mr & Mrs on a Friday night down the Canbury Arms, or the Willoughby Arms, the Wych Elm or the Richmond Park where I was introduced by my grandparents to Guinness and

milk and a horrible ship's biscuit. If the gee gee's or your greyhound had left the trap and romped home, then it was drinks on both Friday and Saturday nights. There would be laughter and a sing song in the pub and through the streets on the way back. Sometimes we would stop off for fish and chips, wrapped in newspaper and hungrily consumed, using our fingers".

Kathleen (front row second from right) with her friends

"Friends, family and neighbours stopped by for a cuppa,

full of gossip and advice (asked for or not)"

"So you see,

we made the most of what we had.

We shared the best,

fought the rest

but were never alone"

Sources
Family history carefully researched by Mike Shaw

Picture Credits
All photos courtesy of the Clements family unless otherwise indicated
NLS: Reproduced with the permission of the National Library of Scotland
GE © Gordon Elsden

The Barnardo Boys of Kingston

Both Yvonne and Harry mention the Barnardo boys who attended both St Paul's Primary School in Borough Road and St Luke's Secondary Modern School in Elm Road. They were living in a home in Galsworthy Road, opposite Kingston Hospital.

One of these boys, by the name of Leslie Thomas, had lost his father when the ship that he was serving on was torpedoed in the South Atlantic. Some months later, in 1943, his mother became ill with cancer and soon died. Leslie was separated from his younger brother and sent to the Dr Barnardo's home in Kingston, which the boys called Dickies. In his book "This Time Next Week: The Autobiography of a Happy Orphan" (1964) Leslie takes up the story: *A small, pointed wind blew the rain into my face. It was March and I had been 13 just a few days before. I shuffled along beside the man who had brought me, and when he turned in at the gate of the Dr Barnardo's home in Kingston upon Thames, I followed.*

Then I stopped. It may have been only for seconds, because the man was walking on, but I know I stopped and looked up at the vast building. A quick loneliness came over me, like a pain. No boy has ever felt so much by himself as I did in that moment.

Strange as it seems, in those first weeks at Dickies, there came on me a sort of settled happiness.

After that first pang of apprehension, I never again felt afraid, nor continuously unhappy. There grew from this ugly old place, with its dripping rooms, hollow dormitories and riotous boys, a sense of warmth, of familiarity, of fun; of fellowship that was strong and real.

Dickies' boys were a rollicking, war-like tribe, united by their bond and the constant adventure of keeping one move ahead of the Gaffer, as Mr Gardner, the home's superintendent was known.

Dr Barnardo's home for orphan boys at the Dalziel of Wooler House on Galsworthy Road
© Peter Higginbotham

He was not a man you could love, the Gaffer, but he was a good man in his narrow way. He was growling and grey, thin, and with a slight stoop. If the stoop was slight, his cynicism was large. He was entitled to it. Forty of his 60-odd years he had occupied with boys, and he had an all-embracing distrust of anything in short trousers.

Even when you are only a boy, for an unexpected moment you can get mixed up with history. One spring afternoon I saw a car, as jet and as smooth and shiny as a rounded beetle, stopped at the kerb near Dickies, a crowd of boys bunched at its side, chewing industriously, talking and laughing.

In front of the car were three motorcyclists, armed with revolvers, which they showed the eager boys.

There were two men in the rear seat, one in Air Force uniform, the other in khaki with fingers of medal ribbons over his pocket. His hair was sparse and when he grinned his mouth was like a banana.

I had seen him in the newspapers — he was a general called Eisenhower. He was saying: 'OK, this is the last pack. Who wants it?' I had poked my head down to look into the window. He said: 'Here, son, you have the last one.' He gave me a packet of chewing gum and I thanked him. Then the car slid away.

That evening the Gaffer caught me with the gum. 'I've told you boys time and again,' he snorted, 'that I won't have you talking to men — and especially American soldiers'.

One night not long after that, I heard the slow grind of an aeroplane, or what I thought was one, overhead. Abruptly the voice of the plane stopped. There were ten seconds or more of drifting silence. Then far away, but clear, came an explosion. Flashes like wings of big white birds flew across the dormitory. Guns began to bite into the dark outside and the air-raid siren sounded.

We clattered downstairs out into the crashing night and down the hole into the air-raid shelter.

That was the first night of the flying bombs. Every day they fell. We lived like moles, rushing out from our shelters to grab meals while we could. One evening in chapel, we were nearly obliterated by yet another missile skimming the roof and crunching somewhere much too close.

When we had picked ourselves up, the Gaffer ordered us to run for the shelters. As we passed the food store, Breadcrumb grabbed my arm.

'Blimey,' he said. 'Look. They've gorn and forgotten the door.' The food store was gaping. We flung ourselves through the opening.

We were in an Aladdin's cave of prunes, figs, eggs, sausages, condensed milk, sugar, butter and Lyons' fruit pies. We loaded our pockets and our jerseys with good things, then fled into the shelter just as another bomb shattered the air.

The bombs flew every day and night. The Gaffer, ancient and brave, used to come tearing through the shrapnel and the hideous noises, fall down the entrance to the shelter and make sure we were all accounted for.

Then out he would go into the danger and run on his elderly legs to another shelter. He was a hard-old bastard, but he would have perished willingly rather than have had any harm come to the roughest, rowdiest young criminal of the 150 boys in his care.

Leslie Thomas went on to become an accomplished writer with a number of best-selling novels including "The Virgin Soldiers" published in 1966.

Leslie Thomas playing with the Barnardo's football team, pictured with the ball

Picture Credits

Dalziel of Wooler House - www.childrenshomes.org.uk

Bevans – The Butchers in Richmond Road, Kingston

1810: It is unlikely that Reuben Bond, a victualler supplying food and provisions to the ships that docked at the Thames port of Gravesend, would ever have considered that several generations later, his descendants, the Bevan family, would still be supplying provisions (mainly meat) to the residents of another Thames-side town, Kingston.

When he finally passed away in 1826, at the age of 60, Reuben was buried in St George's church in Gravesend, the same church that holds the grave of Pocahontas (1595–1617), the daughter of a Native American Chieftain, who was to become the first American to visit England.

His son, Reuben William Bond (1792- 1861) became a butcher and lived with his family in Milton, Gravesend. Reuben's son, Richard, (1820-1895) continued the profession of butchery and on 7th April 1861 he is recorded as having a shop and home at 20 East Terrace in Milton, Gravesend, accompanied by his wife, Harriet and three children including a daughter Clara, aged 4. Clara would continue the family butchery trade and maintain the shop at East Terrace to the end of the century, despite marrying Alfred Bevan, the son of a wealthy foundry owner. It was Clara who passed the butchery knowledge and skills of her family onto her son Reginald (Alfred) Bevan (1885-1937). Reginald left the Thames Port of Gravesend and established a number of butchers' shops in the South East of England.

The shop opened by Reginald in 1929 at 136 Richmond Road

In 1929, Reginald rented a butcher's shop at 136 Richmond Road in Kingston upon Thames. Here he remained until his death in 1937. At this time, meat was plentiful, and people consumed a lot of it. Lamb from New Zealand and beef from cattle raised on the vast pampas plains of Argentina were especially popular with the British people.

On his father's death, Ronald Alfred Bevan, 28 years old, took over the running of the shop. Some two years later, Ron was called up to serve in the Royal Navy. His wife Beatrice, supported by Mr Edwards the manager of the shop, Mr Fred Poulton the Shopman and Miss Page, the bookkeeper, continued the day to day running of the shop. Fred kept a monkey at his home and, many years later, this provided much entertainment to Ron's son, Peter, when he went round to see him.

HMS Quorn in 1940 (IWM)

Ronald Bevan, Chief Petty Officer

HMS Quorn was a Type 1 Hunt-class destroyer commissioned on the 21st September 1940. Part of the 21st Destroyer Flotilla at Harwich she was tasked with convoy protection, anti-shipping and patrol duties. Quorn would stay with this flotilla for the whole of her commission. In April 1941 Quorn was superficially damaged by two delay-action bombs that exploded 20 metres (66 ft) from her port quarter. In April 1942 Quorn hit a mine that blew a 9 by 15 feet (2.7 m × 4.6 m) hole in the port side of the ship. She was towed to Sheerness where repairs took 4 months to complete. On 13th October 1942 Quorn was one of the five destroyers that intercepted the German auxiliary cruiser Komet in the English Channel. Komet was sunk and two M-class minesweepers were heavily damaged and set on fire.

Ron was subsequently posted to the destroyer HMS Quorn where he served as a Chief Petty Officer, working as the Naafi manager. Mr Coughtrey, the owner of Tudor Stores, on Tudor Drive was at the time also serving on HMS Quorn with Ron. They survived many "*Battle Stations*" and became close friends after the war.

Ron's eldest son Roy (Alfred) was born in January 1943 while Ron was still serving on HMS Quorn. Roy's younger brother Peter was born three years later in 1946 and his sister Peggy several years after. During the war, Roy and his mum (Beatrice) were living over the shop in Richmond Road.

In June 1944 Ron transferred ashore to become a Naafi area manager. On 3rd August, HMS Quorn, while serving as an escort for convoys as part of Operation Overlord (the Normandy Landings), was hit and sunk by a human torpedo. Those that survived the initial attack spent up to eight hours in the water before being rescued, and many of these perished. Four officers and 126 ratings were lost, many of whom had been companions of Ron.

Returning to Civilian Life

Ron was fortunate to be discharged as soon as the war ended in 1945. At this time, there were five to six butchers between their shop and Kingston railway station. Yet in 1948, despite this competition, Bevans was selected to be the official butcher to the XIVth Olympic Games that took place in London. Many of the athletes were provided with accommodation in the former army camps located within Richmond Park.

In the early 1950s, Ron and Beatrice and their two boys moved into a house in Garth Close backing onto the Borstal. Occasionally they would see the lads climbing over the fence, endeavouring to escape.

Ron worked hard and also became the president of the local branch of the London Meat Traders Association which held meetings in the Kingston Hotel opposite the Kinema Cinema.

When Roy was a little older, the family moved to a bigger house on Richmond Road near the entrance to Latchmere Road so that Ron could walk to the shop. Roy and Peter attended Arundel House School in Surbiton, (the former Boys' Prep School) before Roy transferred to Ewell Castle School.

Memories of the local area

Pavey's Dairy, essentially a bottling plant, was located in Richmond Road opposite the Shell Petrol station (and now occupied by the physiotherapist). The full bottles were loaded in crates onto a horse drawn cart. The horse strained to pull the heavily laden cart up the ramp that ran alongside the dairy. Whenever the boys saw the milkman, they would shout out "*Hello Nobby*" and get a cheery reply. Peter recalls that his mum would send him out to collect any horse droppings to fertilise their garden.

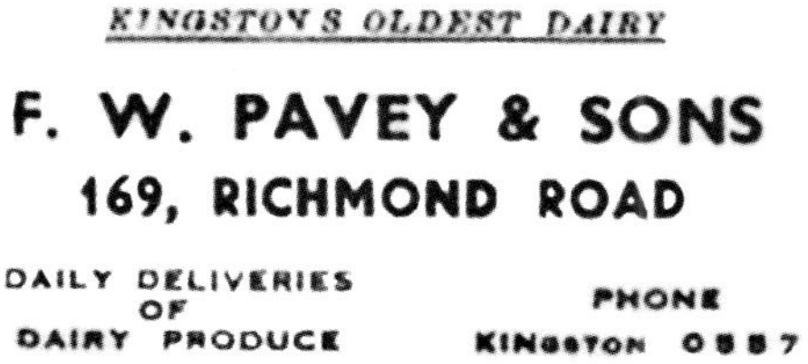

The Power Station by the river produced a lot of soot. All the housewives needed to check the direction of the wind before putting their washing out. Roy was present when King George VI and Queen Elizabeth opened the Power Station in 1948.

The opening of Kingston Power Station by King George VI and Queen Elizabeth in 1948.
Pathé News

Learning the Trade

Both Roy and Peter began helping out at the shop when they became teenagers, plucking turkeys before Christmas and helping to clean the shop at the close of business on Saturdays. Roy recalls pulling the wooden work blocks onto the pavement and scrubbing them down with hot soda water. The shop had six boys delivering meat on their bicycles in the local area, as far north as Richmond. Occasionally Roy and Peter also helped out making deliveries. Peter remembers piling the front tray, high with orders, to be delivered around the local streets. At some of the bigger houses that they supplied, he was firmly requested to go round the back to the tradesman's entrance.

At this time, many people spent up to a third of their income on food and meat was an important part of the diet. A joint of meat would last a number of days. A roast on Sunday, a cold cut on Monday and perhaps a mince dish on Tuesday. The supermarkets were not yet well established and business for independent butchers was good.

Meat remained on rationing until 1954. Because food was rationed everyone had the correct amount of food for a reasonably healthy lifestyle. Strangely enough, offal was not available to the general public during the period of rationing. Roy recalls the brass plate that they had on the wall outside the shop which simply stated "Sorry, no offal".

People at the time bought what they needed to eat in the next few days. There were no freezers and so food was consumed as it was bought and most of it was eaten.

On leaving school at the age of fifteen, Roy had wanted to join the Merchant Navy, employed as a butcher. Yet there was a business to run and Roy and his brother Peter were expected to continue running the shop in Richmond Road.

After three years working in the shop, Roy went to Smithfield College, located next to the Meat Market where he studied for two years. Just opposite the entrance to St Barts Church, near the meat market, he discovered a disused underground station, that had previously been used to bring meat into Smithfield Market.

Underneath Smithfield meat market there is a tunnel with disused railway tracks still in place. You can still see the original "holes in the roof", of the tunnel that allowed meat to be hoisted up from the railway wagons straight into the market. The tunnel complex was featured in the Bond film, Skyfall.

Roy really enjoyed his two years at the Smithfield Meat College and as well as qualifying as a master butcher, was well prepared for a career in the trade. After College he spent nearly three years working for the Fatstock Marketing Corporation (FMC) with a variety of jobs including the grading of animals from the various farms and preparing joints of meat for M&S. He was at the time earning £8 a week. However, an offer of £14 a week to work in his father's shop in Richmond Road could not be turned down. Yet, this was to prove the end of his free weekends with a weekly routine governed by the trade.

Peter left home at the age of 15 and went to work for a livestock supplier in Petersfield, Hampshire. Living in digs, these were three fabulous years where he learnt a lot about the trade. He really enjoyed working with livestock and his wish was to become a qualified livestock buyer. Unfortunately, it didn't work out as planned and he returned to work in one of the meat wholesalers in Kingston. He was later invited to work in the family shop with his father and brother.

In 1963, Ron joined a delegation of twenty butchers, representing the meat industry in England, on a tour of livestock farms and abattoirs in South America.

The shop in the 1960's

Working in the shop in the 1960s

Looking back at their time in the shop both Roy and Peter recall that it got very cold during the winter because the door was always open. With the cold breeze whipping in, Roy often ended up with chilblains on his feet. The front window, on occasions, was frozen from the inside and Peter had to jump up to scrape the frost off. The only salvation was an enamel mug of hot tea.

One of their staff, Miss Miller set a very high standard in the shop. She used to keep the place spotless. On Monday morning she arrived on her bicycle, wearing a brown coat. She then got down on her hands and knees and with a bucket of hot water and soda beside her, proceeded to scrub the entire floor. This completed, she then meticulously polished all of the woodwork and the brass weights and handles throughout the shop. For the remainder of the week, Miss Miller wore her white coat and in this kept a close eye on all of the accounts and any customers who were outstanding. Nevertheless, if a customer came in with a late order requiring a delivery that same day, she would go out of her way to make the delivery on her way home on her bike. Peter recalls that she was a very efficient and committed woman who worked with them for more than thirty years until she retired.

Peter enjoyed travelling with his father to Smithfield Market, once a week, to buy poultry and game that included rabbit, hare, pigeon, partridge and venison. Occasionally they had the opportunity to buy venison that had come from Richmond Park.

They bought the majority of their meat from well-established meat wholesalers in Kingston. There were at least ten in the area of Kingston each with their own area of specialisation. At midnight lorries loaded with carcasses of meat would arrive at the wholesalers and by midday it had been sold.

Roy normally visited the wholesalers between 6 and 7 in the morning to purchase Argentinian beef and New Zealand lamb and pork. Before joining the EEC in 1973, Britain imported vast amounts of meat from Argentina and NZ and the Pool of London was chocka-block with merchant ships. Membership of the EU resulted in all imports of meat from Argentina and NZ being loaded with high tariffs and this put a stop to it all. Pork was supplied locally because there were so many pig farms in the area.

Ron, Roy and Peter in the 70's

On returning to the shop with his purchases, Roy and the other butchers then broke down the carcasses into various retail cuts, with the intention of selling them all by Saturday evening. This was on occasions back breaking work. Sides of beef that were carried by two men could weigh more than 300lbs. A quarter of beef, weighing around 150lbs, was carried by one man, slung over his back.

Peter remembers that every Christmas they worked especially hard. In December, they collected the turkeys in their Morris Minor delivery van. The van was full to the gunnels with little room for Peter to sit on the passenger seat. They always had a first-rate window display with turkey and game and illuminated lights. Out front, they had another display of turkeys which had to be put out every morning and brought back in at the end of the day. Peter's fingers got so sore plucking turkeys. To meet all the orders, they occasionally worked through the night, so as not to let their customers down.

Butchers in the past had their own jargon, which was simply words used back to front, that wouldn't be picked up by the customers.

gel	***leg***	***dlo***	***old***
yenom	***money***	***off to the knab***	***Bank***
knab	***bank***	***Pick up the enoph***	***Phone***
xis dna owt	***two and six***	***Kool ta taht lrig***	***Look at that girl***

Working all hours in the shop, Peter could measure time by the flow of Hawker staff that made their way along Richmond Road, past the shop, early in the morning and then back the opposite way of an evening. They also always knew when the K's were playing at home by the steady trickle of supporters, clad in red and white, making their way to the ground and the mass horde who left it at the end of the game.

When Ron died in 1986, the business passed to his sons Roy and Peter. They worked hard to differentiate the quality of their meat from other butchers and supermarkets. Roy attended a number of butchery schools in Europe to better understand how Dutch, Swiss and German butchers prepared their meat to provide more exciting and innovative cuts along with the skilful preparation of appetising marinades. Against the trend, they established the basis of a successful, expanding business.

Leander Sea Scouts

Roy and Peter were both enthusiastic members of the Leander Sea Scouts at their base by the river on Lower Ham Road.

At the age of twelve Roy applied to join but had to pass a simple test. He was rowed across to the other side of the Thames from Leander. Fully clothed he then had to jump in and make his way back across the river to the scout HQ. No buoyancy aid, no safety line. However, he got across and so began a wonderful adventure with Leander, as did Peter a few years later.

The original Leander Scouts HQ by the River (on right of the photo with mast out front). © Historic England

Roy enthusiastically attended meetings on Tuesday evenings and Saturdays. At these meetings it was the responsibility of an appointed patrol, in rotation, to cook for the entire unit. The patrol leader would decide on the meal and they would go off and buy the food and cook it.

Peter remembers the troop forming up outside, at the beginning of each meeting, standing to attention while the colours were hoisted to the top of the mast. Many of the scout leaders had been in the forces and they taught the boys how to march and conduct themselves smartly on parade. One Sunday a month, the unit would muster on London Road in uniform to march down to St Peter's Church for Church Service. They felt proud to be part of Leander.

The troop had 12-foot dinghies equipped with sails and oars. At the age of 16, Roy and a fellow scout took the boat on the outgoing tide to Lambeth. Here they moored alongside a Motor Torpedo Boat and waited for the next outgoing tide. Some six hours later they would continue their journey down the river, stopping once more on the change of the tide at Greenhithe on board HMS Worcester. Eating and sleeping was determined simply by the timing of the favourable tide. Carrying with them all their provisions, including a small tent and a Primus stove, they would find a suitable place ashore to cook their food and catch some sleep. The last stretch was the wide-open estuary of the Thames running with the fast-flowing tide to their destination at Southend. Here they made fast at the end of the pier. Working the incoming tides to their advantage they then slowly returned to the Leander HQ at Kingston.

Photo of Roy (2nd from right) in the Leander sea scouts

On one such trip, when Peter was also on board, they endeavoured to cross the estuary, just east of Southend, and got stuck on a sandbank, which just happened to be within an army firing range. An army DUKW (six-wheel-drive amphibious vehicle) duly appeared and a livid and very vocal NCO, on board, left them with no misunderstanding of their transgression and his displeasure! Before leaving, he ordered them not to move away from their current position, under any circumstances. Being well and truly stranded on the sand bank, the boys quietly considered that they weren't about to go anywhere! They spent some of their time making lunch, though Peter doesn't recommend potatoes, boiled in saltwater!

On the tidal stretch of the Thames, the river was full of barges and tugs charging busily all over the place. On occasions the powerful wash from the tugs threatened to overturn them. Peter remembers one occasion when faced with a strong tide, they had to make fast next to Traitors Gate. Yet, while undertaking these journeys, Roy, Peter and their fellow scouts were experiencing a great adventure.

When Roy later became a Venture Scout, he took boats to sea in home waters. The unit had a 5-ton cutter moored at Portsmouth harbour. In this they spent a lot of time, exploring the south coast and the Isle of Wight. On one occasion when they brought the cutter up the Thames, Tower Bridge had to be raised to accommodate its tall mast.

The unit also had a 26-foot fibre-glass boat that they sailed over to the Channel Islands and Brittany. Roy was proud to be in Leander Scouts and through all of the challenges he learned how to look after himself. "*If you were an active member of Leander, you were someone special*".

Peter recalls a wonderful journey taking a narrow boat along the Grand Union Canal all the way to Birmingham to attend the Scout Jubilee Jamboree. They had all sorts of bumps and scrapes but somehow managed their way through. Summer Camp was an exciting time. A furniture van was hired to convey the unit dinghies, kayaks and equipment along with thirty scouts, who all piled in the back, to travel to their destination. So began Summer Camp!

Those years in Leander were truly a great adventure and in some way for Roy, made up for the career that escaped him, in the Merchant Navy.

Peter simply reflects; "*Happy Days!*"

Sources

Family history carefully researched by Mike Shaw

Picture Credits

All photos courtesy of the Bevan family unless otherwise indicated
IWM ©Imperial War Museum

A Proud Latchmerian – Owen Walter

In 1933, Harry Walter moved with his wife, Gladys, and baby son, Owen, to a Victorian house at 7 Osborne Road in North Kingston, just opposite his parent's house (No. 8), where he had been born. In total, the Walter family lived in Osborne Road for about 150 years. Harry worked at Hawkers in Canbury Park Road, making the wooden fuselages of the Hurricane fighters that would shortly be put to great use.

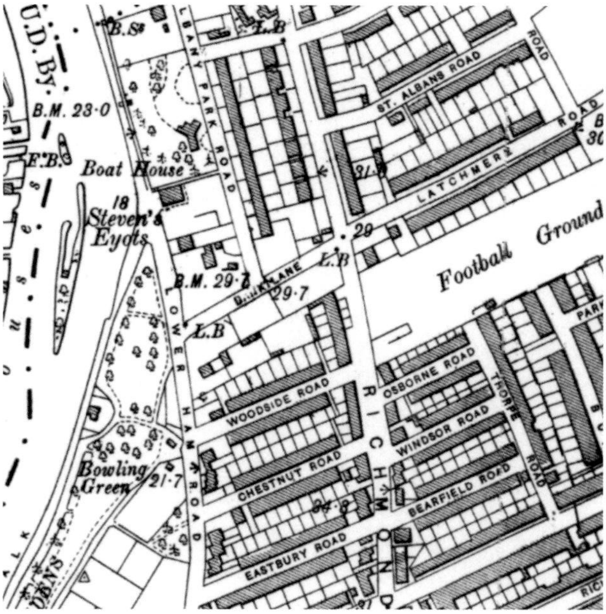

Top Left: *Eastbury Road*

Top Right: *View outside 50 St Albans Road*

Above: *The Canbury Shop in Richmond Road*

Left: *1933 Map showing Osborne Road that ran adjacent to Kingstonian Football Ground* NLS

The Radio

An EKCO radio was all they had at home in the way of entertainment. Prior to the war his father, who liked dance band music, regularly tuned into a Dutch radio station called

Hilversum. Owen felt that he was brought up on the music from this Dutch station. During the war they could no longer receive Hilversum but they loved listening to ITMA with Tommy Handley. It was a good morale booster and kept them going.

The War

Owen was seven years old when the war started. There was an evacuation of children at the beginning of the war, but Owen was only evacuated for three months. 1939 proved to be the phoney war. During this time many of the children had private lessons in houses rather than going to school and Latchmere School was half empty.

They had a Morrison shelter inside the house which had a quarter inch thick top with a mesh around the 4 legs. It was like a zoo cage with the animals outside and the humans inside. When the blitz first started, they had a small cellar with three steps down. He and his brother could just about stand up but their mum put down a mattress for them to help make it more comfortable.

Owen remembers lying in the cellar in the blitz, the guns getting louder and louder as the enemy bombers approached. While inside an Anderson shelter, you could clearly hear the thud of the shrapnel landing in the soft ground. The blitz lasted for fifty-six consecutive nights when large formations of bombers cast a shadow over London. He wasn't frightened by the bombing. If anything, he and his friends thought that it was rather exciting.

Anderson Shelter in Durlston Road

The nearest bomb fell on the opposite side of Richmond Road between St Albans and Durlston Road. The houses there were destroyed and later replaced by a small block of flats.

Recruiting office in King's Road

I recall standing outside Tews, the Tobacconists in Richmond Road (now Jagger Print) with my mum chatting to Mr Tew. I saw a Junkers 88 bomber coming down Richmond Road chased by two Hurricanes. The plane was very low and I could clearly see the front gunner and the pilot. Mr Tew, who was a member of the home guard, dashed inside the shop to get his rifle but by the time he came out the bomber had gone. The bomber later crashed in Leatherhead.

In 1943 Owen moved up to Richmond Road School. In 1944 Richmond Road School was used to accommodate the labourers who were making the bomb-damaged houses safe. Owen therefore transferred to St Luke's School in Elm Road.

Towards the end of the war in 1944, the V1 flying bombs known as doodlebugs descended on London nearly every day. As a result, there was another evacuation.

In September 1944, a V1 flying bomb landed on the allotments of Latchmere Recreation Ground and caused extensive damage to the windows and roof of Latchmere School. Ironically, the houses of Latchmere Lane which had also lost all their windows had only just been visited by the window cleaner!

Anne Bott, another pupil at Latchmere School whose father had a shop called Mason's in Richmond Road, had a very narrow escape that afternoon. She was cycling home from the polo stables on the east side of Ham Common where she enjoyed spending her spare time. Anne was carrying a sack of chaff, for her rabbits, on her handlebars and had a precious hen's egg safely placed in her pocket. The air raid sirens had begun to whine, but over that she heard the dreaded rattle of a flying bomb. Suddenly, realising that the bomb was coming down, she threw herself off her bike onto the pavement in Latchmere Lane and instinctively wrapped her arms around her head. The bomb exploded as she hit the pavement. Fortunately, she was in dead ground at a slightly lower level than the allotments on Latchmere Recreation ground where it had landed. She was therefore shielded from the immense blast:

Mr Bott in the doorway of his shop, Mason's at 152 Richmond Road next door to the café which is on the corner with Osborne Road

I clambered up and stood; a brief silence was followed by the clatter of cascading roof tiles and shortly after by wailing housewives who ran out of the houses opposite and fell into each other's arms. No notice was taken of me; the egg in the pocket of my navy school mac was broken – a sad mess. I looked towards the allotments and saw a man stumbling from left to right. He was, I'm sure, very close to the crater. All there was to be done was cycle home with a tale to tell.

Alan Cookson's dad worked at the Canbury Park Road factory building Hurricanes. Alan remembers standing in the rear garden of his house with his father watching RAF bombers flying over in huge formations to Germany. He clearly remembers his father telling him, *that's a thousand bomber raid.*

Memorial stone at the junction of Park Road and Kings Road

Owen recalls that with V1 Flying bombs you could stand outside and watch them but with the V2 Rocket bombs, you had no warning at all.

On Monday 22nd January 1945 at 3pm, Owen left school to go for piano lessons with Miss Barratt who lived in Park Road. Only shortly before, at 2:35pm a V2 rocket bomb, carrying about 1 ton of explosive, had landed at the junction of Kings Road with Park Road and obliterated her house. Fortunately, she was out shopping at the time. Eight people living in the houses were killed and another one hundred and seventeen injured. More than two hundred houses were badly damaged, 33 destroyed completely. The post office run by the Eastwoods was destroyed. There had been up to twelve people standing at the trolley bus stop in Park Road. Fortunately, the bus had picked them all up and headed off before the bomb landed. Owen recalls walking along Kings Road and seeing fire hoses from the fire engines strewn all across the road.

Above Left: *VE Day celebration in St Albans Road*

Above: *VE Day celebration in Cranleigh Gardens*

Left: *Ladies of Canbury Park Road take a break from VE party preparations in Canbury Park Road*

On May 8th Victory in Europe day was celebrated by many families holding street parties. Games followed for the children with dancing for the adults in the evening. It was a great day of celebration throughout the country.

Flooding in Canbury

The winter of 1947/48 was exceptionally cold with plenty of snow. When the snow melted there was a flood and Canbury Gardens disappeared under water. The water was very deep and extended up Bank Lane. Owen remembers walking through a flooded Canbury Gardens and sinking into the soft earth of a flower bed. Every time there was a lot of rain, there would be a flood under Kingston Railway Bridge.

Water under the bridge at Kingston. In ancient times the Latchmere Brook would have carried this water to the Thames

The Austin 7's would always get stuck there. The railway line had followed the original route of the Latchmere Brook to the river. With the brook now filled in at its southern end, there was no natural outlet for the water.

Kingstonians – The K's

Owen joined the supporters club of Kingstonians in 1946 and attended most games. Many years later, in 1960, he went to Wembley to watch the K's in the Amateur Cup final, though they unfortunately lost to Hendon. They had a large grandstand and one of the best football pitches in Surrey. It was a lovely time with a great atmosphere at the Richmond Road ground. It was a very sad loss to the local community when the last match was played in January 1988 and the cheers and jeers of the K's supporters gave way to the relatively quiet activity of a suburban housing estate.

Above: *Painting by Frank Walter of Kingstonian fans at the Richmond Road ground that ran parallel with Latchmere Road and Osborne Road*

Left: *The Kingstonian Ground looking from the west.* © Historic England

Owen believes that the Kingston authorities have, over many years, been guilty of a lot of vandalism with old buildings thoughtlessly, unnecessarily and in some cases illegally pulled down. He reflects, *Kingston Town has sadly lost its soul.*

Picture of the K's after winning the FA Amateur Cup final in April 1933. Ye Olde Post House, an ancient gabled building was originally an Inn called The Crane where ambassadors often lodged when the Royal Court was at Hampton Court. It was later the County Military Headquarters of the Parliamentarians during the Civil War in the 17th Century. It was demolished in 1954

Picture Credits
All pictures courtesy of Owen Walter unless otherwise indicated
NLS: Reproduced with the permission of the National Library of Scotland

Pioneers of Aviation (Sopwith, Hawker, Camm, Hooper & their People)

When once you have tasted flight, you will forever walk the earth with your eyes turned skyward, for there you have been, and there you will always long to return. Leonardo da Vinci

The Kingston Roller Skating rink

In 1912 the Latchmere Brook, long since buried, ran underground down the east side of Kingston Roller Skating Rink that faced onto Canbury Park Road, a road packed with small Victorian terraced houses. It was, in fact, the Latchmere Brook that had established the boundary of this plot of land that had in turn, defined the strange projection of the roller rink from the road.

Skating had by now lost its allure and the rink was offered for sale or lease. Yet, the building's place in Kingston's history was about to be realised when it came to the attention of a dynamic, wealthy young man by the name of Tommy Sopwith. Tommy who only two years before had taught himself to fly at Brooklands racing circuit, had established a small aircraft workshop at Brooklands. Here he had been joined by luxury motor yacht engineer, Fred Sigrist. They needed more room to build aircraft and the roller rink was ideal. With a large flat wooden floor without the interruption of columns, it was perfect for chalking out full size templates of aircraft structures for the woodworkers. Furthermore, the rink was close to the River Thames and Kingston had an abundance of skilled boat and coach building craftsmen for hire.

Kingston roller skating rink. "Buttons", the boy wearing his rink uniform can be seen standing outside the entrance. Buttons was retained by the new employer as an odd job boy and worked on until he was 80

In December 1912 Tommy Sopwith took a 14-year lease on the roller rink for £300 a year. In June they had been joined by a 23-year-old motor mechanic by the name of Harry Hawker. Hawker, had been born in Moorabbin near Melbourne in Australia, the son of a blacksmith. Harry Hawker was desperate to fly and so he traded in the cost of his £50 return fare to Australia for flying lessons from Tommy Sopwith. Displaying remarkable aptitude, Harry Hawker gained his aviator's certificate within a few days. This aptitude enabled him to become the test pilot and a fellow designer within the dynamic Sopwith team. He would soon become one of the legendary pioneers of manned flight.

Harry Hawker flying at Brooklands

Tommy retained the rink page boy who had been nicknamed Buttons from the metal buttons on his uniform. Buttons, otherwise known as John (Jack) Whitehorn lived just around the corner at 2 Elm Crescent and his mother Catherine worked as an attendant at the Cinem Palace Cinema. In 1913, Jack joined the small team of the newly fledged Sopwith Aviation and with the exception of Tommy Sopwith, would go on to become the longest serving employee of the Hawker Siddeley Corporation.

Some of Britain's most famous fighter aircraft started life on drawing boards at Canbury Park Road and were built in the two factories at Canbury Park Road and Ham. Sadly, the enormous contribution of the people working in these two factories, in the defence of this country, has been very much overlooked.

Yet, thanks to the sterling efforts of the Kingston Aviation Centenary Project Team under the guidance and hard work of David Hassard and Bill Downey we have, on the website at *www.kingstonaviation.org*, a comprehensive account of the history of the Sopwith and Hawker Aircraft factories in Kingston and Ham. The detailed information has allowed me to provide this overview of those two factories that were constructed between the Latchmere Brook and the River Thames and of a few of the many people who had the opportunity to work in this great organisation.

Recognition

Harry Hawker carried out regular test flights on the grass in the middle of Brooklands motor racing circuit next to the sewage farm. Occasionally the planes crashed next door and the pilots experienced a relatively soft landing, if not a little messy! Having gained the attention of both the army and the navy, orders were being placed as Hawker continued to push Sopwith planes to their limits and break numerous records.

On the outbreak of war in 1914, both the Army and Navy quickly came to realise that aircraft played an essential role in intelligence gathering to provide the location and disposition of enemy troops and vessels. Those reconnaissance aircraft soon needed a shield of fighters to protect them against enemy fighters with increasingly powerful guns. The pilots had originally been issued with revolvers to shoot at enemy pilots. Other allied aircraft would later be developed to be deployed in the bombardment, strafing and general harassment of advancing enemy forces, U-boats and the Zeppelin airships that were sent across the channel to bomb London and east coast ports. The reality was that, despite the

At 5 am on Tuesday 7th April 1914 a Tabloid floatplane was towed half a mile from the factory in Canbury Park Road to the Thames slipway in front of Turk's boathouse on the Lower Ham Road

Sopwith's Tabloid floatplane making a fast run by Petersham Meadows on 8th April 1914. It lifts off the water between Eel Pie Island and Glover's Island

size and power of the adversaries, a military force without eyes in the air was operating blind. Demand for ever more manouverable, robust and better armed aircraft increased as the war progressed. Within this highly demanding, fast changing and, for the pilots, extremely deadly environment, the Sopwith Aviation Company became a leading supplier of military aircraft to the Allied forces during the 1st World War.

Between 1913 and 1916, to keep up with substantial demand from both the Royal Flying Corps (RFC) and the Royal Naval Air Service (RNAS), Sopwith bought up more and more houses and land in Canbury Park Road and Elm Grove and steadily expanded the aircraft factory to form the Sopwith "Island" factory.

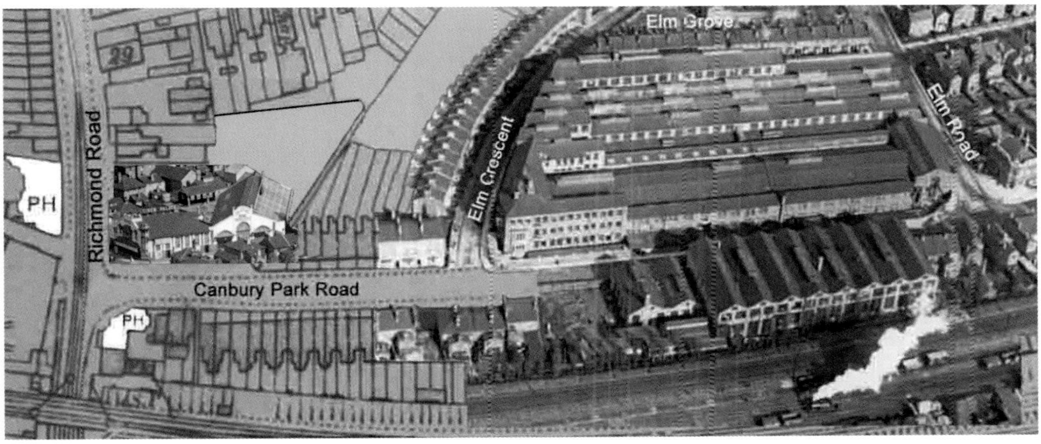

The Sopwith/Hawker factories overlaid on a 1911 map of north Kingston. Far left is the Cinem Palace Cinema (later the ABC Cinema) and next to it is the roller rink that was leased in 1913 to build Sopwith planes. The Sopwith factory island then rapidly grew through the 1st World War. The Canbury Arms pub can be seen far right at the junction of Elm Road with Canbury Park Road

In early February 1914, the First Lord of the Admiralty, Winston Churchill, toured the factory at Canbury Park Road as part of his familiarisation with his suppliers and to take a close look at the Sopwith Tabloid in which he had personally taken an interest. In 1915, Churchill supported the disastrous Dardanelles naval campaign and the military landings on Gallipoli, which ultimately led to a dreadful and pointless loss of life. Ironically, his First Sea Lord, Jacky Fisher, who disagreed strongly over the Dardanelles campaign, was living just down the road at Langham House on Ham Common. Nevertheless, Churchill had quickly seen the potential for aircraft to secure a strategic military advantage and he was relentless in his support of the development of the aircraft factories

Harry Hawker's courage and risk-taking continued to defy belief. On the afternoon of Saturday 27th June 1914, he was displaying a Sopwith Tabloid at Brooklands after a motor racing event. He reached the top of one of his slow loops at a height of about 1,000 feet and the plane's forward momentum came to a halt. Spectators then watched with increasing anxiety as the plane appeared to fall sideways, before dropping nose down and plummeting in a spin. At a mere 200 ft above the ground the machine was seen to flatten out and then drop into a wood to the east of Brooklands airfield. Officials and spectators set out on an immediate search for the wrecked plane with everyone fearing the worst. While the search was underway, Harry Hawker suddenly reappeared on the back of a motorcycle. It transpired that his aircraft had clipped the top of the trees then dropped through branches, which had cushioned his fall, before landing on saplings in the undergrowth with the wings folded over Harry's head. This dreaded spin was known as Parke's Dive but Harry believed that he knew how to get out of it as he was one of the very few who had escaped its fatal hold. The following day with very anxious members of his team looking on, Harry took a Sopwith Scout up to 1,500ft and deliberately put it into a spin. The machine "hung on its tail, slowly rotated and entering a spin, down it went. Then quite suddenly the turning stopped, and the spin became a straight dive that preceded a perfect landing. Asked what he had done, he replied, *I did nothing, absolutely nothing. I took my hands and feet off everything and as I thought came out of the spin and found myself in a straight dive.*

On the penultimate day of 1914, just short of his twenty-seventh birthday, Tommy Sopwith married the Honourable Beatrix Mary Leslie Hore-Ruthven. Her brother Sandy, who had won a VC in the Sudan in 1898 was a close personal friend of Tommy and it is through him that they had been introduced. Beatrix was nearly 17 years older than Tommy and already had six children by two previous marriages. Her eldest daughter was just two years younger than her new husband. Tommy, with his pet brown bear Oonie, bought a large house for them all in Cobham.

On 25th May 1915 Liberal Prime Minister H H Asquith formed a Coalition Government with the Conservatives. One of their conditions was the dismissal of Churchill as the First Lord of the Admiralty. His First Sea Lord, Lord Fisher, had resigned twelve days earlier, horrified by the failures and loss of life in the Dardanelles. Yet Churchill was a sad loss to the RNAS whose development he had robustly supported. Following his sacking as First

Lord of the Admiralty, Winston Churchill, headed out to the battlefields of Flanders to do penance and *take an active part in beating the Germans*. Here he witnessed at first hand the true horror and danger of the war.

Thanks to her great niece, Sandra Baker, we have, via Kindle, access to the diary of 20-year-old, Connie Webb (*A Wartime Diary 1915 – 1916 by Isabel Constance Webb*). This is a highly readable account of Connie's day to day life by the river in Kingston and at Sandbanks in Dorset during the 1st World War. Connie was the eldest daughter of Edmund Webb, an accountant with the Prudential Assurance Company. She had two younger sisters: Irene, aged 17 and Cynthia called "baby" aged 5 and a younger brother called Jack. In 1915, they lived at Albany Park Lodge with a large garden supporting magnificent cedar of Lebanon trees, overlooking the River Thames. Edmund Webb had rebuilt this house on the land of the Albany Club which had burnt down in 1911. The Turk's boathouse was located next door.

The Sopwith planes were tested locally from the slipway of Turk's boat house next to the Thames and from Thorpe Road Football Ground, later the home ground of Kingstonians

Edmund Webb had this house built on the land of the Albany Club which burnt down in 1909

The terrace and garden overlooking the River Thames. The magnificent 18th century cedar of Lebanon trees are still there

The Sopwith team were at the time using the slipway of Turk's boathouse for Harry Hawker to test fly their naval floatplanes along the stretch of the river, heading east, from the boathouse to the half mile tree on the Lower Ham Road. This was less than half a mile from their factory in Canbury Park Road.

On Sunday 5th December according to the entry in Connie's diary:

When we arrived home, we were met in frantic excitement by Irene who said that a water-plane was to go up at 2 o'clock. Wasn't it lucky for me, it being on a Sunday, otherwise I shouldn't have seen it. It was gorgeous, such a bit of excitement in my present drab existence, and I have quite lost my heart to the aviator! Don't know whether it was Hawker or not. We dashed over our dinner, running out several times on false alarms, but at last descended to the towpath, and found a tremendous crowd there, also many friends...... Irene was very disappointed that her naval officer was not there, in fact there was only one sailor there, but several of Sopwith's men, also Jack Highland, looking quite dashing on his motor-cycle. The water-plane was by the water's edge, and presently a quiet looking, unassuming young man pushed his way quickly through the crowd and climbed into the machine. It was the aviator! It seemed strange to see him get in so unconcernedly, somehow, him being a real hero, and all that; one would have expected much more pomp, somehow.

Sopwith Schneiders outside the roller rink in Canbury Park Road

It seemed rather pathetic to see him; he was so young and slim. I thought he had the air (to me, at least) of a martyr going to his doom – he might have been going to his death. No doubt he felt all right, really. He was dark, and nice-looking, and when he had buttoned up his long, warm brown coat (quite an ordinary, unprofessional looking one, there was nothing "swanky" about him) and had pulled a kind of leather hood over his head, which covered his ears and his chin, and gave him the appearance of a knight with his visor up, he was quite irresistible! A prayer for him came from my heart when the machine rose into the air. I'm a frightful coward myself and could never have done that but admire tremendously those things when a man (especially young and handsome) does them. There is an immense fund of hero-worship in me. When the propeller started it made a gale and blew all the people's hats about, the water-plane skimmed along the river and then rose as gracefully as a bird into the air. Everything went off successfully and we saw some splendid flights; he did the spiral and upside-down flying sometimes. Do hope he has plenty of money, poor darling; he should have had a fur coat instead of that brown one.

Harry Hawker with a floatplane in front of Turk's boathouse. The long tall wall and cedar trees behind belonged to Albany Park Lodge. Connie and her sisters sat on top of this wall in milder weather to watch the Sopwith team testing their aircraft

A Sopwith Baby being tested on the Thames near Canbury Gardens. This was used by the Royal Naval Air Service

Monday 13th December 1915

Dada is a "special constable", also Mr. Headley (!!!). Dada has to guard Sopwith's. Hours 6 – 10 four evenings a week.

Saturday 15th January 1916

Irene saw her little naval lieutenant quite a lot the last time the water-plane came down, he and another officer and the airman, Hawker, sat on the seat under our wall and examined papers, and every time Irene went by (which she did pretty frequently!) they all smiled at her! Fancy "getting-off" with a celebrity like Hawker!! I hear he lives at Kingston.

Friday 18th February

Mr. Headley is a special constable now, like Dada, and goes on duty at the "Sopwith Aviation Works" from 6 till 10, also. Last night a man wanted to get in but did not know the password. Mr. Headley refused to allow him by. "It's a nice thing when I can't get into my own works!" laughed the man. It was Sopwith himself! Dada says he is always forgetting the word, and that once Hawker, the chief pilot, came up to him (Dada) rather apologetically to say he did not know it. Dada said, "That's all right. I know your face".

Saturday 19th February

I had a lovely view of Hawker this time. I stood on a bank just above his car. He has to be carried ashore from his machine, which is rather undignified! Then he pushed through the crowd, taking off his flying-cap as he came. He has very thick, rather rumpled-looking black hair, and is not so nice-looking without a cap. He is just irresistible in the flying one with ear pads. But he has a pleasant face and smiled at some little ragamuffins who said something to him, so I'm sure he must be nice! Then he climbed into the little grey two-seater and took the wheel, Irene's little lieutenant climbed in next to him."

On Friday 25th February Connie Webb watched from the smoking-room window in Albany Park Lodge:

Several days ago, some water-planes were brought down, and remained in the snow. This afternoon three were sent up. The ground was covered with snow, and a thick sleet was falling. Felt so sorry for Hawker. Could see him climbing in and out of the machines.

Monday 28th February

Hawker had recently narrowly escaped a serious accident and had hurt his arm against a tree – he 'wore' it in a splint.

A friend was telling me how clever he is; that's why Sopwith makes him try all the new machines. Whilst testing one at Brooklands the other day something broke (I think it was a part of the propeller) when he was in the air, but he kept his nerve and brought the aeroplane safely down. We used to hear a great deal of Hawker in the days of exhibition flying. I think he took part in the Aerial Post, and also won second prize in the Daily Mail contest. If that is the same one as our riverside hero, he is no end of a celebrity.

Saturday 4th March

The water-plane again, and I had quite a good view of Hawker. Irene and I walked past on our way to the town, and as the machine was just coming down, we stopped to watch. Hawker had on a short black oilskin coat instead of his long brown one and of course, the fetching cap. He really is very nice-looking and has a splendid profile. His front face is not so good, but it is very pleasant and he has very nice dark hair and eyes.

Sunday 5th March

A most eventful day. Two water-planes went up in the morning, and of course, being Sunday, there was a tremendous crowd… Sopwith was there with his widow (though Dada says that story is all a myth!). Ever so many naval officers were present and of course strings of motors (the Sopwith men never seem to go anywhere except 'en automobile')…..Dulcie said that he (Hawker) and several other naval officers were all standing quite near. They all seemed to be very proud of him (Hawker) and made a great fuss. I'm afraid he'll get thoroughly spoilt, if he isn't already; and were all laughing and so jolly. Dulcie says that Hawker was very gay and that when he looked round with a smile on his face, straight at them, he was perfectly irresistible! I think that it is the fact of his being such a romantic hero and wearing such becoming things that attracts me, perhaps, as his face is not frantically handsome. He is quite attractive looking, however, and has such a jolly, boyish air. I wonder whether that is partly owing to the black shade on his upper lip, which from a distance looks as if he has a little subaltern's moustache.

Dulcie and I had a ripping view of him when he came down the second time. He had a dark suit on today, under his oilskin (you see, I notice all these details) and after he had slid out of the funny, tight sort of little cubby-hole in which he sits, he stood on one of the planes (I believe that the professional name is "decks" and that one can only stand on certain parts) for some time, laughing and talking to two of the men. Dulcie and I were standing on the upper bank just above his car; he came and stood underneath us, taking off his flying-cap and putting on an ordinary one, then he got into the motor and a friend sat beside him….

That afternoon, another water-plane was sent up and I was rather sorry to miss it. It seemed to be rather a failure for, after skimming along the river, it failed to rise and came back again.

"I suppose they will send that one back to the works," remarked Mrs Salamensen, "surely they won't send it up as it seems to be a wrong one." "I should think not", answered Dada, if anything goes wrong with it whilst it is in the air the pilot will probably lose his life".

Notwithstanding that, Hawker tried it again until at last it rose in the air properly. I do think he is brave. The risk may not have been as great as Dada thought, but anyhow there is always danger in testing an untried machine, especially one that seems to be a bit wrong. I think that he should wear some sort of uniform. At present there is nothing to distinguish him from a slacker, while he is much braver than some of these men who swank about in an officer's uniform, but who have only volunteered for home-duty and who would have a fit if they had to go to the front.

Alice says that Hawker has rooms in Gibbon Road (poor man!) and that when Sopwith wants him to test a water-plane some of the men are sent round to rout him out! I wonder why they send the water-plane up on Sunday. The crowd must be very inconvenient. Mr. Heath thinks it's because Hawker is so busy now and that is the only time he can spare. If he has also to test the water-planes from the Sopwith Works at Old Mill and also at Southampton, in addition to the main works at Kingston, and also aeroplanes at Brooklands, he must be fully occupied.

Thursday 9th March

Two water-planes were by Turk's. Sopwith was there, and several naval officers. The machine would not start off at first when it was floating on the river and some man called out a joking remark to Hawker, who replied in the same vein. It seemed such a light-hearted sort of way to take the affair, though no doubt they are all so used to it that they don't think of the danger….

When the water-plane came back, Hawker got out and lounged about, talking to the other men for quite a long time. I could have had the most lovely view of him, and yet I hardly looked at all. Irene, I, Baby and three other ladies were almost the only people looking on, and I felt so horribly conspicuous. All those wretched Sopwith men stare so, and I was afraid they thought that all I was there for was to look at Hawker (which, being the truth, made me feel more guilty!). All girls are supposed to feel romantically inclined to airmen, and no doubt they all think we are smitten with him, as we turn up so regularly.

When the propeller started of course the usual wind blew and I could see those wretched Sopwith men all looking at us and laughing, hoping our skirts would blow up and that they would see sights and visions, no doubt!

A very smart lady drove down in a lovely Rolls Royce and Sopwith went back with her.

Thursday 16th March

Four or five water-planes are down by the river. It is quite a long time since the last were here, and now they have come with a vengeance!

Friday 17th March

We came back via the river and saw the second water-plane come down. Hawker got out and talked for some time with the naval officer-with-the-drawn-face. During the conversation Hawker looked round at us smilingly several times. A very convenient thing to do. I couldn't smile back at him, with all those cheeky Sopwith men there. We watched another machine go up and return, and then strolled along the tow-path and up the river steps. It was 12.30 and another lovely spring day, so we stayed in the garden by the river, watching Hawker get into the fourth water-plane. As he rushed past along the river, he looked right round at us and I smiled broadly.... We saw some lovely exhibition flying on that last machine. It never went out of sight, but circled about in front of us, doing spirals, corkscrews and curves in the regular Brookland manner. I don't like to see the machine turn right on its side and almost upside down like it did. We were really very lucky to see it, people used to pay ever so much to see the same thing done at the aerodromes. Hawker has never done so much of this show flying with the water-planes before. Then he came flying down the river from the Kingston end and we thought he might be going to land. But he kept on, and it looked as if he were heading straight for us standing on the wall. Apparently just in front of us the machine rose abruptly and went right over our heads, seeming as if it brushed the cedar tops. Irene said she wondered if he did it on purpose because we were there! ...... I hope he didn't hear the chorus of shrieks and gasps that arose when he flew over! I have never had a more thrilling moment. To see it heading straight for us, (when it always goes straight on past) and then go so close over our heads and over our very own cedars! A lady who was standing beneath us on the towing-path laughed immensely, partly at the excitement and partly at ours and our remarks. Hawker flew up to a great height and then commenced the loveliest corkscrew down and passed by us on to Turk's boathouse. We saw him get out and drive off in his motor, and then went into lunch, feeling as if we mustn't grumble if we saw no more flying for another month!

The Sopwith team planned to test their prototype biplane Scout at the Thorpe Road Football Ground in Kingston that ran parallel with Latchmere Road (later used by Kingstonians). Close to Sopwith's factory, these grounds were suitable for engine running and taxying trials. Harry Hawker used this same football ground to test fly the prototype Sopwith Pup.

Above *The backs of the houses are on the south side of Latchmere Road*

Right *Staunton Road when photographed from the other side*

Saturday 18th March

My heart is encircled by a cold band of dismay and apprehension... Two of the Miss Pierponts told me a dreadful piece of news. They heard that these are the last of the water-planes and that henceforth Sopwith's will devote themselves only to aeroplanes! I suppose that will mean that Hawker will always fly at Brooklands, or some such place, and we shall never again see the naval officers. Their work here will be ended. Heavens! What will Irene and I do without the excitement, and nothing to look forward to?

Sunday 19th March

If these two are to be the last of the water-planes it is rather fortunate for us that they are "wrong uns". Hawker tried one this morning, which was a failure, so he will have to come again to try them, I hope. He looked around at us as he went up the river. The machine hardly rose at all this time, and a man tore along the bank with a coil of rope as soon as he saw the machine was not flying. I am sorry for the pilot if he falls in about this time, for the river is in flood and there is a terrible stream. Hawker drove away as soon as he brought the machine back.

Monday 20th March

Sopwith men still tinkering about with engines, propellers, etc. of w-planes by Turk's. Spring commences.

Saturday 25th March

Two more water-planes at Turk's.... It rained while Baby and I were returning from the town (Kingston) this morning and we took shelter under a shop shade. A man came from the direction of Sopwith's and stared at me and "beamed" as if he knew me by sight. I wondered if it could possibly be Hawker or Irene's lieutenant in mufti. He was rather short, good-looking, and went up Gibbon Road! And wore a brown suit. Nothing particular happened at Turk's this afternoon. Dada talked to Turk about the flying, and they both spoke about Hawker's cleverness. The latter drove off in his motor (after taking up two machines). We heard the crowd all talking about some aeroplane that was to be sent up from the football ground, and after the fun was over by the boathouse, everybody streamed thither. There was a great crowd in the field, and everybody was roped off by the fence. We only saw the important people from a great distance (Irene's lieut. etc) standing round the aeroplane right in the centre of the field. Several motors drove in, and as one came up all the little boys shouted, "Here comes old Hawker!" so they all know him by sight.

Connie with Jack, Irene & Baby
Courtesy of Sandra Baker

I caught such interesting scraps of conversation. "Yes, he is very skilful – quite a young man, I believe" – "Yes, from Australia or New Zealand". "No, he'll go up just as he is." – "Oh yes! Strapped into the machine." "Yes, I've been up myself." The machine ran along and rose up beautifully and we saw some splendid flying. First of all, he rose up to a great height, and then did the most wonderful loops I've ever seen. The machine rose up perpendicularly, turned round on its back, curved and then somehow turned the right way again. This was the real upside-down flying. Baby was afraid that he would get the blood to his head. It was most wonderful to watch, but I hated to see it – it looked ghastly and frantically dangerous.

He repeated this, three or four times, and then flew out of sight. How sweet of him to show the crowd something instead of disappearing right away. Wonder where he was going to?

Wednesday 29th March

One of the large old willow trees has been blown down this end of Canbury Gardens, and there is hardly a fence left standing. Dada said that there was rare fun at Sopwiths, everything being blown about like ninepins, even the sentry boxes going over.

Thursday 6th April 1916

At last! Three water-planes down by the river once more. About 12.45, just as I was putting my (gardening) tools away and generally tidying up, I heard the sound of the propeller. Irene, I and Baby all rushed down to our old place under the cedars and were just in time to see Hawker go by. He looked right round as if to see if we were there, and then again. The water-plane never went out of sight and we saw some lovely flights. He was over our head most of the time and we saw spirals and curves galore. At one time it took a straight, downward dive towards our house and I ran under the cedars, being an arrant coward in the matter of things overhead. Lunch was announced at this time, so I had to miss some of the flying, but Baby and I both rushed out again when we heard the water-plane coming back along the river. Hawker looked round again at us several times – Baby waving valiantly – and I could swear he smiled. It seems the most improbably ridiculous thing to think, and yet I do wonder whether, if he had looked and not seen us in the garden when he went by, we should have seen such lovely flying overhead? It's the second time it has happened, you see! People rush up to him with congratulations after some flight, especially girls.

Friday 7th April

The day of departure. I felt sad at parting from Irene and our pretty home. The remaining water-planes had not gone up before we went.

Here ends the last entry of Connie relating to her life at Albany Park Lodge, watching over the river and the antics of Harry Hawker and the Sopwith team. The family left the house in Kingston to spend the summer in Bournemouth and Sandbanks.

One evening, later in the month, Harry Hawker was stopped by a Police Sergeant for failing to display an off-side headlight on his motorcar and not carrying his driving licence with him. A week later at the local Magistrates Court he was fined £1 and 5 shillings respectively for the two offences. The Surrey Comet who ran an article on the incident titled "Famous Flying Man Fined" quoted Harry Hawker as saying he was always anxious to comply with the law.

On 19th April 1917 King George V and Queen Mary visited the Sopwith factory in Canbury Park Road with the Maharaja of Bikaner. They spent an hour and a half reviewing the workshops and the Sopwith triplanes under construction, guided by Tommy Sopwith, General Manager Reg Cary and Works Manager Fred Sigrist.

19th April 1917 Visit by King George V & Queen Mary

When Churchill's battalion was amalgamated with another, making his command redundant, he returned to England and once more took up his seat in Parliament. Having witnessed at first hand the appalling slaughter and conditions on the front, he was even more vociferous on the failings of the government to supply enough munitions and aircraft to the armed forces. On 20th July he was sworn in as Minister for Munitions and a member of the War Cabinet. Flight Journal magazine was quick to acknowledge the importance of this appointment.

Following the decision to expand the RFC from 108 to 200 squadrons, one of Winston Churchill's first actions under the Defence of the Realm Act was to approve the building of National Aircraft Factories. One of these referred to as *The National Aircraft Factory No.2* was to be located on 38 acres of Dysart Land, known as Ham Lands, beside the Thames, just a mile north of Sopwith's factory in Kingston. It was built through the winter of 1917 and Sopwith Aviation secured the lease of the factory.

Local Councils, including Ham District Council, raised strong objections to the establishment of a permanent factory. Nearly £150,000, had already been contributed by the County Councils of London, Surrey and Middlesex, the Local Authorities and individuals, "for the express purpose of preserving the amenities of the River Thames". They therefore urged that the works should be of a temporary character only.

Winston Churchill, taking into account their objections, decided that the factory had to be constructed on the chosen site but as far as possible from the river and it would be classified as a temporary factory to be removed immediately after the war. The Government valuer assessed the 38-acre site and valued it at 6d per sq. ft taking into account that the factory was *practically in the country with no tram or rail facilities for workers and the river at this point was only suitable for barge transport.*

November 1917 Marriage of Harry Hawker & Muriel Peaty

On 14th November 1917, Harry Hawker married Muriel Alice Peaty at St Peter's Church in Ealing. Harry and Muriel had met in Richmond Park in April 1915. Muriel was stranded in the park in her little car after running out of petrol. She had mistakenly topped up her tank from a petrol can that had contained water. After being initially turned away, Harry returned in his Gregoire car and helped Muriel get her car going. He later tempted her with the opportunity to drive his 27/80 Austro Daimler and accompany him on regular fast Sunday drives to Brooklands. For their honeymoon, touring the West Country in their car, Harry had "saved petrol from all quarters" and fitted a stand with a large gas bag on top of the Gregoire which only lasted for about ten miles but gave the impression they were complying with the petrol rationing.

1918 Harry Hawker putting on a display in his Sopwith Camel over Kingston Market

The Sopwith Camel, the successor to the Sopwith Pup, was introduced on the Western Front in 1917. Although Harry Hawker had made the handling of the Sopwith Camel appear effortless, the fighter had by now gained a reputation as both a "vicious" plane in the hands of novices and an exceptionally manoeuvrable fighter in the hands of an experienced pilot. It accounted for more enemy kills than any other allied fighter during WW1. The biggest problem was that novice pilots were not being sufficiently trained to fly the Camel, let alone engage in air to air combat. More novice pilots died during take-off and landing than in aerial combat throughout the War.

2nd Lieutenant William Palmer. On his gravestone are engraved the words: "Fly on, dear boy, from this dark world of strife on to the land of promise, into eternal life."

One such young pilot, William Palmer, of 37 Latchmere Road, is buried in the graveyard of St Andrew's Church in Ham. On September 15th 1917, 2nd Lieutenant Palmer, having passed the initial two flying tests, only had to complete a final solo flight to earn his long-coveted wings. Just as his plane touched down at the end of the flight the engine caught fire and burst into flames. William was severely burnt before he could be pulled from the plane. He died some four hours later of his injuries. He was twenty years old.

Towards the end of the war, Major William "Billy" Barker, a veteran Canadian pilot, with 46 victories notched up in a Sopwith Camel, was returning from a 10-day refresher course on fighting conditions over the Western Front in his new Sopwith Snipe, fresh from the production line in Canbury Park Road. Crossing the enemy lines at 21,000 feet, he identified, attacked and destroyed an enemy plane. Unusually careless by his own admission, he was bounced by a formation of 15 Fokker D.VII's. In a desperate battle descending through the skies, he was wounded three times in the legs then his left elbow was shattered. Despite this, he managed to control his Sopwith Snipe and shoot down three more enemy aircraft before crash landing his severely damaged Snipe inside Allied lines. His life was saved by the men of the RAF Kite Balloon section, though six months later he was still not fit enough to walk the few paces necessary to receive the Victoria Cross at Buckingham Palace. These four victories had brought his total to 50. He was awarded the VC, DSO & Bar, MC & Two Bars. His Sopwith Snipe aircraft was recovered from the battlefield and is now preserved at the Canadian War Museum in Ontario.

Major Barker next to his Sopwith Camel

On 1st January 1918, eighteen days before his 30th birthday, Tommy Sopwith was created a Companion of the Order of the British Empire "in recognition of his outstanding contribution to the war effort". Five months later Reginald Cary, the Sopwith General Manager was awarded an OBE and Harry Hawker was made a Member of the Most Excellent Order of the British Empire for his special service to the Empire.

With the new National Aircraft Factory No.2 at Ham in 1918, Fred Sigrist more than doubled the company's workforce to 3,500 with the recruitment of injured soldiers, older men and nearly 1,000 women who were plucked out of service and their homes to play a critical role in the manufacture of new combat aircraft, Sopwith Snipes and Salamanders, in parallel with the Sopwith Dolphins being produced in Canbury Park Road.

The new recruits were each put through a fast training programme to enable them to perform one or two skilled tasks. For many women, this was liberation from mundane jobs and they soon came to prove that they could do many manual jobs as well, if not better than the men. These women also appreciated that pilots who were fighting for their lives in the skies over France would depend on their special care and attention in the construction of these planes.

The Sopwith Directors realised the value of a Sports and Social Club and were quick to embrace the inclusion of their staff, both men and women, in a wide range of sporting activities.

In September 1917, the Sopwith Company organised a Workers' Sports Day at the Old Kingstonian's Sports Ground at Norbiton. Over 3,000 people turned out to watch a long day of sport. There were races for ladies, veterans and boys, races against other local munitions workers, a one-mile relay against teams from Vickers and Napier plus handicapped races against county and international champions. The 100 yards final was a dead heat between Club Secretary Vic Derrington and Jack Whitehorn, the Skating Rink door boy, known as Buttons.

Sopwith Aviation Athletic Club ladies team win the 80 stone tug-of-war

May 1918 brought about the occasion of a special football match between a team representing Kingston Aircraft Works (Sopwith) wearing maroon shirts with white knickers and Martinsyde Munitions Works football club wearing blue shirts and white knickers. The teams included players who had previously played with Brentford, Bristol City, Manchester City and Southampton football clubs.

At Stamford Bridge football ground on 6th July the Sopwith Aviation athletic club ladies team won the 80 stone tug-of-war against teams from the rest of London's many aircraft companies. These women were now making an important contribution to the war and also having some fun!

Salamanders being manufactured at the Ham Factory

In October 1918 King George V sent his niece HRH Princess Arthur of Connaught to visit the Sopwith factories in Ham and Canbury Park Road to meet the women working in the offices and the woodworking, doping, fuselage assembly, sheet metal and streamlined wire departments. She spent some time with them afterwards at the Sopwith social club in Norbiton.

Major James McCudden VC, DSO & Bar, MC & Bar, MM and Croix de Guerre

Tragically, on 9th July Amelia McCudden of "Pitlochry", 37 Burton Road, Kingston lost her third son in battle. Major James McCudden aged only 23, had enjoyed a remarkable career, all the more exceptional because he had started off as a mechanic in the Royal Flying Corps. At the outbreak of war in 1914 he flew as an observer before training as a fighter pilot in 1916 and claiming his first victory in September. Within two years he had achieved 57 victories and been promoted to the rank of Major, leading more than 78 offensive patrols. Awarded the VC, DSO & Bar, MC & Bar, MM and Croix de Guerre (France), he received more awards for gallantry than any other British airman serving in the First World War. He was also one of the longest serving.

On 3rd July he collected his new aircraft, an SE5A from Farnborough, and on his way to France to take command of 60 squadron flew over his family home in north Kingston before circling over London at 17,000 feet for an hour. Six days later, McCudden died when his aircraft crashed as a result of an engine problem, just after taking off.

HMS Furious, originally commissioned as a Royal Navy cruiser, with more than a little tweaking to her superstructure, became the world's first aircraft carrier that could both launch and recover aircraft on her decks.

On 19th July 1918, she was stationed in the North Sea tasked with destroying the Imperial German Navy's airship sheds at Tondern in Denmark. Two waves of Sopwith 'Ships Camel' bombers set off from the ship in the early hours of 19th July for the 35 mile journey to the Tondern sheds. The youngest of the pilots in the second wave was 19-year-old Flight Sub Lieutenant Toby Yeulett, who had completed his education at Tiffin Boys' School in Kingston in 1915. His heavily laden aircraft lost a wheel during take-off.

RNAS Flight Sub Lieutenant Toby Yeulett. Courtesy of the Casey Family

All three Camels in the first wave located the airship sheds and dropped their 50lb bombs. The largest shed was engulfed in flames up to 500ft high within a minute. The smaller sheds were also hit. Initially caught unprepared, the defending troops, were ready for the second formation. Amid a torrent of anti-aircraft fire, two of the Camel aircraft bombed the undamaged sheds and hit a pressurised gas tank wagon. Toby Yeulett, was the last to arrive, racing low across the airfield in an attack on the railway line and damaging a high-tension wire with his top wing. The attack was all over by 4.50am. Both of the Zeppelins in the largest shed were destroyed. Six small Sopwith Camels had completed the world's first successful bombing raid from an aircraft carrier but now they needed to get home. Not having enough fuel to get back to HMS Furious, two of the planes ditched near one of the supporting destroyers and were rescued. Three other pilots landed their planes in enemy territory in Denmark and were all captured.

The body of the missing 19-year-old Toby Yeulett was washed up on the Danish coast five days later. He only had minor injuries: head cuts, some bruising and a broken nose so it is assumed that he ran out of fuel, crashed in the sea and drowned. He was buried with ceremony in a local Danish cemetery. He posthumously received the Distinguished Flying Cross.

If the attrition rate of aerial combat on the Western Front wasn't enough, 45 squadron were beset with a serious outbreak of flu in early October 1918. Two pilots died and many were incapacitated.

By the end of the war, Sopwith Aviation had built 16,237 aircraft including 1,847 Sopwith Pups, 5,747 Sopwith Camels, 5,466 1½ Strutters (many built under licence by French manufacturers) and various other fighters making a total of 32 different Sopwith designs. Sopwith aircraft made up 23% of the RAF's total aircraft, far outnumbering any other commercial design team. On the front line Sopwith aircraft accounted for 30% of the 3,522 aircraft with the British Army in France and 69% of their single-seat fighters. Sopwith aircraft also accounted for 25% of the 1,281 aircraft with the Royal Navy including all 265 of their wheeled "Ships Aeroplanes".

The Surrey Comet described the reaction to the armistice: *On 11th November 1918 around 11am, sirens were heard in the distance and eventually one in Kingston town centre confirmed the good news that the war had come to an end. Within minutes the town was a blaze of bunting in the spanking breeze with national flags alongside those of the allied nations. Itinerant vendors appeared with barrow loads of flags, children waved small flags, girls wore tri-colour ribbon in their hair or bows and rosettes in red, white and blue. The streets thronged with people bent on making holiday and some workers from Sopwith's Aviation Factory who had downed tools in ebullient glee passed through the streets in a motor van carrying an effigy of the Kaiser. It was not all rejoicing, there was a ghost at the feast, the mourning attires and sad set faces of many women told their own sorrowful stories and the hearts of all those anticipating the return home of those near and dear to them went out in deep sympathy to those who had experienced the tragedy of war in its bitterest form. During the afternoon the bells of the Parish Church continued to peal, residents and shop keepers ignored the restrictions on showing lights, the shades were removed from the electric tram cars which whizzed through the streets like fairy palaces and in the evening all the places of entertainment were crowded to fullest capacity.*

The Ham Urban District Council was now informed: the Minister of Munitions has decided that he would not be justified in treating the National Aircraft Factory at Ham otherwise than as a permanent factory.

By the end of the war Sopwith Snipes, Dolphins and Salamanders were being built in large numbers but as soon as the war ended, most orders were cancelled, leaving huge stocks of unwanted components. Faced with considerable uncertainty, the Sopwith Board decided to plough much of their profits and accumulated reserve funds into turning their Canbury Park Road factory over to volume motor-cycle manufacturing alongside low-volume production of civil aircraft, adapted from existing military designs.

The wreck of the Sopwith Atlantic being displayed at Selfridges

They also planned to secretly start building an aircraft capable of allowing Harry Hawker to win the £10,000 prize for the first non-stop flight across the Atlantic. On 18th May 1919, Harry Hawker and Kenneth Mackenzie-Grieve took off from a field outside Mount Pearl in Newfoundland in a 350-horsepower plane called the Sopwith Atlantic. Several hours into the flight they lost use of the radio and then the engine began to overheat. After 14 hours of flying they ditched in the Atlantic. With nothing heard for a number of days, they were given up for dead. The Australian poet, A.B. "Banjo" Paterson, wrote a poem in tribute, "Hawker, the Standard Bearer". A week later a Danish freighter SS Mary, which had rescued them but didn't have a radio to announce the rescue, finally delivered a message that they were alive. A British destroyer HMS Woolston was sent to collect them and took them to Scapa Flow. Their rescue triggered huge national rejoicing and a parade in London. Debris from the plane was displayed at Selfridges. King George V awarded the two men the Air Force Cross, and the Daily Mail gave them a consolation prize of £5000 pounds for flying more than 1,000 miles.

The Government sold the aircraft factory at Ham to Leyland Motors for the refurbishment of nearly 3,000 RAF Leyland trucks and later the manufacture of the Trojan Utility Car and a small truck known as the Cub. During the 2nd World War Leyland used its facilities at Ham for military products from water trailers to munitions. It also built Leyland Lynx army lorries, tank gun turrets and Leyland Centaur tanks.

The Sopwith Aviation Company in Canbury Park Road

Meanwhile in 1920 the Sopwith Aviation Company, struggling to make ends meet, entered voluntary liquidation and paid all its creditors. Not to be deterred, the Sopwith board members immediately established the H G Hawker Engineering Company, the name recognising its brilliant test pilot and joint designer, Harry Hawker. With a small team of only twenty, the company took over all the Sopwith patent rights and bought the roller rink before renting and later buying the Sopwith factory in Canbury Park Road, initially for government contracts for reconditioning Sopwith Snipes.

Harry Hawker OBE, AFC

When the Brooklands racetrack reopened in 1920, Harry Hawker turned his attention to motor racing. At this circuit he was the first to race the Sunbeam 350HP but suffered a burst tyre and spun off the circuit.

On 12th July 1921 Hawker was test flying a Nieuport Goshawk at RAF Hendon when the plane suddenly caught fire in the air as a result of petrol escaping from an improperly sealed carburettor. While attempting to extinguish the fire that was burning his feet and legs, Hawker crashed into the ground. Although he was thrown clear he was seriously injured and died within a few minutes. So ended the life of one of the great pioneers of manned flight.

In November 1923 Sydney Camm joined the Hawker Aircraft Company based at Canbury Park Road as a senior draughtsman. The success of his first design, the Cygnet, led to him being appointed chief designer in 1925. He also designed the Hart and Fury biplanes and more than 3,000 were built through the 1930s, making Hawker very profitable. This success allowed Tommy Sopwith to buy other British aircraft companies and form Hawker Siddeley Aircraft. Through much of the 1930s, the majority of the aircraft in the RAF were designed by Camm in Kingston and mostly built in Kingston or other Hawker Siddeley factories.

Sydney Camm seen here at Windsor Model Aeroplane Club during circa 1915. Looking on are his wife and two young sons. His favourite hobby was making model aircraft

Camm went on to design 52 aircraft, of which a total of 26,000 were manufactured. Robert Lickey, an engineer who worked for Camm at Hawker Aircraft recalled:

Camm was a very difficult man to work for, but you could not have a better aeronautical engineer to work under… Camm had a one-tracked mind – his aircraft were right, and everybody had to work on them to get them right. If they did not, then there was hell. With regard to his own staff, he did not suffer fools gladly, and at times many of us appeared to be fools. One rarely got into trouble for doing something either in the ideas line, or in the manufacturing line, but woe betide those who did nothing, or who put forward an indeterminate solution.

A 1924 aerial photo showing the expanded Hawker factory, and the original factory that was located in the roller rink behind the Cinem Palace Cinema on Richmond Road

The Latchmere Brook defined the eastern boundary of the roller rink and can be seen emerging from its underground culvert on the eastern side of the East Surrey Regiment Barracks. © Historic England

The Hawker Hurricane was Sydney Camm's most famous plane, a fighter that was crucial to winning the Battle of Britain. In 1933 at his drawing table in Canbury Park Road, Camm designed a high-speed interceptor monoplane that used a Rolls-Royce 1,000 hp (Merlin) engine. The prototype aircraft was built, across the road, in the experimental workshop in what is now named Siddeley House and first flew at Brooklands in November 1935

Believing in the performance and capability of their new fighter, the Hawker board invested in the tooling to start production of 1,000 aircraft before they had received a contract from the Government. This foresight ensured that when the war with Germany started, there were already sufficient Hurricanes in service in 1940 to help keep the Luftwaffe at bay during the evacuation of Dunkirk and the Battle of Britain. The Hurricane was the RAF's first fighter to exceed 300mph, the first with 8 guns and the first with a retractable undercarriage. Although the Spitfire tended to take the glory, it is the robust, easier to fly

1930s aircraft production at the Canbury Park Road Hawker Factory

Hurricane that reliably kept pilots in the air, engaging enemy planes. More than 10,000 Hurricanes were built at Canbury Park Road, Brooklands and a factory at Langley.

Camm introduced an aluminium monocoque rear fuselage with the Hawker Typhoon and a lighter weight high altitude fighter the Hawker Tempest. With a top speed of over 450mph and four 20 mm cannons, the Tempest shot down more German V1 flying bombs than any other type, saving thousands of British lives. The Hawker Typhoon meanwhile, played a major role in the D Day invasion and the subsequent advance into Germany.

One of the few surviving Hawker Hurricanes that is now part of the Battle of Britain Flight.

In 1948, needing to adapt to the new era of jet fighter production, the Hawker Company purchased the Ham Works from Leyland Motors for £500,000 to consolidate its manufacturing base. The Canbury Park Road factory remained in use by Hawker Aircraft into the 1960s.

Knighted in 1953 with Sir Thomas Sopwith, Sir Sydney Camm was equally adept at designing jet aircraft and more than 500 Sea Hawks and 2,000 Hunters rolled off the production lines.

June 1946 A Hurricane fighter being paraded through Kingston

Above and left *1948 The Ham Factory recently purchased by Hawkers from Leyland Motors*

Below left and right *Hunter Assembly at the Hawker Factory in Ham*

From the profits of the sales of the Hunter jet, Hawker Aircraft built an iconic office block on the front of the factory looking onto the Richmond Road, that reflected its standing within the aviation industry. Completed in 1958, the building featured an imposing central marble entrance hall that served a central staircase that led to the directors' offices on the top floor. Entrances and staircases on either end of the building led to the commercial, financial and design departments and another staircase at the back of the building connected the commercial offices with the factory floor and the production department.

The imposing office block built on the front of the Hawker factory in Ham from the profits of sales of the very successful Hawker Hunter Jet

Ralph Hooper, a long-time resident of Ham, consolidated Hawker's fame when he designed the vertical take-off P1040 which developed into the unique Harrier Jump Jet. After seeing this aircraft fly vertically, backwards and sideways, Tommy Sopwith declared that he had now seen it all. More than 800 Harriers and Sea Harriers were built for the RAF, the Royal Navy, the Spanish, Italian and Indian navies and the United States Marine Corps. These later models were jointly produced with McDonnell Douglas in America.

Ralph Hooper OBE

Chief Engineer Ralph Hooper then went on to direct the design of the Hawk advanced trainer and light fighter which achieved sales of more than a thousand aircraft around the World. This remains the display jet used by the Red Arrows.

February 1988: Celebration of the 25th Anniversary of the first vertical short take off landing (VSTOL) on a ship with the Hawker (P1127). The ship was the HMS Ark Royal and Bill Bedford OBE & AFC was the chief test pilot of Hawker Siddeley from 1956-1967. Photo courtesy of Ralph Hooper

Lured by the reputation of the quality of their apprenticeships, Richard Cannon applied to Hawkers for an engineering apprenticeship. He was successful and in October 1951 at Canbury Park Road he began a long, productive and very rewarding career with Hawker Siddeley.

Richard initially began work in the treatment department and after nine months training in both Fitters and Machine workshops he was delighted to be given a position in the Installations Department, designing and testing systems such as fuel and cabin conditioning. In 1955 he was awarded the *Best Apprentice of the Year* trophy.

After one year's valuable experience in the Stress Office, Richard embarked on a two year post graduate course at the Cranfield College of Aeronautics. When he returned to Hawkers, he joined the Research and Development department, a much sought after career posting.

Richard reflects: *It was extremely satisfying to work in a company that had been associated with Tommy Sopwith, Sydney Camm, and Ralph Hooper. Hawkers produced so many world beaters and 21 countries purchased the Hunter. It really was an incredible achievement to sell Hawk and Harrier military aircraft to the United States.*

He recalls that although Hawkers didn't pay the highest of salaries, they did treat their staff very well. Of the five employees that joined the R & D Department with him in 1959 only one had left by the time of the closure of the factory in 1992. During this period, he was involved in working on three fabulous aircraft, the Hawker Hunter, the Harrier and the Hawk.

At the Ham factory, Hawkers had several restaurants/canteens on site which included the works canteen for people on the shop floor, the works staff canteen for foremen and charge hands, the weekly staff restaurant for people who worked in the office but were paid weekly, the monthly staff restaurant for more senior people and the silver grill for the heads of departments and directors. Richard, in turn used the weekly paid and monthly paid staff canteens. For a highly subsidised payment that was deducted from his salary, Richard enjoyed a very good meal every day, comprising a starter, a main course and a sweet. Now long since retired, Richard continues to enjoy his main meal each day at around 12:30pm.

Richard was an active member of the Hawker sailing club and over many years took on various committee roles including Commodore, Treasurer and Sailing Secretary. Employees of Hawker's could join the sports club for a small charge then join any of the sections that interested them for another small charge. The sailing club had a purpose-built club house behind the Hawker sports and social club, overlooking the river and built their own slipway into the Thames.

From Spring to Autumn, immediately after finishing work, he made his way directly to the sailing club two nights a week. They carried out training on Wednesday evenings and races on Fridays. The club owned 3 SigneTs and members personally built five SigneTs one of which was for the use of the club. Richard is still sailing his SigneT today (in 2020) at the age of eighty-five.

The Hawker Sports Club by the River Thames with SigneT ST368 and prizes/trophies won around 1980. Crews Guy Addis, Roy Melsom, Tim Wild, and helm Richard Cannon

Richard worked for Hawkers until the very last day that the factory in Ham was open in 1992. He reflects that it was a very sad day when they started to demolish the magnificent office block on the front of the factory, that had meant so much to so many people in the area.

Yet, Richard considers himself very fortunate to have enjoyed a lengthy, interesting and very rewarding career at Hawkers, part of a large family. Although they had many challenges, some of them very demanding, it had also been great fun.

Top left *Hawk Assembly*
Above and left *Harrier Assembly*

Note from Author: *Living in Tudor Drive in the 1960s and 1970s I was familiar with the Hawker tide that swept up and down the road twice a working day. In the morning before 8:30 a stream of Hawker employees, many of the men wearing suits and carrying briefcases walked up Tudor Drive to the Hawker Factory at the top of the road. At the end of the working day back they would return, day after day, year after year throughout the length of my childhood. Many of our neighbours were long term employees of Hawker's, Derek Avery, Graham Galton to name just two. My mother Eileen Elsden, worked at Hawker's for more than 15 years and my sister, Frances's, experiences there for more than 10 years, after leaving school, set her up with the foundation of a successful career.*

A GR9 Harrier from 800 Naval Air Squadron takes off from HMS Ark Royal
Credit: Ministry of Defence – Open Government Licence

Between 1975 and 1980, I was fortunate to get summer holiday jobs working in the Personnel department of Hawker Siddeley at the Richmond Road Factory in Ham. When I first started in 1975, I was made the odd job boy of the department. Amongst other routine tasks, I had the opportunity to carry notes and memos to the secretaries of the directors on the imposing and very silent golden mile (on the top floor), the less tranquil silver mile (a floor below) the design office and the factory floor where they were assembling double seater Harrier jump jets for the US Marine Corp. On my first day, I was seated at a desk at the back of the large, open floor personnel office when I was approached by the secretary to the personnel director. Very politely, yet firmly, Rosemary asked me to sit at the next desk. Half an hour later, an elderly, rather stooped gentleman with quite prominent ears took his seat at the desk where I had been sitting. He introduced himself as Jack, formerly known in his youth as Buttons from the roller-skating rink in

Canbury Park Road, who had been employed by Thomas Sopwith so many years ago. Jack, 79 years old, lived at 14 Tudor Drive and was a passionate member of the Hawker's bowls team. Every evening in the summer he would be found at their immaculate green at the thriving Hawker's sports club, located between the factory and the river. The sports club is still there, now owned by the YMCA. Unfortunately, the grass square is nowadays a ghost of the bowling lawn, that provided so much entertainment for so many members of Hawker's! Over the next six weeks, at our desks at the back of the personnel office, I would often chat to Jack. He told me about the excitement of towing planes down to the river for Harry Hawker to put them through their paces and his passion for all the sporting activities organised by Sopwith's and later Hawker's. Looking back, I wish that I had been a little more inquisitive and documented more of his stories.

Hawker Aircraft Head Office and Works in Ham

For most of the 20th century, the aviation business that bore the names of Tommy Sopwith and Harry Hawker had served as the largest employer in Kingston, providing jobs and long-term security to thousands of local families. Sopwith/Hawker apprenticeships were very much sought after and they gave many a school leaver a solid start in life. Furthermore, the Hawker sports and social club, with its fabulous ground by the river, supported a multitude of sports and social activities for the entertainment of many Kingston families and provided an uplifting, wonderful sense of camaraderie amongst its members.

In 1977, when Hawker Siddeley was nationalised by the British government to become part of British Aerospace, the company owned half of Britain's aircraft industry. Fortunately, Tommy Sopwith who lived to the age of 101, did not have to witness the closure of the Ham

Sir Tommy Sopwith CBE (1888 - 1989)

Harry Hawker MBE AFC (1889 - 1921)

factory by British Aerospace in 1992 and the demolition of that wonderful iconic building, that had so proudly represented the might of British aviation. It is sadly missed!

Picture Credits

All photos courtesy of David Hassard and the Kingston Aviation Project, unless otherwise indicated.

From Orchard to Housing Estate

c1926 aerial view overlooking Ham Farm & Orchard, Fernhill and the Leylands Factory. Courtesy of Ian Hazleden

c1937 aerial view showing Tudor Drive stopping at Latchmere Lane. The route of the Latchmere Brook can be seen in the distance at the top of the picture. © Historic England

c1947 aerial view showing Ham Farmhouse centre left in front of St Andrew's Church. Tudor Drive & Barnfield Avenue are well established. © Historic England.

Close up of Ham Farmhouse with St Andrew's Church and Ormeley Lodge behind. © Historic England.

Church Road & Ham Farmhouse by S.J.Lansdale

The new Richmond Park Estate, that consisted of about 830 houses, was built on Ham Farm, land previously owned by Lord Dysart of Ham House within the urban district of Ham.

In April 1933, the urban district of Ham had ceased to exist, and this southern part of Ham was transferred to the authority of Kingston. Lord Dysart sold part of the land of Ham Farm to G T Crouch Developers and the new houses and roads of the Richmond Park Estate quickly emerged.

Promoting the Richmond Park Estate.
Courtesy of Don Chetland

1948 aerial photograph showing Ham Parade and Ham Farm Courtesy of David Hassard

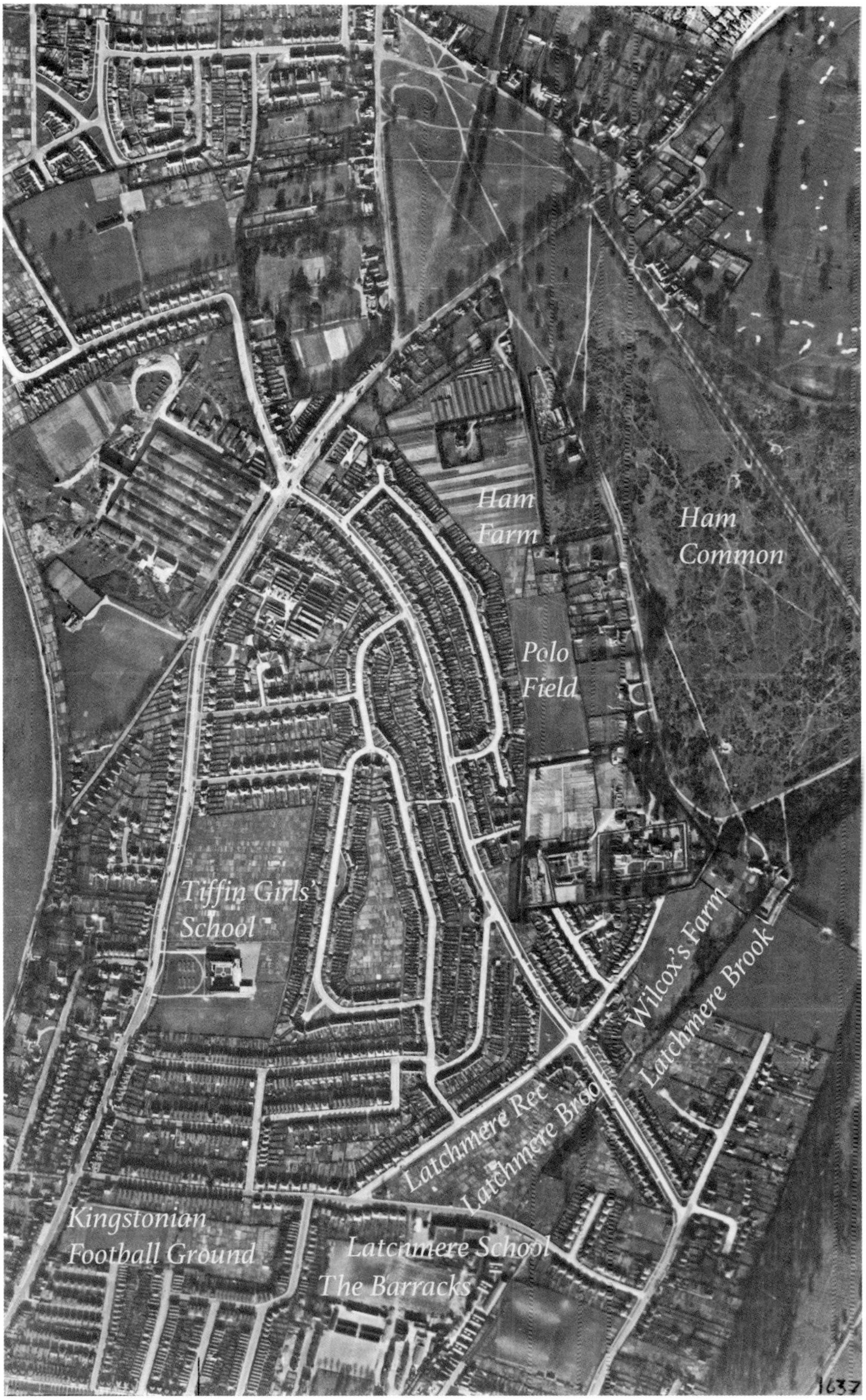

1944 RAF Reconnaissance aerial photograph showing Ham Farm & surrounding area © Historic England

Taking the Name of the Brook – The Latchmere School

Hurricane over Latchmere School painted by B. Withams.

Within four years of being opened, Latchmere School was cast in the shadow of the 2nd World War. Many of the children were evacuated. All of the male teachers were enlisted and the female teachers had to take turns watching out for incendiary bombs landing on the school during night time bombing

The Latchmere School emblem designed by Mr Pearson. It features steps leading up to a doorway. At Latchmere, students can climb the steps and open the door to learning.

The school, completed in 1936, faced onto the Latchmere Recreation Ground (known locally as the rec) that had been gifted to Kingston Corporation by Lord Dysart under the Richmond, Petersham and Ham Open Spaces Act of 1902. Behind the school was the East Surrey Barracks. The noises from the rifle range and drill square made an interesting distraction for the school children, however, the rank odour from the pigsties, attached to the Barracks, wasn't so pleasant. The culverted Latchmere Brook determined the eastern boundary of the school.

The school was a single storey building with a large enclosed quadrangle containing a grass lawn surrounded by a covered walkway that fed into each of the classrooms. The classrooms had large picture windows which allowed plenty of light and added to a sense of spaciousness.

Latchmere School took many children from the new Richmond Park Estate as well as children living in the streets of north Kingston as far south as Eastbury & Bearfield Roads. Children living further south continued attending Richmond Road and St Paul's Primary Schools.

Mr F A Pearson was the headmaster of the junior school from its opening on 31st August 1936 to April 1958. He was fondly remembered for his puppet shows and he was also a very good artist. His nickname, though not to his face, was Polly in tribute to his beaked nose. He was remembered by many students for being the only master that used the cane. Though the use of the cane is frowned upon now, it was at the time an accepted means of discipline in most of the schools in the country. By all accounts, Mr Pearson used it sparingly and created a more relaxed and creative environment for the children at Latchmere than many other junior schools.

When the school opened it had eight female teachers and two male. Miss Stanbridge became the headmistress of the infants school for children aged between five and seven.

The War 1939 – 1945

All the male teachers, with the exception of Mr Pearson, were called up during the war. Air raid shelters were built at the back and front of Latchmere School. When the air raid sirens sounded, the children picked up their pencils and books and accompanied the teacher to the shelter. They stayed there, working, until the all clear sounded. Each night three female teachers were on duty, along with Mr Pearson, to take turns doing a fire watch with stirrup pumps and water buckets ready, in case any incendiary bombs were dropped on the school. They rested on camp beds in the staff room and took it in turns to keep awake. The following morning, they started teaching at the usual time.

Mike Eaton who went to Latchmere school in 1941 remembers:

From the playground at the rear of the school we used to look through the railings directly onto Kingston Barracks. We could see the soldiers cleaning their weapons and quite often the soldiers would come over for a chat and show us how to pull cloth through the rifles to clean the barrels. We could also see a corner of the drill square and hear the men being put through their paces.

1945 Classes and Teachers of the Junior School

Headmaster - Mr Pearson

1A Miss Madley	44 pupils	1B Mrs Dowling	44 pupils
2A Miss Booth	46 pupils	2B Miss Audric	45pupils
3A Miss Owen	44 pupils	3B Mrs Arthur	41 pupils
4A Miss Wills	48 pupils	4B Mrs Howard	38 pupils

1C Miss Bayliss (30 pupils in special class)

1948 - Teachers at Latchmere Juniors School

Back Row : Mr Branson, Miss Baptie, ??, Mr Townsend, Miss Crowe, Miss Audric, Mr Price

Front Row : Miss Madley, Mrs Dowling, Miss Bayliss, Mr Pearson, Miss Wills, Miss Booth, Miss Owen.

Miss Madley was a popular teacher who enthusiastically recited all the verses of The Cataract of Lodore by Robert Southey to the children in her class. Below is one of the many enchanting verses of the Poem.

The Cataract of Lodore

From its sources which well
In the Tarn on the fell;
From its fountains
In the mountains,
Its rills and its gills;
Through moss and through brake,
It runs and it creeps
For a while, till it sleeps
In its own little Lake.
And thence at departing,
Awakening and starting,
It runs through the reeds,
And away it proceeds,
Through meadow and glade,
In sun and in shade,
And through the wood-shelter,
Among crags in its flurry,
Helter-skelter,
Hurry-skurry.
Here it comes sparkling,
And there it lies darkling;
Now smoking and frothing
Its tumult and wrath in,
Till, in this rapid race
On which it is bent,
It reaches the place
Of its steep descent.

Latchmere School

In 1937, Owen Walter went to the newly opened Latchmere School. In later years he wrote a very interesting book called 'Latchmere School – The First Ten Years'. This book is still available from the school reception.

Aerial photograph taken in the late 1940s showing Latchmere school from the west and the prefabricated houses that were built on Latchmere Recreation Ground, opposite the school. © Historic England

The Infants School

Although his sister Eileen and his cousins Joyce and Eva went to St Paul's Infants and Junior School, John Hayward and his cousins Pat and Jo were among the first children to go to Latchmere School which had opened only two years before in 1936. John and Pat were both quite rebellious. In 1953, Anne Sloan, his niece, began at Latchmere School. In view of the reputation that John had established for himself, more than ten years before, Anne was relieved that her surname was not Hayward!

Anne's first teacher was Miss Pert who taught in a wooden classroom at the back of the school next to the Barracks. Miss Pert, in her early 20s, was lively and enthusiastic and helped the children settle into the routine of school life very quickly.

In the second year Anne was with Mrs Horsley in a hut on the west side of the school near to Latchmere Road. She remembers that Mrs Horsley was a kind and sympathetic lady who, on a cold winter's day, would warm the children's milk around a stove in the classroom so they wouldn't have to drink it cold. She was quite slim with glasses and short curly dark hair, similar in age to Anne's mum. She was very keen on country dancing and ran classes with her husband, who played the accordion. Years later when Anne met her, Anne was amazed when Mrs Horsley appeared a lot younger than she expected.

Anne remembers: *The headmistress of the Infants at the time was Miss Stanbridge, an elderly stern lady. Whenever she entered a classroom, she hung her cane up on the cupboard door. That immediately changed the atmosphere in the class.*

Miss Stanbridge and her cane were partners during her regime as head teacher of the infants. She often carried her cane around with her and threatened that if anyone broke the rules, the cane would be used. Quite scary for a five-year-old! The threat sufficed.

Anne remembers the two sisters, the Misses Crowe who worked in the school office, one for the juniors and one for the infants:

They liberally dispensed Dettol to bathe all the cuts and grazes which were incurred in the playground during break. In fact, their small office smelt of Dettol. The Miss Crowe, who looked after the infants, had a kind and gentle demeanour and the children all felt comfortable going to her for help. The Miss Crowe who looked after the juniors was a lot sterner, more brusque, and the children were quite wary of her. They drove to school together in a Morris Minor.

Carole Richardson started at the infants in September 1949. She was part of the generation of war babies and there were more than 40 children in each class. She recalls Mrs Danks, who one Christmas asked if Carole's dad (a greengrocer in Tudor Drive) could get her some bananas which were still difficult to get hold of.

The Headmaster of the Junior School, Mr Pearson

Anne Sloan recalls: *The headmaster, Mr Pearson, was totally committed to the school and all of the children in it. He was aware of his nickname (Polly) and whenever he signed his autograph, he drew a bird like a cockatoo.*

As headmaster, he selected one boy and one girl, a different one each day to be his monitors. It made us feel very important. When not running errands around the school, he taught us to play chess and encouraged attendance at a chess club at lunchtime.

The children were genuinely quite sad when Mr Pearson retired. He had taken a real interest in the children and the school. After his retirement, he came back into the school after a long trip to Africa, or maybe South America, and showed my class a photo of a bird, just like the one that he drew next to his autograph.

Teachers of the Junior School

Owen Walter remembers: *Miss Booth was the strictest of the teachers and terrified most of the children. If you stepped out of line you got a ruler over the back of the legs or a rap over the knuckles. We all sat in a state of fear and trepidation and very much paid attention. Well, all except for John (Hayward), who couldn't help but provoke Miss Booth on a regular basis, much to the fascination of the other children in the class. Apparently one of the first topics of conversation for Joan W. and her mother after school was "what did John get up to today?"*

John Hayward recalls: *I really didn't get on at school and Miss Booth tended to bring out the worst in me.*

Mike Eaton remembers: *Miss Booth, who was a bit of a stickler, was not averse to giving a rap over the knuckles with a ruler.*

In the 1st year of juniors, Anne's teacher was Mrs Dowling. She was one of the older teachers with her dark wavy hair secured in a bun at the nape of her neck. She managed to balance a firm handling of the more boisterous boys with a gentle welcoming approach to the class. Anne enjoyed having her as a teacher.

Miss Simon was Anne's teacher in the 2nd year. She was one of the oldest teachers with white hair and a foreign accent. She always pronounced "And" as "An" which always brought Anne up with a start because she thought that she had been caught for not paying attention. They had *fun time* on Friday afternoons when members of the class were invited to sing or tell stories.

In her 3rd year, Anne Sloan considered herself lucky to have Mr Townsend as the class teacher. He was very popular with the children and this was for Anne, a special year at Latchmere. The children in the class responded well and did their best for him. Occasionally he would show films on a projector in the main hall. He left the school for a while but then came back as headmaster. (*Apparently, he had done his wartime service in the Royal Navy. When he returned to the school, he was well tanned. He was a handsome man and very popular with the Mums!*)

Miss Owen with brown hair and a slight build was affectionately remembered by many of the children at the school for being a gentle, cheerful and caring teacher who gained the co-operation of the children without ever shouting at them. She joined the school in August 1937 and stayed at Latchmere until her retirement.

Anne Sloan: *The other 4th year teacher was Miss Owen. She was a lovely teacher who took the girls in my class for Needlework every Thursday afternoon. I remember making a pillowcase by hand while we listened to a story on the radio. Many years later, I met the niece of Miss Owen. Apparently, Miss Owen, who was very creative, had really wanted to be an artist but her parents insisted that she should be a teacher. I was told that there was a beautiful work by Miss Owen on display at St Mary's Church in Wareham, Dorset.*

For her 4th year Anne really hoped for Miss Owen but instead, her class got Mr Branson: *What a change from Mr Townsend! Mr Branson was quite scary and used to throw chalk at us if we weren't paying attention. When I got an interview following my 11+, he told me "wonders will never cease". This was the only year at Latchmere that I did not enjoy.*

Carole Richardson recalls: *Mr Branson, one of my class teachers, had quite a temper. He would throw board rubbers or chalk at the children. In anticipation, we would lift our desk lids to block the missiles.*

Miss Wills was very understanding and could easily soothe down a class and let incidents blow over. Bill Waddell was taught by Miss Wills in Class 4A. She filled Bill with amazement because she had travelled to Switzerland and had, in her classroom, wonderful picture books.

Miss Audric had auburn hair that was plaited and curled round like headphones. She was a support teacher who taught music, country dancing and nature studies. She played the violin, the piano at assembly and endeavoured tirelessly to teach many children how to play the recorder. Anne Sloan thought that she was a bit nutty: *she used to sit on the grass in the quadrangle at breaktime, sometimes doing her hair or grooming her dog, called Patch, that occasionally she brought into school.* Miss Audric also took a group of children on a youth hostelling trip.

Miss Alexander was a craft teacher and Carole R remembers that she taught the girls to knit a pair of sleeve extensions for a jumper (not that they had any use for them!)

Mr Edmonds was a teacher who had spent a lot of time in the army. Carole Richardson recalls: *He could be easily diverted to tell us one of his many wonderful stories. "Sir will you tell us about your time in Africa" and off he would go.*

Discipline

As soon as the war began many of the male teachers left to join the forces. John Hayward remembers Mr Pearson, the headmaster, standing at the school gate in the morning with his cane twitching, to clip anyone who arrived late.

One day after he had been squabbling with Janet G, who lived in Kings Road, they were both sent to Mr Pearson. He gave John three strokes of the cane on his left hand then asked him to put out his right hand. John was expected to take the punishment of Janet G because Mr Pearson didn't cane girls! John never spoke to her again.

John's cousin Pat, who was in the same class, was even wilder than him. She was a fiery girl with red hair and would fight anyone. She lost her temper one day and threw an ink well across the classroom. John wasn't sure what happened to her after the incident because she refused to talk about it: *None of the younger ones were angels*, recalls John.

Overall John hated school. Unsurprisingly, he was caned quite a few times while he was there.

When Owen Walters was about 9 years old, he was involved in a tussle with another boy resulting in him encroaching on the grass, which was out of bounds. He was summoned to the headmaster's office and caned twice on his hand by Mr Pearson. He clearly remembers that it stung a lot.

Mike Eaton managed to avoid getting the cane at school, though, on occasions he might get a rap over the knuckles or have chalk thrown at him.

During Anne Sloan's time at the school, caning was the exception rather than the rule. Mind you, the weekly average of strokes administered had significantly reduced after her Uncle John (Hayward) had left the school.

Ink Wells, Fountain Pens and Chalk Boards

Two children shared a wooden desk with a lid that lifted. Ink wells were located in the top corners and these had to be filled by an ink monitor. In the early days they did not have fountain pens, just a nib on a wooden shaft.

By the time that Carole Richardson arrived at the school: *All of the children had simple fountain pens. An ink monitor had to fill up the ink wells. They were also given green blotting paper which the boys folded up to soak up all the ink in the wells. This created a mess which they then had to clean up.*

Mike Eaton recalls, *some of the more mischievous boys would dip the ends of the plaits of the longer haired girls, who were sitting in front of them, into the ink wells.*

Mike also remembers, *many of the teachers had beautiful flowing handwriting on the chalk board.*

Milk Monitor

Every morning, each of the children would get a small bottle of milk holding a third of a pint. It was a good job being a milk monitor. You collected the crates and handed out the milk and if you were lucky you could get another bottle.

Owen Walter shown holding a teddy bear during the milk break

Walking to School

Carole Richardson who lived in Tudor Drive recalls: *It was an easy journey, each day, from my home above the shop on Tudor Parade, down Hollybush Road then across the recreation ground. I don't remember my mum ever taking me to school or collecting me.*

School Lunches

Carole remembers, *there was a canteen at the opposite end of the school (a low level white prefabricated building) with a pervasive smell of stewed meat. All the food was freshly cooked. Fish was served every Friday, usually with bones. Meat pie and stew were also common fare. There was always a pudding and on good days, jam sponge pudding with custard or butterscotch tart. Looking back, I always think of the catering team, as "Wholesome cooks with white overalls and hats"*

Christmas Concerts

Bill Waddell recalls the first Christmas concert that he starred in at the age of about seven: *I was delighted to get a role as one of the Kings in a production called, "We three Kings", as I would be able to wear a crown. What I hadn't expected was that I would also be wearing a voluminous pair of knickers. On the night of the production I had to be cajoled onto the stage in front of all the proud parents but tightly wrapped up inside a cape that hid my face. I could hardly breathe!*

Anne Sloan: *Mr Pearson also wrote the scripts for the school Christmas Pantomime. One year, my class performed a sketch called "Old King Coal". I played Queen Fuela alongside Princess Anthracite! I had to dress up for the part and wear high heels. Unfortunately, as I was crossing the stage in front of all the parents one of my heels caught in a gap between the floorboards and brought me to a dead stop.*

Empire Day previously celebrated at Latchmere School on the 24th of May each year. Courtesy of K. Drake

Picture Credits:
Photos courtesy of Owen Walter unless otherwise indicated

Sources
Personal interviews with former students
Latchmere School – The First Ten Years by Owen Walter.

Serving the Crown – The Eaton Family

Mike's father, Frederick, far right with his parents, brothers & sisters. Frederick's father was one of Queen Victoria's gamekeepers in Windsor Great Park

Frederick Eaton was born on 6th November 1891, the son of one of Queen Victoria's gamekeepers in Windsor Great Park. Here, he and his wife raised two boys and four girls within the embrace of a relatively comfortable lifestyle. Fred attended a school in a village in Windsor Great Park that was exclusively for the children of the staff employed in the Park. His father ended his days as a lodge keeper in the Park. Was it through his connections with the staff of King George V, that gained Fred entry into the 2nd Battalion of the prestigious Coldstream Guards on the outbreak of the 1st World War?

Despite the devastating losses incurred by the Regiment in the valley of the Somme, Fred somehow survived and ended the war in the more benign landscapes of Italy and Malta.

Moving to Kingston Upon Thames

After the war, Fred joined the Metropolitan Police Force and married Marjorie. Marjorie was a State Registered Nurse, having specialised in midwifery. At this time there was no National Health Service and it cost a few shillings every time that you called a Doctor out.

Fred in the field uniform of the Coldstream Guards

The majority of families could not afford this. A landed family had engaged her as a District Nurse to support the inhabitants of East Hagbourne in Berkshire with the use of a tied cottage. She dealt with their day to day health problems, their injuries, delivered their babies and laid out their dead.

Michael (Mike) was born in November 1936 and a year later Fred managed to purchase a house in Barnfield Avenue on the Richmond Park Estate for about £350. Fred was employed as a Police Constable in V Division working shifts at Richmond Police Station and on occasions patrolling around Ham and Petersham. He used to cycle every day to the police station.

Mike recalls that his father was a quiet man who kept himself to himself. He had a powerful vice-like grip, obviously useful in the police force. One of Mike's regrets is that he never had the opportunity to speak to his father about the war. In reality, he saw very little of him. Fred worked shifts and spent a lot of his free time working on their two allotments, one in Fernhill and one in Petersham. During the war years he was also employed as a local air raid precaution warden, equipped with a stirrup pump and responsible for putting out fires caused by incendiary bombs. In the spare time that he did have, Fred was an active freemason.

Having been a guardsman in the Coldstream Guards, Fred was meticulous in preparing his police uniform, polishing his boots and folding his cape in a certain way. Mike clearly remembers helping his father by polishing the metal buttons of his tunic in the warmth of the kitchen, listening to the wireless. It was a rare moment of quiet camaraderie between them.

A lifetime of polishing buttons from the Coldstream Guards to the Metropolitan Police

At this time people had to work otherwise their families could starve. There was little in the way of support. Workers were rarely late. If they were, they would be docked pay. They also never took a day off, unless really necessary. A job was extremely valuable and essential to pay the bills. As soon as the weekly pay packet was received you paid the government what you owed, then you paid the rent or mortgage. Money was then allocated for food for the children and then the adults. If there was any money left it was put towards clothing and shoes. There was no way of getting credit so if you ran out of money, you went without until the next pay day when the cycle started again.

Unfortunately, when Mike was still at Latchmere School, his mother, who had been a heavy smoker, collapsed in the front garden from a stroke. Mike was sent away for three months but when he returned, his mother, though physically recovered, was a different person. Life was never to be the same again. He had to take on increased responsibility, helping to clean the house and occasionally doing the shopping. As Mike recalls, *from that moment, I had to stop sodding around.*

Neighbours

Their next-door neighbour was a retired sea Captain, Mr D who used to smoke a pipe. His son Frank, who lived with him, was also ex-Navy but during the war he worked at Leylands factory on the Richmond Road. Frank grew tobacco plants in his garden and dried them upstairs in the boxroom (small bedroom). Home consumption only!

Mr Wing, two doors along was also a police officer based at Richmond. He and Mike's father cycled together to the station when they were on the same shift. His daughter gained entrance to the Royal Ballet School at White Lodge in Richmond Park.

Another neighbour was a park keeper based at Ham Gate Lodge whose son Tony also went to Latchmere School.

Mr Gardener, who lived opposite, was a film director. He had an Allard Sports car which was quite a sensation in the area. His daughter Jane was very attractive. Mike recalls, *all the boys fancied her.*

Barnfield Avenue

Mike recalls that their house was sparsely furnished with stained wood floorboards. The small kitchen that extended slightly to the rear of the dining room by a few feet had an Ideal boiler, heated by a coke fired stove. The stove had a round top in which you fed the coke to top up the fire. It had a door at the bottom from where you started the fire and cleared the ash.

Mike and his mates took it upon themselves to forage for fallen branches in Ham Common and Richmond Park as kindling for their fires. To avoid being seen going through Ham Gate, they climbed over the wall with their spoil.

A pipe connected the boiler to the bathroom directly above: *The stove got very hot and you didn't want to accidentally put your hand on it.* The fire was kept permanently going to heat the water in the boiler. Mike's father was on rotating shifts (6-2, 2-10 and 10-6) and so he needed to wash and shave at different times of the day before going on duty. This made the kitchen the warmest room in the house and here they often gathered in the winter, listening to the wireless.

The kitchen had a gas cooker and a ceramic (Belfast) sink with a wooden draining board. A wooden flap with an enamel top served as a work area and a small cabinet held plates bowls, cups and saucers. The floor had a mixture of ceramic black and white square tiles and lino running all the way through the hall.

The dining room at the back of the house next to the kitchen had a table with four chairs and a sideboard. It also had two easy chairs facing an open fire with a wooden fire surround and a mantelpiece. This was usually the only fire in the house because there wasn't enough fuel to light another. Wooden French doors within a bow shaped frame, opened out to the rear garden

The front living room was rarely entered by Mike. It tended to be reserved for aunts or anyone posh who came around. It had an oblong carpet laid on top of the wooden floorboards in the middle of the room. This had a similar open fire with a grate and a tiled (brown/cream) fire surround. A mirror was placed above the mantlepiece which supported two brass candlesticks. *These were polished pretty regularly*. It had two easy chairs and a two-seater settee with a small table under the window supporting an ornament. A nice bronze ornament, of a famous brown greyhound called Mick the Miller, was placed on the windowsill. A bay window with the two opening side windows overlooked the front garden and the street.

Upstairs, there were two double bedrooms and a tiny box room in which you could just about fit a bed and chest of drawers. Each of the double bedrooms had gas fireplaces, though Mike never recalls them being used.

One day while visiting his grandmother he was curious about the gas lamp, mounted on the wall. He poked the delicate mantle and to his horror, it disintegrated: *I got my arse smacked something terrible.*

The bathroom was quite modern for the time with a bath and wash basin. His father would shave with a cutthroat razor and would strop the blade on a strap kept in the bathroom.

The toilet, Mike's occasional place of sanctuary, was a separate tiny room.

The wooden boarded stairs were covered with a carpet runner down the middle, secured tight with wooden carpet rods.

Mike's mother washed towels and linen in the bath and clothes in the large Belfast kitchen sink. To get rid of the water, she used a mangle. They had to feed the sheets in carefully, mindful not to get their fingers trapped as they turned the handle. The clothes were placed on a washing line but in the winter, when it was freezing, they were as stiff as boards when they were taken off the line.

Devices

They had electricity but aside from all the lights, the only devices that used electricity were the wireless, an electric iron and a Hoover vacuum cleaner. The plugs were connected to two wires, red and black (no earth). In the back room, there was a wind-up gramophone with his mother's records of classical violin music.

On the wireless in the kitchen, they only heard official news. To find out what was going on you needed to go to the cinema (Granada or Regal) and watch Pathé News. From 1943 to 1946 they listened to Workers' Playtime which was broadcast live from a factory canteen "*somewhere in Britain*' with a well-known celebrity providing the entertainment.

On weekdays in 1949 and the early 1950s they listened every evening at 6:45 to Dick Barton Special Agent. It had a catchy theme tune and every episode ended with Dick Barton in a precarious predicament. They were left to wonder how he would get out of it. Throughout his childhood they never had a telephone or television in the house.

Back Garden

The back garden had a Bramley apple tree that provided an abundance of fruit that would last them all year. There were fruit trees (apple, pear and Victoria plum) in the back gardens of many of the houses on the Estate. These had been part of the original orchard of Ham Farm. However, much of the fruit was going to waste: Needs must, so Mike and his mates went scrumping over the fences to collect the fruit: *I was afraid that my father would give me a right telling off if I got caught, especially as he was a police officer. So, it was important to be ready to leg it fast.*

Food and Meals

As a child, Mike kept rabbits and made quite a fuss of them. When the rabbits reached a certain age, his father adeptly killed them and put them in the pot. They also kept chickens which would scratch and peck within a wire netting enclosure in the back garden. This provided a regular supply of eggs.

His father had two allotments, one on the site of the current Tiffin Girls' School, another in Sandy Lane in Petersham. He grew potatoes, carrots, onions, cabbages and runner beans. Mike remembers his father bringing a large bag of potatoes back on the rear carrier of his push bike and two bags full of vegetables, suspended from the handlebars. With the produce from the allotments, they were remarkably self-sufficient and coped tolerably well during the war. Nevertheless, Mike recollects that the food was very limited and dull during his childhood, owing to rationing during the war and for a long period after. The rationing also affected their clothing and until 1951, Mike only had a bib and brace outfit to wear to work.

In the morning they often had milk porridge. They never had sugar because his mother reserved the ration for making cakes. They had tea without sugar and sometime later, Camp coffee which was an essence of coffee that they poured out of a bottle with a spoon of condensed milk.

Dinner at midday was the main meal with vegetables from the allotments. For tea they occasionally had jam on bread or bread covered with condensed milk. Mike remembers a milk pudding that he enjoyed. It could have been tapioca or semolina with a blob of jam. He energetically mixed the jam to make a pink sweet pudding. His mother made jam from the plums that sometimes came from the trees in the gardens and the blackberries that they collected from Ham Common.

Fruit and tomatoes were bottled in Kilner jars, tomato was turned into chutney and onions were pickled.

You could get a bit of fish during the war at a wet fish shop in Kingston with its distinctive marble slabs covered with fresh fish on ice, and white ceramic tiles on the floor. His mother warned him to keep out of the streams of water that flowed out of the shop and across the pavement to the gutter. At this shop, his mother bought herrings which were very cheap and occasionally winkles which they would extract with a pin. This had a certain novelty factor but didn't do much to relieve hunger. Occasionally his mother bought sprats in Kingston Market then fried them in a pan. This was a favourite meal.

A real treat was roasting chestnuts. On special occasions they made pancakes and apples that were coated with toffee and not forgetting toffee fudge!

Leisure

His father made him a wooden sword and a tomahawk. He also had a pistol in a holster. He often played cowboys and Indians then moved onto Robin Hood and knights in armour. With these few props his imagination knew no bounds and with his friends, they had wonderful adventures.

Mike's father acquired a football for him. Mike took it to Ham Common and immediately become popular with all of the Ham lads: *We would throw our coats down to make two goals and then play a match, thirty-a-side. If you got three kicks in a game, you were doing well.*

The gravel pits in Ham were a dumping place where they could find pram wheels and fruit crates, to build go-carts. He and his mates also became really proficient at building bikes.

Christmas

They had a tree with a few lights and glass baubles and paper chains across the ceiling. On Christmas Day, he would invariably receive an apple and a tangerine, a low value coin, a small chocolate, a toy in a stocking and a Rupert annual.

Shopping and Ham Parade

They very rarely went into Kingston as most of their needs were satisfied by the shops on Ham Parade. The shops during and after the war had very little variety of food and sweets.

His mother had a large shopping bag. She first went to the greengrocer's and he placed the potatoes in the bottom of the bag. This was followed by carrots and cabbage. The ration of meat was wrapped in greaseproof paper as were the fish and the butter. There was very little wasted packaging, hence only a single metal dustbin.

Ham Parade at the north end of Tudor Drive in 1947 © Historic England

Jock's Café was a double fronted café where Costa coffee shop is now located. Workers from Leylands routinely dashed in there for a quick mug of tea and a bun. His mother wouldn't let Mike go in.

On Ham Parade, towards the Common, they had a local fish and chip shop, close to a butcher. Some of the butchers had their own slang that only they knew. Mike tends to think that one of their expressions translated as: *Give the lady the joint that has been in the window.*

Denbys was the local grocer on the parade. But they had to be registered with them to get their rations, if they were available. At the time, biscuits came in large tins and inevitably a number of the biscuits would be damaged. The grocer then made up smaller bags of broken biscuits and these could be bought cheaply "off ration". This was their one opportunity to enjoy biscuits. At the time butter was also rationed. A small wedge was cut from a large slab of butter and patted into a square then weighed. It was then wrapped in grease proof paper and carefully placed in the top of his mother's shopping bag.

Towards the end of his childhood, Mike returned bottles of Corona lemonade and Tizer to the off-license, Threshers on Ham Parade and received 2d for each bottle.

Mike and his friends, at school, swapped their comics to get maximum coverage. One would get the Beano, one the Dandy and another the Hotspur. In this way they would get to read all of the weekly comics, which otherwise they could not afford.

Cigarette cards were also highly prized, and they spent much time swapping cards and building up their collections. Mike recalls the brands of the period - Weights, Tenner, Gold Flake, Woodbines and Craven A. His mother smoked Capstan full strength which Mike recalls well: *Evil buggers they were!*

Left *Courtesy of Owen Walter from his personal collection*

Above *Not from Owen Walter's personal collection!*

Tradesmen

Because of the restriction on the supply of petrol, all the deliveries by the milkman, baker and grocer were done by horse and cart. Milk was delivered to the doorstep by United Dairies. In later years, the horse pulled cart was replaced by an electric van. They needed to be home when the milk was delivered. Otherwise, in the summer the milk would go off and in winter the birds would peck the top to get at the cream.

When Mike was 11, he did a paper round on his bike for the newsagents on Tudor Parade. He got up at 6:30 and carried a large bag, packed full with copies of the Mirror, Mail, Express and Telegraph to deliver along Tudor Drive, Barnfield Avenue, Cardinal Avenue and Aragon Road. It took him an hour each morning before school, and he earned about 4 shillings a week. Many people had a newspaper delivered in those days.

Mike also did an evening paper round for the Ham Parade newsagents. He delivered copies of the Evening News, Evening Standard and the Racing Gazette to Lancaster Gardens &

Lancaster Close. The flats and stairs in the close were hard work with a full bag. For this round, which took about forty-five minutes, he earned about 3 shillings a week.

The Cardinal was the only pub on the Tudor Estate. Mike remembers a cart pulled by two large dray horses. The men unloaded wooden barrels of beer then rolled them through an open trap and down a ramp into the cellar.

The coalman stopped his horse-pulled cart in front of the house. He kept a bull terrier attached to the back of the cart. While the coalman carried the heavy sacks of coal into the back gardens and emptied them into the coal bunkers, the terrier discouraged anyone from pinching his coal from the cart.

They also had two metal dustbins, one for ash and one for normal rubbish. These were emptied once a week by dustbin men coming down the back alley. The dustbin men would open their rear gate, come down the path, collect the dustbin, throw the rubbish in the back of the lorry, then return the empty bins.

Pig bins for waste food were distributed around the neighbourhood and outside the local school and factory canteens. These were routinely collected and taken to local pig farms to feed the pigs.

Mike's father repaired their shoes and boots himself. He would get a big piece of leather that he would sew onto the shoe. He waxed around the seams and then hammered metal studs into the soles to stop them wearing out.

Visit to the Doctor

During his childhood every visit to the Doctor cost a few shillings to half a crown, money that they could little afford. His father initially only earned £4 a week. Despite suffering as a child from what was later diagnosed as a collapsed lung, Mike's mother put a kaolin poultice on his chest. This was a thick paste that was heated up, placed on a rag and applied to his chest. It felt and smelt horrible.

The Local Area

In the 1940's, there were a number of blue police phone boxes in the area. One was located where the bus stop now stands in Tudor Drive, opposite Number 98. There was also one on the grass verge on the Richmond Road at the mouth of the passage running between Tiffin Girls' and The Kingston Academy leading to Wolsey Drive.

There was a polo field at the back of Barnfield Avenue where Barnfield Gardens now sits. Here they could watch Jimmy Edwards, a well-known character, with a full moustache playing polo. Occasionally they found wooden polo balls which they used to play cricket.

Walkers Nursery at Ham Farm had large greenhouses where they grew tomatoes. Closer to the polo field, the land was ploughed and planted with cabbages, potatoes and lettuces.

Walking towards Ham Common on Latchmere Lane there was a small farm on the right-hand side (Wilcox's Farm) which had several cows. The farm had a small horse-pulled trap that carried two churns of fresh milk for sale locally. The women of the area came out of their houses with jugs which were then filled from the churns. (*Some years later this farm amazed the local children when it had a llama in its field.*)

On occasions his mother walked them down to the river via Ham and they stopped to look at the pigs that were kept in small smelly holdings. For children, the grubbing pigs were fascinating to watch.

There were no vehicles parked on Tudor Drive or Barnfield Avenue. This was a wonderful time for kids because the roads and streets were so empty. During the war, owing to petrol rationing, many cars had been mothballed in garages. They were propped up on bricks and the wheels hung on the walls to prevent the tyres from spoiling.

In 1947 they experienced a bitterly cold winter and Mike remembers the Thames freezing. The winters were very cold and foggy and some mornings they would wake to find frost on the inside of the bedroom windows: *Sometimes we used to get dressed in bed because it was so bloody cold.*

Ham Common

We used to select slender branches from elm trees to make our bows because the wood had more give. We also made our own arrows and would have battles over the Common.

Mike remembers at the age of 12 getting his first air pistol, a Diana: *I would have duels with my mates. We stood back to back, advanced 10 paces then turned and shot at each other. Someone was shot through the ear and we were lucky that no one lost an eye. It was strange that half of us, who were up to mischief, were the sons of policemen.*

Kingston Town

Kingston was a bustling, busy working town, characterised as much by its smells as its noise and colour.

If they had the money to travel by bus into Kingston, Mike and his mother walked to the end of Tudor Drive to catch a 65, which travelled from Ealing as far as Chessington Zoo. A single decker Green Line bus that started in Luton travelled via Richmond and the Richmond Road as far as Dorking. They bought a ticket for each journey from the conductor and were charged 2d or 3d, depending on their destination. Pushchairs had to be folded up and placed in the space under the stairs. What a thrill it was to pull the chord running below the ceiling along the length of the bus to ring the bell!

If Mike needed a haircut, they walked into Kingston and stopped at the barbers on the right-hand side opposite the Regal Cinema (later the ABC). Here Mike sat on a highchair and was promptly given a short back and sides.

The Gridley & Miskin Timber yard was located next to Kingston Bridge on the opposite bank of the Thames. Its pleasant odour of freshly cut timber drifted across the river.

A more unpleasant odour came from the tannery, a little further upriver on the Kingston side: *Depending on the wind direction, as we were walking into Kingston, I often said to my mother, "What a stink". It was a sharp pungent smell.*

The market in those days was a proper market. Wet fish stalls, meat, fruit and vegetables. Each stall had its own distinctive smell. The stall holders could add up quick then, even with the added complication of pounds shillings and pence. How quick they could add up 3lb of potatoes, 1lb of carrots... They also had halfpennies and farthings to worry about.

Bentalls was a grand department store. Mike was fascinated by the way that the staff on the counters handled their change. Money was placed in a cylindrical metal container with the bill. The container was then placed inside a metal pipe behind the counter that fed into an overhead network of pipes. With a whoosh, off it disappeared to the cashier's office. Shortly afterwards, it magically returned, with the correct change inside. Every year at Richmond Road School, Bentalls offered a scholarship for one of the children to get a much-coveted job at the store.

Woolworths was another large store with wooden floorboards and in later years, amazing sweet counters packed full of vibrantly wrapped sweets at the front of the store.

Respect

All the boys had school caps and Mike always wore his Latchmere cap when he went to school. If he met an adult, he was expected to doff his cap as a mark of respect.

St Andrew's Church

The church sat on the edge of the Common, clearly visible from the main road which gave it presence. The church was important locally, whether you were religious or not, and the Reverend Mr. Beard, was very active in the local community. He was a very likeable and popular man.

One Ascension Day, Mike was excused school to attend the church choir. After the service Mr. Beard took all the boys to Ham Common to play football and he treated them all to ice creams. These were bought from an ice cream man with a small fridge on the front of a bicycle.

Mike joined the scouts that were run by the church. The scout master was Mr Cockburn.

In those days the vicarage grounds were extensive. Camping was a big thing in those days and a lot of fun. They learned to make shelters and fires, cook and tie knots.

Mike also played in St Andrew's Church football team. Every Sunday they used a pitch near the Ham Rover's pitch on Ham Common. Before the match they had to carry their goal posts down from the church to Ham Common and help mark the pitch out.

Years later in 1962, Mike and his fiancé were married at St Andrew's Church. At their initial meeting to arrange the wedding Canon Beard volunteered, *I suppose you want the choir.*

Memories of the War

Mike was aged between three and nine during the course of the war. They didn't have an air raid shelter in their garden and no means of protection in their house. He doesn't know why. On the green near to the house in Barnfield Avenue was a large reinforced concrete air raid shelter which they could use. When the air raid warning went off, his mother put him under the stairs. They hoped and prayed that the bombs would not fall on them.

One day during the war he was standing in the back alley of Barnfield Avenue with his father and Mr Wing who lived next door but one. He clearly remembers looking up in the sky and seeing a great horde of aircraft slowly droning their way across the sky. Mike urgently said, *Dad, there's an awful lot of planes up there. His father briefly looked up then commented, yes, and they aren't all ours!*

On another occasion, Mike clearly remembers seeing a Hurricane or Spitfire engaging a German bomber and shooting it down. The only problem was that the German bomber, fully laden with bombs, then crashed somewhere in London.

Barrage balloons were amazing! Intended to deter low flying planes from bombing with any accuracy they were secured with a heavy-duty cable and flown at various heights over local factories and in Richmond Park.

Mike's Uncle Lyonald had fought in Burma, with the Gurkhas, possibly as part of the legendary Chindits Brigade. When he returned, he was *skin and bone*. He had suffered badly from malaria and his skin had turned yellow. He only lived for a few years after the war. He gave Mike a Gurkha Kukri and told Mike that he only ever slept well in the jungle when the Gurkhas were on guard. Mike didn't get the chance to speak much to him. In fact, he didn't get the chance to speak to many adults: *You remembered what you earwigged*. He has, however, kept the Kukri which throughout his childhood evoked vivid images of surviving in the jungle on a bowl of rice a day, evading capture by the Japanese.

At the time the Leyland factory on Richmond Road had no façade and consisted of what looked like giant Nissan huts with corrugated roofs. Mike remembers the tanks leaving the

Leyland factory. They travelled along Upper Ham Road and then right along Ham Gate Avenue towards the entrance to Richmond Park. After climbing the steep hill leading up to Ham Cross, they made their way through the Park to Robin Hood Gate. From there they had to make the steep climb up Test Hill (Broomfield Hill) before returning to the factory. The tank tracks could quite easily chew up the road.

The boys were continuously looking for shrapnel, though most of it came from the anti-aircraft guns. Some of the Pom Pom guns were housed on railway carriages so they could be moved quickly along the railway lines. Others were located on the high ground of Richmond Park.

The interior of Richmond Park, halfway up the hill, was closed with rolls of barbed wire to prevent access. However, the best chestnuts and cob nuts were inside a plantation opposite to Pembroke Lodge. Mike and his mates would find a way through the fence to search for nuts there. Ironically, Pembroke Lodge was being used at the time by the Phantom squad, a secret unit trained to operate behind enemy lines. David Niven, a well-known movie star, was a member of this squad. He could have learned a thing or two from the boys operating undetected inside the Park!

The Phantom Squad in Richmond Park being inspected by King George VI.

Digital photo in the Hearsum collection from an original owned by Colonel D.T.W Gibson, a member of the Phantom Squad

Let's go and explore: Shortly after the end of the war, aged 9-10 years, Mike and his mates had a dare to get onto the roof of Pembroke Lodge which at the time was being used to store tools. They would enter through a cellar window and climb the stairs up past the large rooms on the first floor, still full of furniture, to a window that opened onto the flat roof. It was great fun walking around on the roof.

One day, at about noon, towards the end of the war, his mother was taking Mike out for a walk. As they passed St Andrew's Church, a V1 flying bomb (doodlebug) flew over and the motor suddenly stopped. Fortunately for them, the bomb glided rather than dropped and headed towards Teddington Lock where it exploded. He will never forget the distinctive rattle of the flying bombs and the air raid sirens that were located throughout the area. Other than this, he was never really frightened: *I never thought it was going to happen to me.*

Latchmere Recreation Ground had been turned into allotments. Towards the end of the War a V1 flying bomb landed on the allotments and caused a lot of damage to the roof and front of Latchmere School. This meant that, for a term Mike had lessons in the large air raid shelters outside Tiffin Girls' School on the Richmond Road. A paraffin Tilley lamp provided the light and they worked with chalk on slate boards. It was cold and damp down there. The children were exhausted, and many fell asleep. The teachers did their best in trying to teach them, but it was a difficult time for all of them.

VE Day Celebration on the Polo Field behind Barnfield Avenue. It was ruined for Mike when he had to recite a poem but forgot half of the lines! Photo courtesy of Owen Walter

During the war, 65 buses had a large bag on the roof filled with gas that powered the engine. The gas was manufactured from burning coke and was more readily available than petrol. Mike still doesn't understand why they got rid of the electric trolley buses that ran in a loop from Kingston down Park Road and Kings Road. They produced no fumes and were relatively quiet!

D Day was a very well-kept secret. It was only when the radio announcer reported, *the invasion is on; they have landed*, that they were aware that it had started.

On a couple of occasions during the war, Mike's mother took him to Bushy Park for a picnic. The American troops were based there and occupied much of the Park. Mike was fascinated to watch them practicing parachute jumps on a static line from a balloon. Within the Park the Americans had also laid a light aircraft strip.

Mike attended an after-school club at Latchmere School. On one occasion they were taken on a special trip to meet the American GIs in the Bushy Park Camp. They were invited into the Troops' Naafi in a large Nissen hut, where each of them was given a bottle of Coke for the first time and a small fruit pie. Mike watched with fascination a game on a small snooker table in which the balls had numbers. He recalls that the soldiers who looked after them were, *really friendly smashing guys*.

Hawker Aircraft Factory in Canbury Park Road

Mike left school at Christmas in 1951 and a year later, started work in the pattern shop in the Hawker Factory in Canbury Park Road. At the time, they were tooling up to make the Hawker Hunter jet, a very successful jet fighter. Sidney Camm, the famous aircraft designer was still working at Canbury Park Road.

Many houses in Canbury Park Road were owned by Hawkers but sadly today there is not much to show the existence of the thriving aircraft factory, that made such a valuable contribution to this country during both world wars.

Smog

Mike recalls cycling to work in the early 1950s with a scarf wrapped tightly around his face to reduce his exposure to the awful smog. On occasions the buses would follow him down the road because the drivers could see only a short distance in front of them.

National Service 1958-1960

Mike's National Service was delayed because he was doing a toolmaker apprenticeship at Venners on Shannon Corner in New Malden, so he didn't begin until he was nearly 22 years old.

Mike, far right, competing as part of a Jeep assembling display team

He trained for National Service running every morning, before work, from Ham Gate to Kingston Gate in Richmond Park and back again. He was also a keen cyclist. This meant that in the cross country he came 5th out of 200 recruits. This level of fitness made life a lot easier for him. He really enjoyed the discipline, sense of purpose and camaraderie of National Service. He also learned to drive in the army. Being part of the Royal Electrical & Mechanical Engineers Jeep display team, he performed with his group at the Royal Tournament.

Mike gained some awareness of what his father must have gone through when, during the last six months of his service, he was attached to a Guards battalion carrying out manoeuvres on Salisbury Plain.

Looking back

Living through the war years and the period of austerity that lasted for over a decade made me both resilient and adaptable. I learnt to take things in my stride and never worried about things over which I had no control.

My imagination and my memory were fully utilised throughout my childhood and this has stood me in very good stead, long into my old age.

Picture Credits

All pictures are courtesy of Mike Eaton unless otherwise indicated

Wartime Children of the Richmond Park Estate

Bill Waddell's Story

In 1938 William Waddell, a serving police officer in the Traffic Division of the Metropolitan Police, his wife Lilly and their six-year-old son Bill, moved from an apartment in Mayfair to a new house at 6 Garth Close, near Latchmere Lane on the new Richmond Park Estate in Kingston. The house cost £650 with £50 extra for a garage. The builder Crouch had offered every twelfth house to serving police officers with a fixed interest rate on the mortgage of only 2½%: *You could put a fiver down and get a house.* As a result, there was a very strong police presence on the Estate.

It was a modern house built to a pattern. They had a Radio Rentals radio set that they rented for many years. On this they could dial into all sorts of stations. They never had a telephone in the house. They only got a television in 1953 to enable them to watch the coronation of Queen Elizabeth.

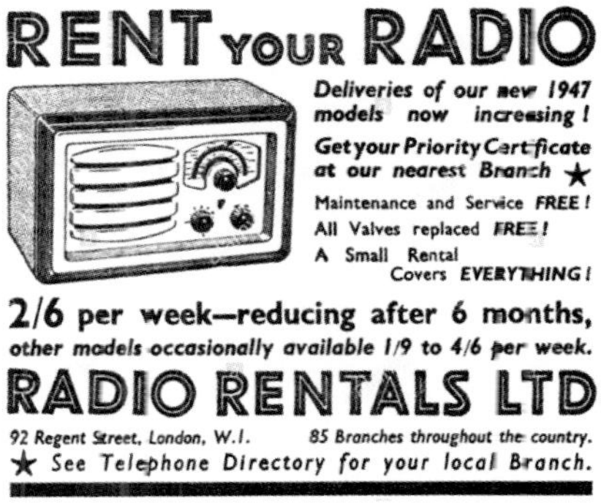

Horace Kenney an actor and writer, lived with his family at number 10. His son James Kenney was a bit of a film star and played Captain Horatio Hornblower in a movie in 1951 and Sherlock Holmes in 1964.

The Richmond Park Estate

The houses at the southern end of the estate had been built on an orchard. Nearly every house had retained a fruit tree in its back garden.

At the end of Garth Road on the opposite side of Latchmere Lane was a small farm.

During the war Bill's mum sent him to the farm to collect goats' milk. Polo ponies were trained on a field behind the stables that ran parallel with Latchmere Lane.

It cost 5 shillings to see a doctor, so you didn't call a doctor unless you were really ill. The local surgery of Dr Kesselson was located at 227 Tudor Drive, the house that many years later, Bill purchased. It had a pharmacy at the back of the house, but the more dangerous drugs were kept under the floor, accessed by a trapdoor.

The Cardinal was a strange pub built at the time that the estate was built with all sorts of Tudor period carvings around the bar.

The War

In 1939 when the war started, they were issued with gas masks and some of the children were evacuated straight away. His father made blackout blinds that sealed the windows.

From 1934 the Bayko construction set was a popular children's toy

Occasionally, when the bombs were falling, Bill joined the family at Number 2. They had a deluxe cosy shelter with bunk beds and an electric heater to keep the shelter warm and dry. Here they would play games. Bill vividly recalls a Bayko construction kit, with a house built on a base with metal pins, that he used to play with while the bombs were dropping.

Children sitting on the large air raid shelter at the junction of Tudor Drive with Latchmere Lane. Courtesy of Owen Walter

Opposite the doctor's surgery, on the green at the junction of Tudor Drive and Latchmere Lane was a large group air raid shelter, covered with a mound of earth and grass with doors at either end. It was invariably full of water.

The German bombers could only carry two or three large bombs, so after hearing the first loud explosion Bill would brace in anticipation for two more explosions. One night a very big bang came from the direction of Ham Common. They waited for the second explosion, but none came. When they went to explore the following day, they found a big crater on the right-hand side of the path (walking from Latchmere Lane). In the late 1950s a large unexploded bomb weighing approximately 200lbs was found on the other side of Latchmere Recreation Ground.

On 16th August 1940, Bill was walking home from school along Latchmere Lane. He heard a racket up ahead of him and, looking up, saw a Junkers JU88, flying very low lining up on the street. In that moment Bill could clearly see, through the Perspex front section of the plane, the machine gunner and the machine gun pointing downwards. He was very shocked. To this day he believes that the only reason the street was not strafed was because it was full of children walking home from school. The plane then banked to the left and flew over the Barracks. His father later informed him that a squadron of low

Junkers JU88 Bombers

flying Junkers JU88's had bombed and strafed the railway station and high street in New Malden killing and injuring many people. (*This was the same bombing raid that had destroyed Eric Lavender's house in New Malden*)

A Centaur Tank built in the Leyland Ham works

Towards the end of the war, Centaur tanks were built at the Leyland factory in Ham. At the junction of Upper Ham Road and Ham Gate Avenue, the road was cobbled to allow the tanks to turn right on their tracks without ripping up the surface. There was an area in the park near Pen Ponds where they carried out controlled detonations of unexploded enemy bombs.

For most of the war, the interior of the Park was fenced off with high barbed wire fences, though you could still take the paths between the gates. Bill would cycle down the path from Ham Gate to the Dysart Gate to go to choir practice at St Peter's Church. This was disrupted when a flying bomb landed near the Russell School inside the park. For some time after, you could see part of the fuselage and the tail fin of the flying bomb beside the path. On the high ground, big navy guns had been placed that could fire horizontally at enemy bombers making their way to London.

One day Bill's father took him to Pembroke Lodge to meet Queen Wilhelmina of the Netherlands, who was briefly living there.

In May 1944, just before D Day, landing craft were stored in the Ham gravel pits. They were there one day and gone the next. Shortly after, Bill recalls seeing wave after wave of Dakotas flying over Latchmere Rec. They all had distinctive white invasion stripes on the bottom of their wings and fuselage to identify them as friendly aircraft.

Bill was a bit of a seeker during the war, collecting bits of shrapnel, all shapes and sizes. He swapped shrapnel for a hand grenade which was a prize possession until his father confiscated it.

The drone of the pulse jet motor of the V1 flying bombs was such a distinctive sound. As long as you could hear them there was no reason to be afraid, which meant that he had a strong urge to run towards them. For the rest of his life, the sound of the air raid sirens made Bill shiver.

In 1945, a V2 rocket landed at the junction of Kings Road and Park Road. The huge explosion killed many people and destroyed a lot of houses. Some boys at Latchmere School told him that the bomb had landed on his house. In a panic he raced home from school on his bike to find his house intact.

One day, as he was walking down Latchmere Lane, he encountered a group of Italian and German prisoners of war digging the road up, supervised by armed British guards. The men, who were probably missing their own families, were very happy to talk to the local people and the children.

Bill was evacuated to live in a cottage on Usk Farm near Middleton in Teesdale, surrounded by the North Pennines. This was great because he didn't have to go to school. Instead he learnt how to milk cows, tickle trout and hunt for rabbits. He will never forget the farmer enticing ravens to fly down and perch on his arm for him to feed them. Bill missed quite a lot of schooling.

St Andrew's to Chapel Royal

Bill was in the choir at St Andrew's. Because of the lack of vitamins from fresh fruit a lot of the children got boils. Bill's baby brother, Kip, was given concentrated orange juice and provided with a gas suit that fully enclosed him. To help compensate for the lack of vitamins, Bill's father gave him fresh garlic to eat. As a result, he was unceremoniously thrown out of the church choir by the choir master, having created havoc during one of the rehearsals. Within a week the assistant choirmaster had invited him to join St Peter's Church choir in Petersham where he earned five shillings a month. Shortly after, he saw an advert in the newspaper for choirboys for the Chapel Royal at Hampton Court. He rode to Hampton Court Palace and met the chaplain and had an audition on the following Sunday. At the age of ten he was accepted into the Chapel Royal Choir in Hampton Court Palace. That garlic wasn't such a bad thing after all!

October 1948 – King George VI inspecting the Steadfast Sea Cadet Corps, Guard of Honour at the opening of the new Kingston power station

Steadfast Sea Cadets

At the same age, Bill joined the Steadfast Sea Cadets in Kingston and became a drummer boy in the band. The Steadfast band was very highly regarded and in 1947 they took part in the Lord Mayors Parade.

A Bicycle made in Heaven

Roads on the Tudor Estate were made of white concrete and edged with tar. You would bump over the raised tar on your bike. On his 12th birthday he received a brand-new Raleigh bike. He thought that he had arrived in heaven and cycled everywhere. One day he was closely following a trolley bus along Kings Road into Kingston when it suddenly stopped. He ran into the back of the bus and the rear board of the bus fell down. Bill continued pedalling furiously knowing that they couldn't catch him.

Lights out

Bill was also the proud owner of an air rifle that gave him a credible appearance that more than compensated for its lack of oomph. One day he decided that it would be a good thing to shoot the streetlight outside his house. Trying to be discrete, he poked the barrel out of the letter box of the front door and took aim. He isn't too sure whether or not he hit the lamp because the barrel was seized by his father on the other side of the door: *Boy, did I get a good larruping!* The air rifle was confiscated never to be seen again.

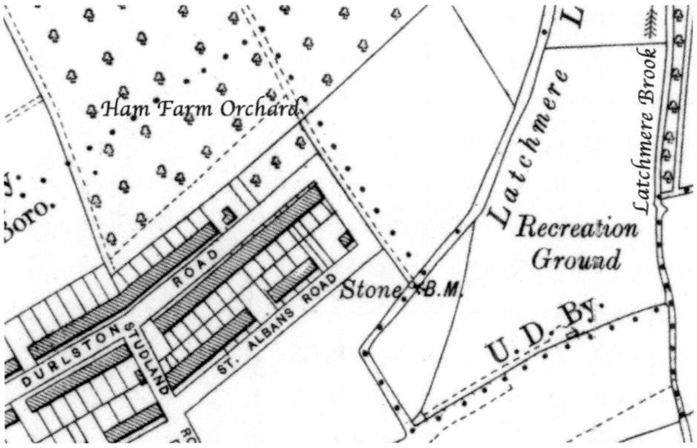

1933 Map showing the orchard of Ham Farm to the north of Durlston Road. NLS

Brian Maskell's Story

Brian was a good friend of Bill Waddell. In fact, he introduced Bill to the Modern school in Surbiton and they were both drummers in the Steadfast Sea Cadet band.

Brian was born in 1932 in Richmond. In the same year his parents moved to 99 Durlston Road in Kingston. At that time, they could look out of the rear bedroom window of their house onto a large orchard that was part of Ham Farm. His mother was extremely distressed when a couple of years later, two tractors dragging chains began to tear down the trees of the orchard to clear the land for the new houses of Wolsey Drive. That wonderful spring carpet of pink and white blossom was gone forever.

1924 aerial photo showing Ham Farm Orchard, north of Durlston Road. © Historic England

Taken from the back garden of 87 Durlston Road. The next building through the orchard was St Andrew's church

Apparently, the south end of the newly established Tudor Drive had been built on land that had formerly been covered by the Hodgsons' Brewery Sports Field and Pavilion. One of the house owners, on this part of the Drive, when clearing out his back garden, ended up filling three lorry loads with empty beer bottles.

The War Years

During the war Brian wasn't particularly frightened about the bombing. If anything, there was an air of excitement. What did scare him was the announcement that letter box tops would be painted with a special chemical. If, following a bombing raid, the paint changed colour then people should immediately don their gas masks.

Although most of the bombing raids were at night, Brian witnessed a number of daytime raids over north Kingston. You could identify the planes by the beat of their engines. In the distance they produced a humming sound. When followed by another wave of bombers the air resonated with the beat of both the near and distant bombers, *da da da da.*

Even at night he could clearly see the bombers. He remembers walking down the path through the common, via Wilmer House and past the church when a German bomber flew very low overhead. There was a huge bomb crater just to the right of this path about 20 feet wide and 15 feet deep. The boys played wall of death on their bicycles cycling around the wall of the crater. They could do this until it rained and the crater filled with water.

The authorities installed an anti-aircraft gun on a trailer at the green at the top of Durlston Road. This fired away all through the bombing raids. The neighbours were so worried about the gun being targeted that they complained until it was removed.

My friends and I liked to play in the wooded stretch of the common to the north of Ham Gate. We used to make dens and climbed up onto the wall of the park. One day, when we were walking back along the narrow path outside the park towards Ham Gate, we saw a man dressed in a raincoat and a trilby hat crouched down by the wall wearing a pair of headphones and looking down at a suitcase that had a long aerial. He saw us watching and told us to clear off.

A few years later, after a house on the Tudor Estate had been sold, the new owners found a German radio device in a suitcase in their roof. This was reported in the Surrey Comet.

Evelyn's Story

Alfred Baker, an accountant and his wife Constance, went and visited 72 Wolsey Drive while it was being built in the mid 1930s. Happy with what they saw, they placed a deposit but in 1937 when they moved in, they were a little disappointed because the rear garden, which was on an angle plot, was a lot smaller than they had expected. The garden was, however, big enough to support an apple tree and a pear tree and it was a good environment to raise their two young children, the youngest of whom was Evelyn, born in August 1932.

Alfred was further disappointed when his business partner let him down resulting in their company going bankrupt. In 1938 with two children, a son aged eight and Evelyn aged six, he joined the RAF. Because of his age he was assigned as ground crew at Biggin Hill.

On Friday 30th August 1940 there was a daytime raid on Biggin Hill.

A group of about ten JU88s made low and fast for Sheppey and then turned south to Biggin Hill where at six o'clock, they hit the airfield with 1,000-pound bombs. Workshops, the transport yard, stores, barracks, the met. office, the armoury, WAAF quarters, and another hangar were wrecked; the power, gas and water mains were severed and all telephone lines north of the camp were cut in three places. Amid the rubble and fires, casualties were very heavy, with thirty-nine dead and twenty-six injured – a number of them in a shelter trench which received a direct hit. Somehow the mess was cleared up and the station put back on an operational footing.

Evelyn's father, aged 32 was one of those who had been in the shelter trench. This was the biggest daytime loss of life at Biggin Hill. Evelyn was only eight.

Following her husband's death and to help make ends meet, Constance took a lodger who was employed at the Leyland factory in Richmond Road.

At the end of the war, Evelyn was able to join in the VE Street Party in Wolsey Drive, but it wasn't quite the same without her dad.

Picture Credits
All pictures courtesy of Owen Walter unless otherwise indicated
NLS: Reproduced with the permission of the National Library of Scotland

VE Day celebrations in Wolsey Drive
Courtesy of Evelyn Baker

The Greengrocer on Tudor Parade & Ghosts

Shortly after the end of the war in 1945, Ben Richardson, from a family of greengrocers in Raynes Park, rented a shop on Tudor Drive Parade. A year later, he also managed to lease the flat above the shop and his wife Connie and daughter Carole, aged two, moved in.

Richardson Greengrocers at 164 Tudor Drive

Fruit carefully displayed in nests of tissue paper

1958 Directory – Tudor Parade residents remembered by Carole

162 Richard Cornwall's – Newsagent managed by John & Mrs Noble

The door was on the angle facing the green grocers. A counter on the far side had behind it several shelves supporting large jars of colourful sweets. At the rear of the shop was another counter covered with newspapers. Tobacco was displayed on the shelves behind this counter. John Noble, his wife and their three children Ann, Christopher and Dianne lived in the flat above the shop. At the back they had, what Carole considered, *a proper garden with grass and flowers.*

164 Ben Richardson - Greengrocer

166 A & M Domestic store with a wooden floor and the pervasive smell of paraffin, which was sold in the shop. Harry Webber had a painting and decorating business and his wife Alice ran the shop with her sister Maud (hence A & M). Alice & Harry Webber lived above the shop.

168 John (Jack) Coughtrey - Grocer & post office. Keith Coughtrey later took over the shop from his father. Jack Coughtrey had served on HMS Quorn with Ron Bevan (Bevans Butchers) during the war. The post office was at the back of the shop.

170 Frederick Green split the shop in two. One half sold toiletries and basic medicine. The other half was a haberdashery shop which sold knitting wool, embroidery, sewing cottons, stockings, gloves & trimmings. Each side had its own distinctive smell.

172 Sid Dornan – Butcher. Sid later split 172 to form two shops, a hairdressers for his wife Joan and a narrow butchers shop retained on the end.

174 The Cardinal Public House. The first landlord was Freddy Higgins and his wife Marie (1940s and 1950s). Then in the 1960s Leo Webb took over with his wife Eve.

Kingston Library, Tudor Drive Branch & Tudor Hall (Bunyan Baptist)

There was a gentlemen's agreement between the shop owners that they would not compete with each other on any product line.

The Cardinal Pub

Carol recalls that every lunchtime, during the 1950s and 1960s, her dad, Ben, visited the private bar of the pub with Sid Dornan, the butcher. Her mum, Connie, never accompanied him. The pub sold Courage beer. Carole remembers the large beer barrels being rolled down through a large trap door into the cellar at the front of the pub.

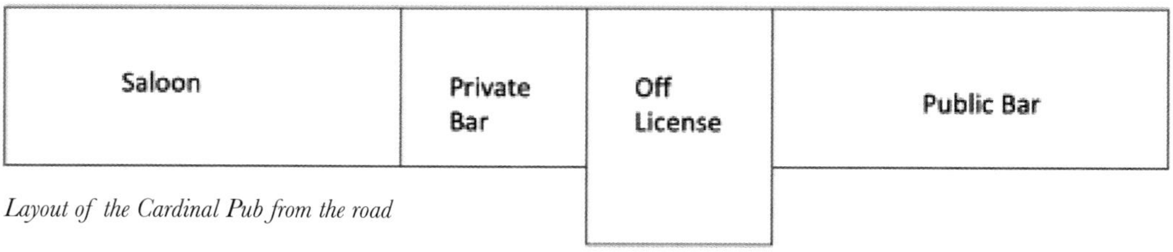

Layout of the Cardinal Pub from the road

The Cardinal in Tudor Drive. It had a twin pub called The Crooked Billet in Ham Street

The Crooked Billet in Ham Street that used to be located opposite the Ham Brewery Tap

The Greengrocers Trade

Ben travelled to Brentford Market four times a week, in an old army vehicle with a cab and canvas-covered iron frame over the platform. Carole remembers her dad telling her that when he had a horse and cart, working from the shop in Raynes Park, he had to be very careful not to get the wheels stuck in the tramlines. Initially, Ben got up at 6am and Carole's mum, Connie, cycled over to open up the shop in Tudor Drive. Carole was looked after in the flat above Coughtrey's store.

Later on, her dad would go to the market a little later in the morning, because he thought that he would get a better price on the stock that was selling slowly. He was very shrewd and a good talker. Carole remembers one of the suppliers telling her: *your Dad is one of the best buyers in this market.*

164 Tudor Parade

At the end of every day, Carole's dad sprinkled disinfectant with a watering can onto the dusty wooden floor before sweeping it thoroughly. She can clearly remember the decorative design of the wood blocks and the very distinctive smell of the disinfectant.

The shop had a large window and inside, a wooden angled display deck covered with green artificial grass. The fruit was taken out and stacked in pyramids, each piece of fruit sitting in a nest of tissue paper, the tissue paper that had wrapped the fruit. Carole's dad carefully twisted and shaped each piece to form the nest. This was a lengthy job but Ben believed that a good window display was very important and he took a lot of effort in making it look good. A rail above the window held bananas on hooks.

Ripening bananas in the storeroom of the Fyffes warehouse next to Kingston Railway Station

The first shipment of oranges, after the war, came over in the late 1940s and there was a queue from the shop all the way down Tudor Drive to Cranmer Road. Customers could only purchase one orange. Bananas were purchased from Fyffes warehouse in Wood Street beside the railway station. The bananas were unloaded straight off the train into the warehouse.

In a stock room, immediately behind the shop, they kept 1cwt (112lbs) woven sacks of potatoes along with carrots and wooden trays of other vegetables and fruit. Later, the sacks of potatoes were reduced to 56lb bags due to the difficulty in carrying and moving them.

Behind the shop was a tiny room with a door that opened onto the yard at the back of the house. In here was an old copper vessel. Carole's dad bought beetroots by the sack-load and boiled them in the copper. As they were being cooked, they gave off a very earthy smell and the water turned a deep purple. Cooked beetroot was very popular with their customers.

The shop had three sizes of brown paper bags depending on whether they were selling soft fruit, tomatoes or mushrooms. Sheets of newspaper were suspended from a hook. This was to wrap potatoes, onions, carrots and greens before placing them directly in the customer's shopping bag. Everything was priced according to weight. Because the potatoes often came in with clumps of mud on them, Ben ensured that the mud was rubbed off by hand to ensure customers only paid for potatoes, not mud. Similarly, carrots had their green tops removed so people weren't paying for what they couldn't eat.

Connie, far left, before the war, at work in the Civil Service

Connie with Carole in the pram in the rear yard of the shop on Tudor Parade

Ben had a large pair of Avery scales with a big scoop to weigh the potatoes and carrots and heavier produce. At the front of the shop he had a smaller pair of scales for soft fruit and tomatoes.

Ben calculated the price of the sale in his head as he was maintaining a conversation with the customer. Carole, herself, later learnt to add up the cost of her shopping as she went around a supermarket.

Customers came every day to buy vegetables for their meals. Ben would refer to his customers, depending on what they bought from him: He would say to Connie,

here comes

Can I have just big ones (referring to potatoes)

Can I have three firm tomatoes

Can I have two Granny Smiths

But if Carole's mum, Connie was serving (and being particularly obliging), Ben's voice could be heard from the back of the shop: *Con, they have to take them as they come!*

On the shelves at the back of the shop they also stocked Bachelors tinned vegetables. In the small garden at the back of the shop they had an old enamel bath which was filled with fresh water to freshen up the greens and lettuces in the summer.

For a two-week period, each year in June, Ben sold strawberries, but it was really difficult to keep them fresh. He had an arrangement with Sid the butcher at the other end of the parade to keep them in the chiller overnight.

He also brought in two or three bundles of asparagus each May. This was a luxury and they kept one of the bundles for themselves for an extra special meal!

Ben monitored his sales carefully and preferred to give Carole 6d to buy a bar of chocolate than for her to take an apple from the shop.

Carole really enjoyed the Cape apples because they were full of flavour. After the UK joined the EU, Cape fruit was not so readily available. Carole's favourite oranges were the Spanish Navel oranges because they were so sweet, but they only got them at Christmas. All the grapes contained pips, and the only time Carole recalls any without pips was a small green grape, which came in from Greece towards the end of the summer.

At Christmas, Ben bought sacks of nuts and Carole helped him weigh walnuts, brazil nuts, hazelnuts and almonds in different quantities to make up Christmas bags. These were white paper bags with a cellophane window so that people could clearly see the mix of nuts.

Ben employed a delivery lad to make deliveries around the Richmond Park Estate that had now become known as the Tudor Estate, owing to the mock Tudor timberwork on the front of the houses. He was provided with a bike with a large tray on the front for carrying the orders.

After the war, people were in the habit of cutting up newspapers for toilet paper. Carole's family used the tissue paper from the fruit wrapping of the Jaffa oranges and so Carole genuinely believed, *we were posh.*

All the produce came in wooden crates or sacks. Ben tended to deal with wholesalers who sourced their produce from farms in Devon and Lincolnshire.

Opposite the parade of shops was open land and they could clearly see the wall of the borstal. Occasionally boys escaped over the wall and fled as quickly as possible.

Cricket

Ben was a keen cricketer and played for "the Crickets", a wandering side that played at some wonderful grounds in the south of England. He used to give a lift to other members of the team in his truck. When Carole accompanied him, she and about ten other children played in the back of the truck while the cricket was being played. On cricket outings, there was always plenty of food and lunch and tea were served at the ground. On the way home there was always a sing song and they often stopped at a pub.

The Crickets with Ben Richardson, front row, far right

Doctors Surgery

This was Dr Bagley at Stokes Hall in Ham Street, with the front door facing directly onto the footpath. Dr Bagley was very approachable and a nice man who knew the families in his practice well and who would always come out for a home visit if required. For a multitude of ailments, Carole remembers her mother heating up a small bottle of camphorated oil in front of the coal fire then rubbing the oil on her body. It smelt wonderful!

Ham Common

Carole spent much of her childhood with family and friends in Ham Common and Richmond Park. On the right-hand side of Ham Gate Avenue leading to the Park (100 yards down) was a small wooden hut, the hut of the Common keeper, a man who patrolled the Common. He wasn't that friendly.

Latchmere Lane

On the right-hand side of Latchmere Lane (walking to the Common) was a white painted stable block and a small house. After the war it appeared that they were building prefabs on every available plot of land. After the stable block were three rows of prefabs, each with their own front and back gardens. There was also a row of prefabs built on Latchmere Rec, facing the school.

Canbury Residents' Christmas Parties

These were arranged by local residents at Christmas for the local children and held at the Tudor Hall. They were great fun, and much enjoyed by the children.

Radio

Radio programmes were a great source of entertainment and very much looked forward to by the whole family. On Sunday afternoon they listened to "Two-Way Family Favourites" that linked army families based overseas with their relatives in Britain.

Other favourites were "Round the Horne", a comedy programme and "The Navy Lark" with Jon Pertwee. In "Educating Archie" Peter Brough, a ventriloquist, had a dummy called Archie Andrews. Looking back, it appears really strange to have a ventriloquist on the radio, but they didn't think about that at the time.

Restaurants

People didn't generally eat out much. Kingston boasted an upmarket restaurant at Nuthalls tea rooms, where Ultimate Outdoors is now located in the Market Place with pagodas by the riverside. Bentalls also had a very posh restaurant on the 2nd floor, with a small orchestra.

Carole enjoyed going to the ABC Café in Clarence Street where she felt very grown up, drinking milk with a dash of coffee. There was also the Black & White milk bar opposite the bus station. Gary's Fish Bar opposite Richmond Road School had excellent fish and chips that always had an outer wrapping of newspaper. Gary was the main frier and his wife was a rather large lady who wore vibrant lipstick.

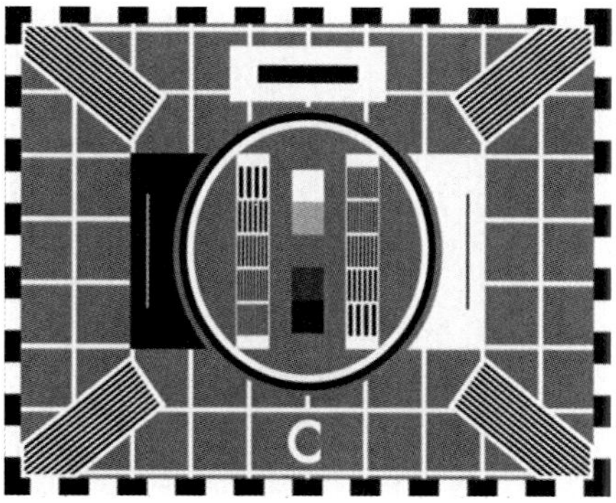

TV

They didn't get their first TV until the mid 1950s. This was a huge cabinet housing a tiny screen which they had to sit directly in front of. They often sat and patiently watched the test card in anticipation of the programmes beginning at 5pm.

TV Test Card in the 1950s

St Andrew's Church

In 1964, Carole and Peter were married by the Reverend Mr. Beard at St Andrew's Church. Canon Beard was a small man with a strong presence. He had a nice sense of humour and they felt very comfortable with him.

John Sentamu was a curate of St Andrew's Church and Chaplain of HM Remand Centre in Latchmere House from 1979-1982. (*He later became the Archbishop of York, which is the second most senior clerical position in the Church of England.*)

A Missed Opportunity

Carole reflects, *Dad had been offered the opportunity to buy the shop and the flat above in the late 1940s for £2,000. Following his well-tested formula, he declined, in anticipation that he would get a better price later on. He never got another opportunity to buy them. When he and Mum finally retired in 1976, after 31 years working in the shop, they unfortunately could not afford to remain in the area and moved to a mobile home in Sayers Common, Sussex.*

Looking Back

Carole reflects, *we always treated elders and teachers with respect and certainly respected the police.*

I had a happy childhood, though, because I was an only child, it was a bit lonely on occasions. I spent a lot of time with the Knight family who lived in Hollybush Road. They had a stall in Kingston Market Place.

At that time, we didn't expect too much. We didn't have a lot of money. Life was a lot simpler and we just got on with it. We made our own entertainment and used our imagination.

Ghosts

In 1964 while discussing their forthcoming marriage plans, Canon Beard told Carole and her fiancé, Peter Smith, that the vicarage was haunted. On one occasion he had been tipped out of bed by the ghost.

Marjorie Lansdale in her small booklet Reminiscences recalled the Poltergeist which caused a stir in the area in the 1950s: *It became a great nuisance in one of the houses in Ham Gate Avenue. I think it must have been Ormeley Lodge and had to be exorcised. It next arrived at St Andrew's vicarage and again caused a lot of trouble, rushing down corridors, pulling clothes off the beds etc. The Vicar of the time, Mr. Baird, refused to allow himself to be worried, but others - housekeepers, curates etc found it impossible to sleep in the house, and again exorcism had to be used. This strange visitation brought us notoriety – it was given a front-page column in one of the big national newspapers and was even mentioned in the House of Commons.*

The path running alongside St Andrew's Church. GE

Malt House Cottage in Lock Road complete with police call box in the far right of the picture. RLS

Michael Willoughby lived with his family in the Malt House at the top of Lock Road. In the 1950s, aged about 13, in the dim light of a winter's evening he was walking past the church on a narrow path with a friend directly behind him,

Suddenly a large chap, wearing dark glasses, appeared and walked straight into me. The force was so strong that I was knocked to the ground. I shouted out in protest but when I looked up the man had disappeared. My friend was looking at me strangely, asking me why I had fallen over. Some 62 years later I can recall the incident so vividly but am still unable to explain what happened.

Picture Credits

All photos unless otherwise identified are courtesy of Carole

GE © Gordon Elsden

RLS: Courtesy of Richmond upon Thames Local Studies Library & Archive

The War comes to Ham

Norman Hill

During the war, Norman Hill was a schoolboy living at 50 Lock Road in Ham. He kept a diary logging all of the bombing raids during the Blitz. It provides a fascinating insight into the disruptive impact of the war for everyone living in this area at the time. This narrative is a true extract taken from the original notebooks which belong to Norman's widow Stella.

Norman and his mum outside their house at 50 Lock Road. Courtesy of Stella Hill

Norman in Lock Road. Courtesy of Stella Hill

22nd November 1940

A raid in early morning, some slight gunfire at beginning. Plenty of planes went over round midday. An early siren sounded just after six. Gunfire started about 10.30 pm. Raid still on at midnight

23rd November 1940

Raid on with gunfire fairly loud, ten small bombs dropped in Ham about 4.30 am. Two bombs in the walk trees, one by Eckit's, one in the dip by the pond, one outside Bendal's front gate, one outside Bensons front gate, one in between Mead and Cleves Road, one in Henner's garden, two in Mead Road. Casualties were Mrs Spiers and Mrs Jux's baby killed, Mrs Jux and Mrs Newman injured. All clear sounded about 9 am and 9.30 am. Puffs of smoke in distance from guns. Lock Road was strewn with pieces of tiles, windows were broken in the houses. Two sirens in the afternoon but all was quiet. A late siren about 8 pm but hardly any guns before midnight.

(Michael Jux and his parents (from Duke's Avenue) were visiting his father's aunt, Louisa Spiers. The explosion, from the bomb that landed on the house, killed both Michael and Louisa and buried his parents under the debris of the damaged house. A leaking gas main caused a fire which the fireman had to urgently attend to before they could set about digging out Michael's parents. MF)

24th November 1940

Raid went on until about 7 am but only a few guns went. Planes have been over this morning, an alert sounded about 1.30 pm, all clear going about 2 pm, but all was quiet. A quiet afternoon. An alert sounded about 6.50 pm ended at about 7 pm. The sirens sounded about 7.30 pm and guns started going at times, but the all-clear went about 10.15 pm. It was quiet until midnight.

25th November 1940

A quiet spell from midnight onwards with no siren, A quiet and foggy morning. An alert sounded about midday and lasted half an hour, nothing was heard in the afternoon except a few time bombs going off. A quiet evening with no alert.

26th November 1940

Quiet from midnight onwards with no siren until about 1.30 pm, when we had a short alert lasting nearly half an hour, but all was quiet. A quiet afternoon with no alert until about 7.30 pm.

27th November 1940

Quiet from midnight until about 6.50 am when an alert sounded which lasted about 65 minutes, but all was quiet. An alert sounded about 11 am and the all clear about 11.30 am. Then there was no activity until about 3.40 pm when an alert sounded, the all-clear going about 4.30 pm. Many planes were about. A lot of time bombs have gone off today. The usual alert sounded about 7.30 pm and the guns were going at times and the raid was still on at midnight.

28th November 1940

An all-clear sounded about 1.30 in the morning. It was then quiet until about 6.15 am when an alert sounded with the all-clear going about 8 am but all was quiet. A quiet morning of no activity. An alert sounded about 12.30 pm and when we were going down to the shelters a German plane with a smoke trail behind it was in the sky with guns going after it. The all clear went about 20 minutes afterwards. It was then quiet until about 2.45 pm when an alert sounded the all clear going about 3.30 pm but all was quiet. The night siren sounded about

6.45 pm but the planes were over and guns going before that. The planes kept coming over and there were not many quiet spells up till midnight.

29th November 1940

Fairly quiet from midnight onwards but a few guns at times, the all-clear sounded about 4 am. At about 12 o'clock a ten-minute alert sounded but all was quiet. Another alert lasted until about 1.15 pm. Another alert sounded about 1.50 pm and lasted till about 2.45 pm. In all these alerts nothing was heard. The nightly alert sounded early at about 6.15 pm. Almost immediately, planes started coming over and every plane seemed to drop a bomb. We went down the shelter and Mrs Giles and family came down as well. This was still on at midnight.

30th November 1940

Raid still on as bad as ever. A welcome all-clear sounded about two o'clock. A big bomb dropped in Lock Road. Greenwoods, Smiths, Elsons, Greens, and one other house are to the ground. Another bomb dropped at the corner of New Road destroying houses in New Road and Craig Road. Two more bombs dropped in Lawrence Road and Broughton Avenue, 6 bombs dropped down the Common, one on Walker's Farm and one on Oak Lodge. A Molotov breadbasket dropped on the Common. We had tiles off and windows broken. Nearly everyone in Ham has tiles off or windows broken. All quiet the rest of the day except for two alerts but all was quiet. We did not have the siren at dusk, but it sounded about 11 o'clock. The all-clear went at 11.20 pm and there was some distant gunfire.

1st December 1940

All quiet from 12 to 12.30 pm when an alert was sounded lasting about 20 minutes, but all was quiet. Two alerts sounded before noon, about one o'clock it was thought that a time bomb was in Darnell's allotments. The engineer came and said it was a time bomb, so we had to clear out. We went down to Aunt Rose's. The traffic was going around the Common owing to a time bomb in Oak Lodge. An alert sounded about 3 o'clock but was all clear about 30 minutes after. Another siren sounded about 7 o'clock and lasted 45 minutes. In all these raids, all was quiet. An alert sounded about 10 o'clock and lasted about 2 hours with slight A.A. fire.

2nd December 1940

An alert sounded about 1 o'clock and lasted till 4 o'clock. Slight A.A. fire. Went to Kingston in the morning for I did not go to school. Dad did not go to work in the morning, still down at Aunt Rose's. A five-minute alert sounded about 1 o'clock. After this, all was quiet until 10 o'clock at night when an alert sounded lasting about 30 minutes. It was then all clear until midnight.

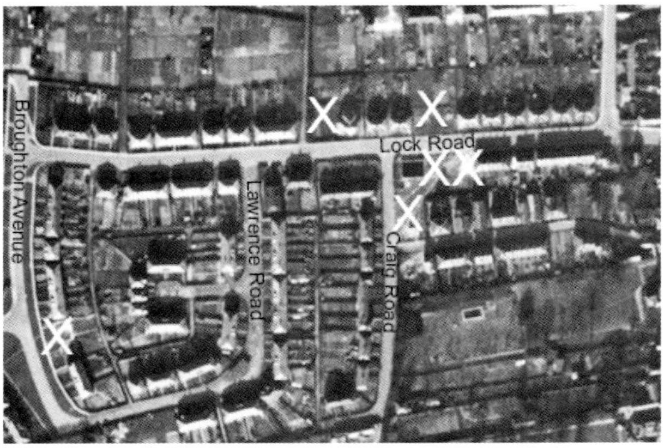

1944 aerial photo showing where houses were completely destroyed. © Historic England

Aerial photo taken in June 1944 showing the Mulberry harbour barges being stored in the gravel pits in Ham in preparation for the Normandy landings. © Historic England

28th December 1940.

Bad night raid. Worst in London for about three months. Fires all around in London.

Nearest bombs round here were in Elm Road, Kingston. Eighty horses were killed when a bomb hit a brewery in London. Two hospitals, a museum and a famous church were hit. Raid ended just before midnight.

Sources
Personal diary of Norman Hill courtesy of his wife, Stella Hill
MF: Information supplied by Margaret Frood. See her blog on the personal stories of those commemorated on the Ham & Petersham Parish war memorial at hamremembers.wordpress.com

The Thames Disappears!

This story was submitted on behalf of Mick Pitt, to 'WW2 People's War', an online archive of wartime memories gathered by the BBC.

It was a warm, sunny Sunday around 1941, and the French windows were open at our home in Kingston, Surrey overlooking the river Thames. With no air raid warning there was a sudden bang. I was 12 years-old and my mother, in the kitchen, vexedly called to my father: "What's he doing now?" She meant me, and I was doing nothing but waiting for my lunch. From our windows we could see a pall of smoke over Teddington Lock, a few hundred yards downriver, where the Thames becomes tidal. We quickly realised it was a bomb. So blasé had the family become about bombs (a hundred fell on our neighbourhood of Ham, so one more could wait) my parents made me sit down to lunch before I was allowed out to investigate.

Neither they, nor my elder brother, bothered to leave the house. But curiosity took me to the Lock. It was astonishing. The river was alive with dinghies and people, surrounded by hundreds of dead fish. They were pulling them from the water — many measuring some two feet - and offering them for sale, supposedly to benefit the War Charity which funded, among other things, aid to our Russian allies. The cause of this impromptu fish market was a stick of bombs, dropped by a German plane, on the Lock. Three or four had fallen into the river without exploding, but one had hit the weir island, destroying it and the sluice gates which controlled the flow at this crucial spot where the Thames becomes tidal. A torrent was pouring over the smashed weir, and concussion of the explosion had killed the fish. When the entrepreneurial trade had subsided I went home to bed, and my father to work on nightshift at the Leyland factory, a few hundred yards upriver from our home, where they built Cromwell tanks.

I awoke when he arrived home in the morning to hear him tell the family in amazed tones: "the river's gone!" We got up to cross the green outside our front windows and stared in amazement. The Thames had disappeared. There was nothing but a tiny rivulet trickling between its broad banks. Off came my socks and shoes and I walked across its bed, some 70 yards, to the Middlesex side. I was soon joined by scores of other sightseers, instant beachcombers of treasures at our feet. There were numerous handbags and handfuls of cash which had fallen, over the years, out of skiffs, rowing boats and punts which recreationally used the river. Revolvers and rifles were also recovered, and beneath Kingston Bridge an empty safe, believed to have been dumped after a successful robbery. I came home with a typewriter, much to my parents' disgust. Apart from its soiled and rusted condition none of us could type.

From Hampton Court lock to Richmond, moored boats had been toppled and damaged, and though the daily tides rose and fell below Teddington Lock, sections upriver remained dry for weeks before the sluices were rebuilt. The bomb had destroyed part of the central island.

Motor Torpedo Boats. IWM

The river was no longer navigable for wartime barges carrying coal and materials up to Oxford. Petrol rationing had turned the Thames into a major highway and Vospers boatyards upriver at Walton, where they built motor torpedo boats (MTBs), could not dispatch their craft to the Royal Navy until the river was brought back to life.

Not a word of the Thames's humiliation ever appeared in the newspapers. Wartime security, denying the enemy satisfaction of publicity, saw to that.

It's not too late to start a new career!

The following story was brought to my attention by Stella Hill whose husband Norman, mentioned previously, followed a banking career after the war. He was a friend of another bank manager whose story follows;

Next time you pass 25 Lock Road in Ham, think of a young army officer, in the midst of the 2nd World War, having a whirlwind romance with a local young lady and marrying her after a week.

That young lady was Iris Mountford, who lived with her family at 25 Lock Road in Ham and worked as a librarian in Richmond. They married on 1st April 1942. Her husband, who had gained some notable success as an amateur boxer in his youth, served as a physical training and jungle warfare instructor in South Africa and India. After the war, he resumed his steady job in the bank and ended up as a manager of the NatWest bank in Thames Ditton.

On retiring at the age of 57, after 40 years diligent service that had been only interrupted by the war, he followed his lifelong passion and tentatively began an acting career. He enjoyed some success and will be fondly remembered for a distinctive role.

Iris's parents continued living in Lock Road until their deaths and are buried in the graveyard of St Andrew's Church. Iris and her husband were together for 57 years until his death in 1999.

Oh, I nearly forgot to mention, the bank manager who became an actor, is better known as Uncle Albert in Only Fools and Horses - Buster Merryfield.

During the war…

The Legacy of Ham's Legendary Boxing Club

Author's note: Gerald Stevens, locally known in Ham Village as the Duke, published a book several years ago covering his childhood memories of Ham and Petersham in the 1950s and 1960s. Dave Morris, a long-standing friend, was quick to point out that Gerald had not included the Ham Boxing Club, which had been a source of discipline, direction, pain, satisfaction and pride in equal measure, for many Ham boys. With the personal recollections of Dave, we have now endeavoured to put this right.

In the 1950s the Ham Boxing Cub shared its domain with Ham Boys Club within a large clapper board structure sitting parallel with Pointers Cottages and tucked out of sight behind Back Lane clinic. It was a fairly basic concrete floored wooden hall with a toilet in a small shed outside. In one corner of the hall there was a small but welcome kitchen that served tea and snacks including baked beans on toast for the members of the boys' club. On boxing nights, Tuesday and Thursday between 7pm and 10pm, it was to prove a more austere environment with the kitchen closed. The first task of the boxers was to assemble the ring in the centre of the hall and set up the boxing apparatus.

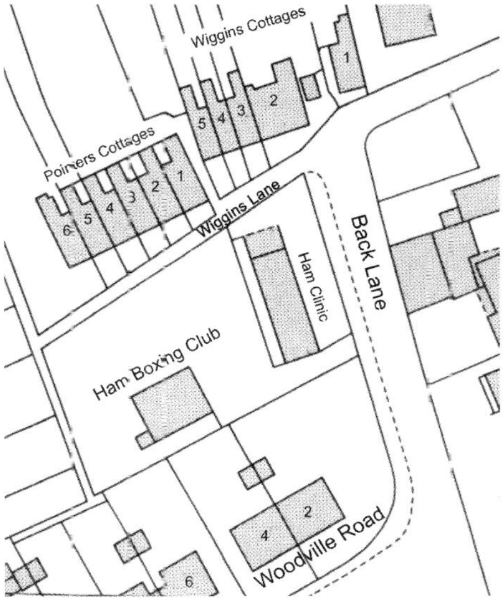

The location of the wooden hut that served as Ham's Boxing Club. Dave Morris lived at 2 Woodville Road and Roy (Nobby) Wills lived at Number 4. They used to jump over the back fence to get to training.

Dave Morris had moved with his parents and thirteen sisters and brothers from Richmond to 2 Woodville Road in 1948, at the age of eight. His grandfather, Percy Morris a Richmond resident, had been an all comer's bare-knuckle fighter in his younger years and his reputation as the *Governor* was imprinted deep on the consciousness of Dave and his brothers. So, when Dave discovered that the wooden structure on the other side of their back fence was the local boxing club, he realised that this had been a divine move. Yet he had to be patient because he could not join until he was nine years old.

Finally, in November 1949, Dave was allowed to enter the hallowed hall of the boxing club. The trainer at the time was George Lovatt. The president was Major McGrath who lived at the Manor House in Ham. At the time he was the Director of Wembley Stadium. Although he had a Rolls Royce sitting in his drive, Dave invariably bumped into Major McGrath at the bus stop while waiting to catch the bus. It appeared that the Rolls was reserved for the use of his wife and her sister!

So, you want to be a boxer, asked George Lovatt, the trainer.

Yes sir, I do.

Call me George. Put on those gloves and let's see you hit that bag over there.

Dave's initial enthusiasm was tempered by the sand-filled bag that felt like concrete and quickly sapped his energy. Nevertheless, George having watched him for a while finally commented,

I think we can do things with you,

and with those few words, Dave entered the revered boxing programme of the club in the company of a band of high pedigree amateur boxers.

Dave Stone

Dave Stone, although a resident of Richmond, learned his boxing craft in the wooden hall of Ham Boxing Club. He then moved to Battersea Boxing Club which was a famous club with excellent training facilities and well established trainers. After leaving Ham Boxing Club, he won two ABA light welterweight titles. The first was with Battersea Boxing Club in 1956. He was then called up for National Service. For the boxers, National Service caused little concern. In fact, after their basic training, the boxers were much sought after by the various regiments. They then spent most of their time training and travelling around the country and in some cases around the Empire, to compete on behalf of their regiment. The record books reveal that a year after winning the ABA title for Battersea, Dave Stone was competing and winning the same title in army colours. In 1958 he turned professional and in his first year won 13 fights, lost three and drew one. In 1959 he won a technical knockout to claim the British Boxing Board lightweight title for the south of England. In the early 1960s he was rated among the top ten British lightweight boxers.

Alex Dunning, who lived in the prefabs, where Ham Close is now situated, was another very talented boxer at the club and excelled both at amateur level and in the army. Dick McTaggart had won the ABA middleweight title, yet Alex went on to beat him three times. Despite having the potential to be among the best, he declined, for his own reasons, to turn professional. He later became a taxi driver.

Charlie Payne was another very promising boxer, but a fluke accident sadly brought a premature end to his boxing career. Yet Charlie maintained his passion for boxing and later became the Chief Inspector of the Boxing Board of Control in the UK. Over the years he worked with many top boxers. A good friend and business partner of his occasionally parked his Rolls Royce outside Charlie's house in Lock Road. It had the registration AM1. Alan Minter later won the unified world middleweight title in Las Vegas in March 1980. Charlie was ringside at that fight, wearing his Union Jack suit and bowler hat.

Roy (Nobby) Wills, a very talented junior boxer, lived next door to Dave at 4 Woodville Road. On 10th March 1951 at Harringay arena, he won the ABA National Schools Championships. He was awarded his certificate and colours by Field Marshall Montgomery. Because his back fence was quite high, Roy used to jump over the connecting fence with Dave's house then the two of them climbed over Dave's rear fence to go to training at the boxing club.

Freddie Spreadborough who lived in Neville Road was a very powerful boxer. Early in his boxing apprenticeship at the club, Dave witnessed Freddie hit a spring supported punch ball. The force of his punch snapped it off the spring and sent the ball tumbling across the floor of the hall.

Living in Stuart Road was Wally Pick who was a bit older than Dave. Dave recalls, he was a big fellow, another very talented boxer who hit very hard. He later owned a wine bar on Richmond Hill.

In the same cohort of young boxers as Dave were:

Paul Cooper, who lived in Lock Road, was in the same class as Dave at St Mary's School in Richmond. He was what Dave would term *a jab jab get on your bike, jab jab dance around the ring, boxer* (which meant that he was on his toes, dancing throughout the bout). Dave believed that he would have made a great ballroom dancer!

Yet another boxer in the same class at school and training with them at Ham Boxing Club was Terry Payne who also lived in Lock Road. He was what Dave would term a good hitter.

His closest friend, Les High, who lived round the corner at 8 Neville Road in Ham, was the final member of the junior section at Ham Boxing Club and also in the same class at St Mary's. Dave recalls that over the years they became like brothers, always having a laugh and egging each other on to a new dare. Les's father was a lorry driver for Ham River Grit Company. A little later he became a ranger in Richmond Park and routinely shot rabbits which he brought back for rabbit pie. Dave was also invited around to join them and enjoy cuts of venison that occasionally became available.

Surrey county colours

Despite having such a wealth of boxing talent from Ham at St Marys, the school gave them little support and encouragement. For the inter school boxing events and championships the boys had to rely on their trainers from Ham to train them and support them ringside. They competed against schools throughout the area including Mortlake School, Gainsborough County Secondary School in Richmond, Ewell Castle School and Fairfield Hall School. It was after an unbeaten event at Fairfield Hall School that Dave received his Surrey county colours.

Training at the club involved a hard physical routine of press-ups, sit-ups and skipping before moving onto the punch bag, punch ball and spring ball with an intense session of sparring to complete the evening. Well, not quite completed, because they then had to dismantle the ring and put all the apparatus away.

George was a tough trainer but a year later, he left the club and his role was temporarily taken over by the club's matchmaker (fight arranger) Jack Saunders. Jack Saunders took the boys under his wing and made sure that they got regular fights at respectable venues. On the afternoon of the event he always reminded them not to eat too much, just a slice or two of toast and a cup of tea. He didn't want them throwing up in the ring after receiving a stomach punch. However, as soon as the event was over, he treated them all to fish and chips. Jack who lived in Murray Road, was a river pilot by trade and towards the end of his career ran boat trips up and down the Thames. After one late night event he was driving home to Ham. It is assumed that he fell asleep at the wheel because his car crashed into the Star and Garter pub in Putney, killing him instantly. He was very sadly missed.

On Sunday mornings the boys of the boxing club ran a circuit of Ham Common then on to Ham Gate through the park to Richmond Gate, down the Star & Garter Hill and back to the club.

Dave's first fight was for his secondary school, St Mary's, at the age of 11, the earliest age that he could legally fight. Although he narrowly lost this fight to Derek Harwood, he then went on to defeat him on two occasions while competing in the Surrey championship for affiliated clubs.

The boys were gradually introduced by Jack Saunders to three round bouts every other week at such venues as Willesden Working Men's Club, Seymour Hall, Paddington Green and Andy Newton's Boxing Club in Marylebone. They also took part in exhibition bouts at Latchmere House and the Star & Garter Home. They managed to get a lot of fights because at the time Dave Stone was boxing for their club and all the other clubs wanted him on the bill. Jack took the view, *If you want Dave, you take all of our lads.*

Dave clearly remembers an event at Willesden Working Men's Club when he was only thirteen. *I was up against a lad, aged 16 who was overconfident. I beat him in the 2nd round.*

Dave was a natural boxer and at the age of 18 became the Southern Counties NABC (National Association of Boys Clubs) champion. Competing in the two final bouts, he finished them both within half a minute.

Yet one by one the experienced boxers of the club were called up for National Service, a gateway to new opportunities and bigger horizons. With the departure of their trainer, the Ham Boxing Club went into hibernation.

Dave was meanwhile taking risks elsewhere. One of the favourite dares of the Ham lads was to jump off Teddington Bridge into the deep water on the Teddington side of the lock.

Having made the plunge, they had to dive to the bottom of the river, grab a handful of mud and come back to the surface to show the mud in their hand. Dave did this many, many times. He recalls however, one occasion when the incoming tide had lifted the river higher than normal. His descent to the riverbed was more difficult and he incurred some discomfort in one of his ears. At the time he thought nothing of it. His close friend, Les was also a good footballer and a keen member of the Ham Rovers Football Team.

Dave finished school at the age of 14. His first job was temporary employment at Bevans Butchers in Richmond Road. He developed a good friendship with the owner's son Roy Bevan. Although it was hard work they would occasionally mess around together when Roy's father Ron was not present. On one occasion they were having a water fight in the cellar and Roy dashed back up the stairs. A little later he came back down, and Dave directed the hose on him. Unfortunately, it wasn't Roy, but his father, the Governor Ron Bevan.

"*You little B…..*", shouted Ron

"Sorry Sir I thought it was Roy"

"Well it ain't"

Dave recalls, *I was frightened to go up again. Mr Bevan was a big man but a really decent man. A little later I heard them laughing upstairs and so I crept up, hoping not to be noticed. It was all soon forgotten.*

Dave has very fond memories of working at Bevans. Mr Bevan kept in touch and Dave spent another 6 months working through a very busy Christmas period.

Dave had yearned to work on a farm, and he spent some time in Wales and nearly three years (1955 – 57) in Wiltshire. It was very hard work for very little pay and in the end his father made him a financially far more lucrative offer to return to Ham and join him in the central heating trade.

In 1958, Dave and Les, along with Pat Slattery, resurrected the Ham Boxing Club. Initially, his dad and Charlie Goode helped train them but soon they were joined by an excellent trainer, Jim Driscoll. Dave, Les and Pat having reached the age of 18 were now classified as seniors. Les had married at very short notice and within a relatively short period of time he had two sons to support.

Jim was a hard trainer and Dave recalls himself and Les running through the park with Jim following on a bike and rapping the back of their legs with a cane when he thought they weren't lifting their knees high enough. One of their other trainers, Fred Hanbridge, had been a prisoner during the war in a Japanese camp in the Far East. He was a strong man, but he had been brutally treated and he used to flinch involuntarily. Charlie Goode was now the matchmaker and Mr Grant, the treasurer of the club.

Back row: Fred Hanbridge, Harry Morris, Jim Driscoll, Charlie Goode, Mr Grant
Front Row: Les High, Dave Morris, Pat Slattery after a gruelling training session

Dave, compared to Les and Pat, was slight in build. Weighing in at the top end of 8 stone he fought in the featherweight class. Les was a heavyweight. Although he was *a little fellow*, Dave hit hard and fast and over time cultivated a solid knockout punch.

Not having an equivalent weight to spar against at Ham, Jim introduced Dave to the Swan Boxing Club at Walton. Here he took part in 3-minute sparring bouts with boxers of a similar weight. In total, Dave boxed 15 rounds with three different boxers, one of whom was called Riley. He remembers Riley well because as the evening progressed Riley gave him a bit of a hammering. At a subsequent event at Woking Football Ground, Dave was matched against Riley. Shortly before the bout, Jim informed him that on the previous occasion he had been deliberately rested for only 3 minutes, whereas the other boxers including Riley were being rested for 9 minutes. *I knocked him out in the 2nd round.* Dave was clear in his own mind that you had to finish off the other boxer before he finished you. If you were to relax once you put your opponent under pressure, he would have the opportunity to regroup and come back at you.

Dave Morris & Jim Driscoll in the Ham Boxing Club

Dave stops Riley in the second round!

One day his trainer Jim, informed Dave that he was taking him up to London to spar with Terry Spinks, an Olympic Gold medallist. If he proved himself, he would be taken on by Terry's trainer, Dave Charnley, who himself had been a highly competent professional boxer. This would put him on a fast-track programme to compete for England and Britain, before turning professional. Dave's dream was now tantalisingly within reach.

Shortly after, Dave fought in the quarter final of the All England NABC Championships at Chelsea Barracks against Billy Davis from West Ham Boxing Club. Dave genuinely believed that he had won the fight but became concerned when they were kept waiting in their corners for an exceptionally long time. The decision controversially went against him by a very narrow margin. Nevertheless, he had acquitted himself well and was gaining invaluable experience. Billy Davis later turned professional and fought Terry Spinks in an eliminator for the British title. He stopped Spinks in the 9th round but dislocated his wrist in the process. His wrist never recovered, and he had to prematurely hang up his gloves.

It was the week before Les's 19th birthday in 1959 that he and Les competed at a venue organised by Bracknell Boxing Club. Dave recalls,

That night we were plagued with bad luck. The bus that was taking us with our support team and close supporters, broke down outside Ascot racecourse. After an hour delay Les, myself, Jim and my Dad managed to get a taxi to the venue leaving the others to follow on. We arrived as the organisers were calling me to the ring to start my fight. Having arrived late we were under pressure to get changed quickly. It was at this point that Les mentioned to me that he had a headache. I told him to withdraw from the fight but to our relief his opponent hadn't turned up. I went to get weighed on the scales but came in one pound too light. Jim Driscoll, my trainer, gave me a hammer head to put in my shorts to bring me within the target weight. This worked but when I returned to prepare for my fight, we learnt that another opponent, a former heavyweight army champion, had been entered against Les. Les's headache had not relented and he sat there very quiet. However, he had previously beaten this opponent and he didn't want to let the side down. He assured me that he would be alright. To this day I bitterly regret not telling our coach, Jim about Les's headache.

Normally once the bell rang to commence the bout, I was so focused that I heard nothing from outside the ring. On this occasion I heard my sister's voice shouting out, "Go on Dave". I then knew that our other boxers and support team had turned up. I won the fight easily.

Les's headache hadn't abated by the time that he got in the ring. Nevertheless, he was making a good fight of it and connected with a right hand to his opponent's jaw. His opponent was now scrambling and threw a desperate punch. It was the lightest of punches and appeared to simply tap Les on the chin. Yet Les dropped immediately, his head crashing onto the canvas. He lay senseless as we looked on in mounting horror. Les never regained consciousness and died the following morning.

I was devastated. My best friend since the age of ten, who had gone through all of the boxing training and the competitions alongside me, as well as those many hours sitting together navigating the monotony of so many boring lessons through the years at St Mary's School was dead. We had shared the dares, the pain, and the laughter and then suddenly, without a farewell, he was gone.

Les left behind a young widow and two children who would never know their father. Bracknell Boxing club organised a series of charity events to raise money for his wife and I competed in two of them. They were the last fights that I would undertake. As a result of Les's death, myself and Pat Slattery had to take a medical. I failed the medical because of a perforated ear drum caused by that descent to the riverbed below Teddington Lock Bridge. This ended my boxing career. It also meant that my option of joining the army was unachievable because I once more failed the medical.

Dave, right, on the way to winning the bout on the night that Les died

Dave having won his last ever fight, a charity event to raise money for Les's wife and boys

That was the end of the golden era of Ham Boxing Club. The Club had built a tremendous reputation among the amateur boxing fraternity. Years later, Dave's brother, Christopher, stopped off in a pub on the way back from Goodwood and got into conversation with a local who had been a boxer. When he mentioned that he came from Ham, the chap replied, *I used to hate having to fight boxers from Ham*, testimony to their reputation at the time.

Dave later accompanied Charlie Payne to many fights at Wembley and was also invited by Alan Minter to the opening of his restaurant in Crawley. Over the years he has met many talented and famous boxers. There is a great sense of camaraderie within the boxing community and Dave has retained a lot of friends in the sport.

Despite the heartache and disappointment Dave has no regrets at taking up boxing. In a way it was in his blood. Yet boxing got him incredibly fit and taught him both discipline and respect for other people. He especially respected all of his adversaries, because they had all taken the courageous step to climb into the ring.

As for all the boys who attended Ham Boxing Club,

they definitely punched above their weight.

Picture Credits
Photos supplied by Dave Morris and Gerald Stevens

Ham – An Ever-Changing Landscape & People

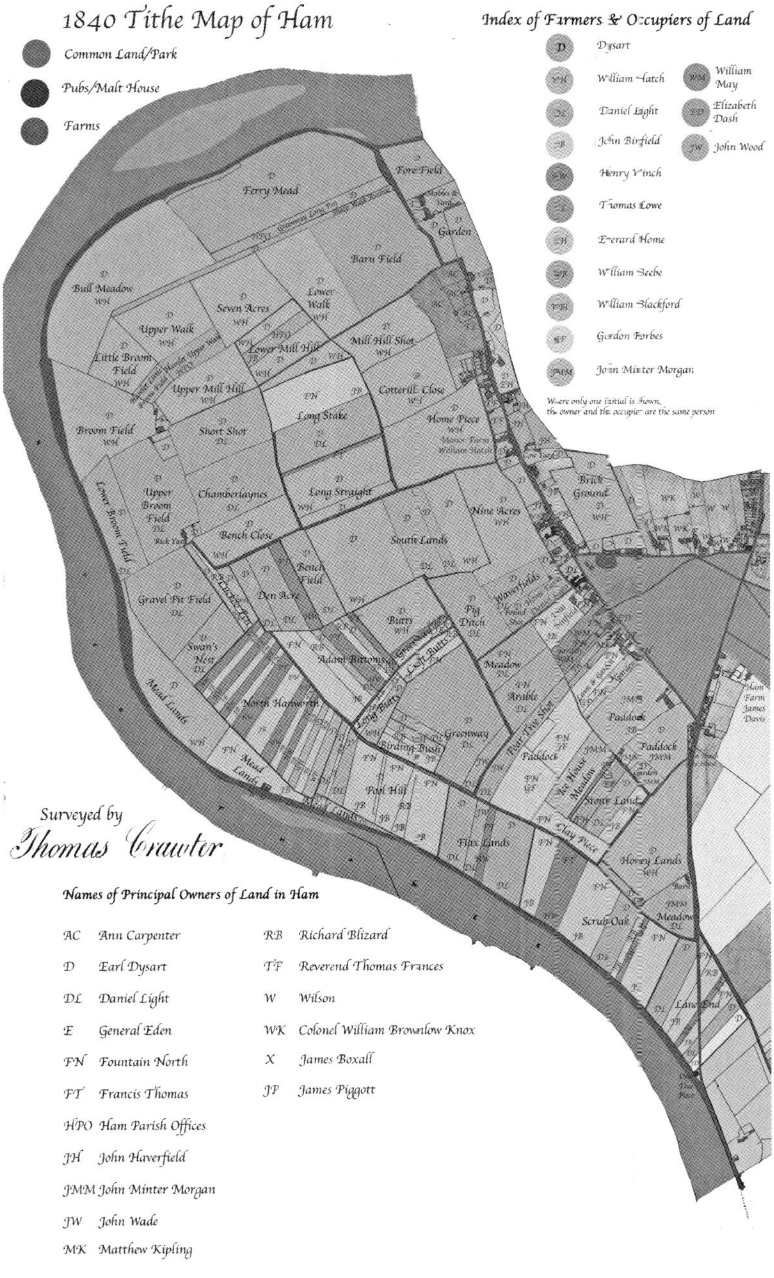

The landscape of Ham created from the original 1840 Tithe Map surveyed by Thomas Crawter. Many of the modern-day street names come from the names of ancient field plots in Ham. © Gordon Elsden

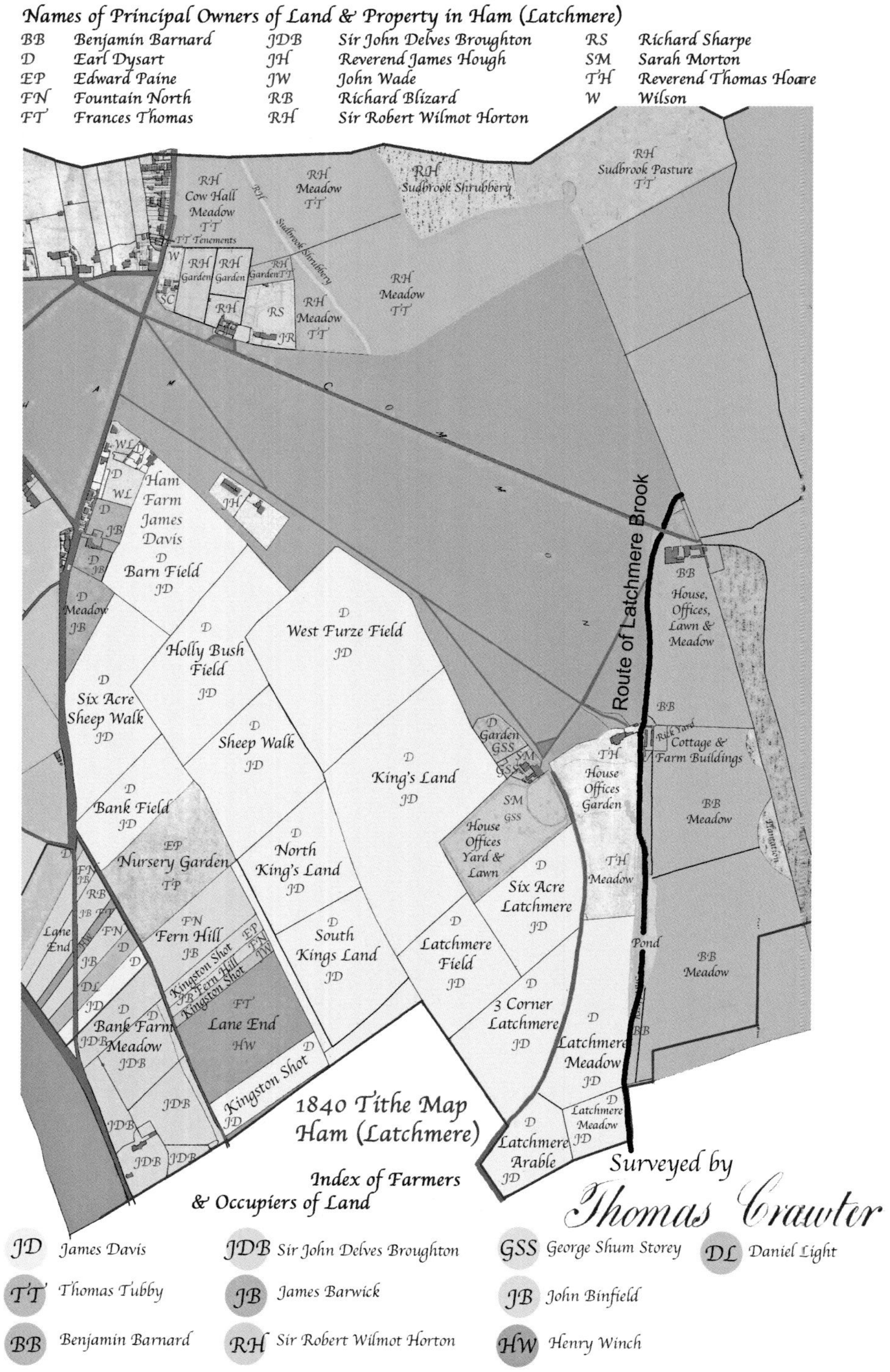

The landscape of the Tudor Estate in 1840 that was at the time in the southern part of Ham. This has been created from the original Tithe Map © Gordon Elsden

A Diverse and Transient Community

In 1841, the rural village of Ham, which included Hatch, held a population of 1,391 people inhabiting a total of 210 houses. 151 people (87 men and 64 women) were sleeping rough in barns, sheds or in the open air.

Only a third of all the people living in Ham in 1841 had actually been born in Ham. This was a pattern that would be repeated over the decades and continues today

---

At this time, the pastoral landscape consisting of 449 acres of arable land and 290 acres of pasture/meadowland supported 119 agricultural labourers. They cultivated a mixture of wheat, barley, oats, flax, potatoes, turnips and the wonderfully named mangel wurzels, which was a type of beet used to feed cattle. *Common land* made up 882 acres and on this, many of the *Common people* grazed their own horses, donkeys, cows, sheep, goats, pigs, geese, ducks and chickens.

Sixteen large houses principally located around Ham Common and along Ham Street were owned or rented by well-off people of independent means: professional men, senior officers serving in the army or navy, and wealthy merchants. These sixteen houses provided employment to 123 governesses, servants, gardeners, laundresses and needlewomen. Employment as a gardener was much preferred to gruelling seasonal work on the land. Around these houses evolved a group of tradesmen that included dairymen, butchers, bakers, grocers, tailors, shoemakers and craftsmen skilled in carpentry, bricklaying, plumbing, as well as blacksmiths and wheelwrights.

A Thirst for Beer

By 1851, the village supported three licensed victuallers: the New Inn on the Common, with the Crooked Billet and Royal Oak both in Ham Street. There were also a further two drinking houses, the Fox and Goose in Petersham Road and the Crown next to the alms house in Kingston Road (now called Ham Parade). The Ham Brewery was located at 103 Ham Street and a large malt house was situated at the southern end of Ham Street, facing the common.

The New Inn

1910 Crooked Billet on Ham Street DW

The Ham Village Centre, previously the Royal Oak

The Fox & Goose on Petersham Road. This was replaced by a small detached building that has since been converted into a private house. RLS

The Crown drinking house on Ham Parade just along from the old alms house opposite the entrance to Parkleys

The Malt House at the north end of Ham Common that blocked the eastern end of Lock Road. RLS

Ownership of the Land and Houses

Lionel, the 8th Earl of Dysart, Lord of the Manor of Ham, owned 485 acres, 66% of the land in Ham. Charles Fountain North was the next largest landowner with 75 acres, mainly located to the east of Ham Common, followed by Sir Robert Wilmott Horton with 55 acres to the north east of Ham Common. There were in total only 77 landowners and of these only ten owned more than 10 acres. Ham Manor Farm, Home Farm and Ham Farm (near the church) were all owned by the Earl of Dysart and worked by tenant farmers.

Ham Manor Farm later known as Hatch Farm then Secrett's Farm after the tenant farmers. Charlotte Hatch is standing outside with her husband Edward Rayne (of Rayne's Park). ©The Rayne family

On the west side of Ham Street was located Ham Manor Farm, containing the original medieval manor house dating from the 1400s and predating Ham House by nearly 200 years. It was undoubtedly an archaeological treasure trove but unfortunately, along with the ancient tithe barn, the manor house was demolished in 1958 to make way for a precinct of shops on the corner of Ashburnham Road and Ham Street, opposite Grey Court School. The cow yard stood on the site of Grey Court School and further east was Bull Meadow where the farm's irascible bull grazed.

A very rare photograph of the original Ham Farmhouse that faced onto what is now Ham Farm Road near St Andrew's Church RLS

A romantic view of Ham Farm which included all of the land now covered by the Tudor Estate and Parkleys. RC

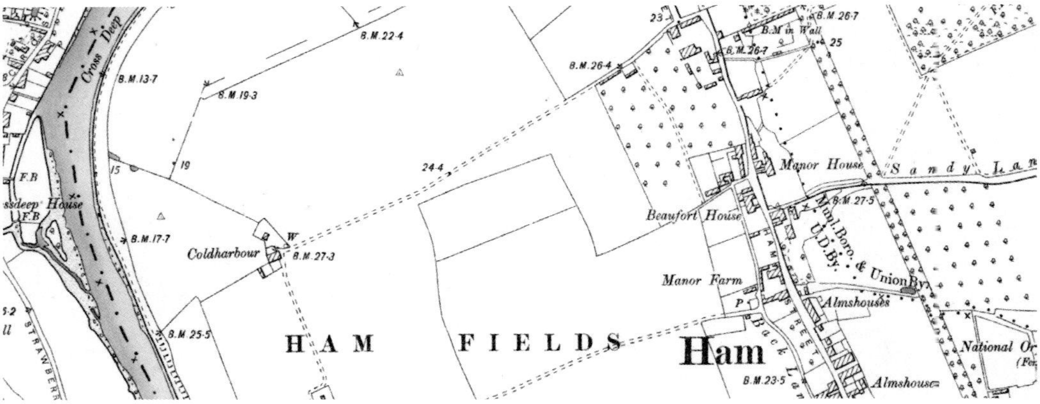

Coldharbour was the ancient settlement of Ham where most of the prehistoric finds in the area were discovered. It is now the site of Thames Young Mariners Base. Sadly, there are no street names in Ham to remind us of Coldharbour's important role in our local history. NLS

A Latchmere Family Emerges

At about this time (1841) William Bliss, aged two, was living in Lambeth, the son of Daniel Bliss, a gas fitter. William followed in the footsteps of his father and with the development of the gas works in Kingston, he moved to Kingston with his family. By 1881 he was living above a shop at 2 Richmond Road, opposite Canbury Lodge and the Railway Tavern, very close to the spot where the now culverted Latchmere Brook originally turned west to flow towards the Thames: the current railway line follows its original course. With the death of his wife, William was supporting two girls Margaret and Beatrice and three boys, all under the age of sixteen.

Ten years on, William had remarried and, with his new wife, was living at 108 Canbury Park Road with Albert from his existing marriage and four younger children. Beatrice who was now 19 years old was working as a kitchen maid in Petersham House, Petersham.

She had unknowingly moved to the other end of the Latchmere Brook, alias the Sudbrook.

Three years later in 1894, Beatrice briefly returned to her father's home at 20 Elm Grove prior to marrying Jesse Slatter on 4th August at St Luke's Church in Canbury, Kingston. Jesse, who was working as a milkman in Ham, had originally come to Ham with his father from Steventon in Berkshire, to seek work on the land.

Shortly after their wedding, Beatrice and Jesse set up home in one of the newly built houses at 13 Evelyn Road in Ham. Jesse gained manual employment as a labourer in and around Ham.

The View from Richmond Hill

At this time, within the Ham and Petersham Dysart Estate, there were 176 acres of arable fields and market gardens, known as Lammas Lands over which rights of pasture were

Members of the Greenwood family working in Lammas Lands. RLS

exercisable by commoners from Lammas day, the 1st August each year until the 6th April the following year. These rights prevented the Dysart Estate Trustees from using this land as they wished and so they applied to parliament in 1896 to have these Lammas rights extinguished by virtue of them having fallen into disuse. The application was rejected.

Lammas Day was originally a pagan dedication of the beginning of the harvest and celebrated the first wheat or corn crop. The early English church later accommodated this celebration and on Lammas Day, loaves of bread, baked from the first-ripened grain, were brought to the churches to be consecrated. The word "Lammas" derives from the Saxon hlaf, "loaf," and maesse, "mass" or "feast."

A subsequent application was made in which these Lammas rights were to be extinguished in return for preservation of the view from Richmond Hill. This struck the right chord and in 1902 the 'Richmond, Petersham and Ham Open Spaces' Act was passed. This extinguished the Lammas rights of grazing by the inhabitants of Ham. In return:

- Petersham Meadows (39 acres) was vested in Richmond Corporation to be preserved as land not to be built upon other than a pavilion.
- Petersham Common (17 acres) was vested in Richmond Corporation.
- Ham Common (125 acres) was vested in Ham District Council.
- A riverside promenade extending from River Lane in Petersham to Half Mile tree in Kingston having a length of 3 miles and an acreage of 52 acres was vested partly in Richmond Corporation and partly in the Surrey County Council. (This is why Thames Young Mariners Base is owned today by Surrey County Council).
- A cricket field of 9 acres to be given to Kingston Corporation. (This is modern day Latchmere Recreation Ground).

The Ham River Grit Company

In 1903 William Brice, a clay merchant and barge owner, was taking a walk along the towpath of Ham when he noticed a small excavation of good quality ballast. After due enquiry, he managed to negotiate a lease with the 9th Earl of Dysart, Sir William John Manners Tollemache, to extract gravel. By 1904, eighty acres were taken over on a royalty arrangement, allowing the installation of plant and machinery to process the ballast into different grades of aggregate and sand.

In 1906, the construction of Brooklands Racetrack, the first purpose-built motor racing circuit in the world, required an enormous quantity of large stones. The Ham River Grit Co. won the contract. The excavated stone was carried by barge to Kingston, unloaded into carts and taken to Kingston Station, where it was transported by train to Weybridge Station. Here it was unloaded onto carts and then transported to the construction site in Weybridge. The Brooklands Racetrack opened in 1907.

As building increased in London, the output of The Ham River Grit Co. had to increase to meet demand. The company gained permission to clear a cutting through the towpath in order to utilise the tidal waters to bring barges to the pits. Approval was also obtained from the Thames Conservancy to build a wharf and a light railway which went along the towpath to load the barges.

Monday 19th June 1911 – Taking the dog for a morning walk past Lord Dysart's Docks in Ham Lands. This location is where the channel now enters Thames Young Mariners Base from the river close to the ancient settlement of Coldharbour. ©SHC

A Contrasting Portrayal of Ham

An early 1900s postcard showing children playing beside Ham Common Pond. Yet, life wasn't always so pleasant for some of the children in Ham. RLS

The Times Friday 1st May 1908 (page 16)

CHILDREN ASLEEP IN A PIG-STY.—At Kingston yesterday two little children, Henry Gee, aged 10, and Daisy Gee, aged 11, of 6, Lock-road, Ham-common, were charged on remand with being found asleep in a pig-sty on the allotments in Kingston-road, Ham-common, early on the morning of April 23, and with not being under proper control. When the children were found by Police-constable Cheeseman they said they did not want to go home as their father had threatened to kill them, and Inspector Thompson, of the National Society for the Prevention of Cruelty to Children, at the last hearing stated that he found the girl with scratches on her neck, which she said were caused by her trying to cut her throat with a razor, as her father had often threatened to do. Robert Gee, the father, who is in the employ of the Ham Urban District Council, was now summoned, at the instance of the N.S.P.C.C., for ill-treating and neglecting the children on several occasions, but when his name was called he failed to appear. Police-constable Cheeseman said that when he served the summons upon Gee he used most filthy and abusive language. The bench issued a warrant for his arrest. The chairman said that several applications had been received by the bench from persons willing to adopt the children, but they were of opinion that the best course to take would be to send the children to the workhouse, and to ask the guardians to consider what should be done with them.

The First World War

By 1911, Jesse and Beatrice Slatter were still living at 13 Evelyn Road along with their three children, Gertrude Alberta, Jesse and Elizabeth, all under the age of eleven.

When the First World War broke the dam of peace in 1914, Jesse was already 45 years old. Within a year, measured at only 5 feet ½ inch, Jesse answered the call to arms and joined up in the Army Service Corps. His labouring strength and stamina was in great demand in the construction of thousands of miles of trenches and tunnels in the heavy soil of Flanders Fields. Fortunately, he survived the war and returned to 13 Evelyn Road physically intact in February 1919.

1909 Evelyn Road in Ham. RLS

Their daughter, Gertrude married Harold George Clark on Christmas Day in 1922 at St Andrew's Church. In November 1923, a son, Keith George Clark was born in Cedar Lodge, Ham Street. This house, situated next to Cut Throat Alley, had the famous mulberry tree in the garden.

Ham Lock was constructed between 1922 and 1923 to accommodate the barges that cleared the pits. (It now forms part of the Thames Young Mariners site owned by Surrey County Council. You can see it clearly on the riverside walk past Thames Young Mariners Base in the midst of Ham Lands).

Market Gardens and Farms

Early 1900s image of Ham Fields and the path to Ham leading from Teddington Lock. Courtesy of Keith Mulberry

In 1925 Eric Parker published a book titled "Highways and Byways in Surrey" and includes a nostalgic recollection of Ham: *I never saw Ham until one day, walking out from Kingston, I suddenly found myself in the fruitful spaces of market gardens and farms. It is the suddenest change. Kingston with the oldest memories of all Surrey towns, is as new and noisy as a thoroughly efficient service of tramways can make it; and then, within a stone's throw of bricks and barracks, you come upon acres beyond acres of level farmland, bean fields and cabbage fields and all the pleasantness of tilled soil and trenched earth and the wealth of kindly fruits. When I saw the fields by Ham on a hot day in August there were country women gathering runner beans into coarse aprons, stooping over the clustered plants, the humblest and hardiest of workers on the farm.*

1927 aerial view looking west and showing the expanding gravel pits of the Ham River Grit Company. Bottom left is Secrett's Farm with the original manor farmhouse of Ham that predated Ham House by 200 years. To the right, extending into the fields, are Wiggins and Pointers Cottages. Bottom right is the Manor House and slightly to the left facing onto Ham Street is Beaufort House ©Historic England

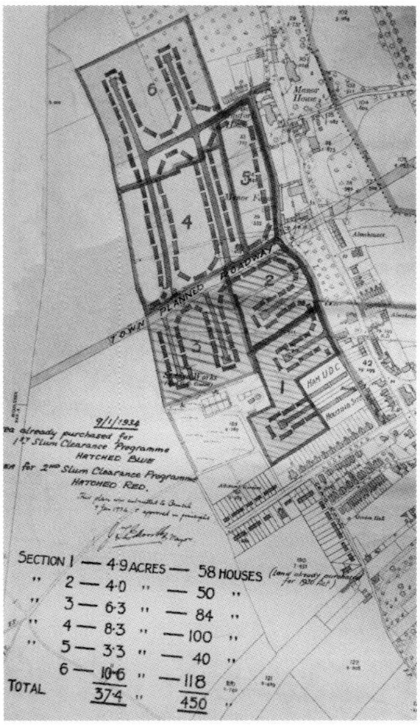

January 1934 – Allocation of land for new council housing in Ham. RLS

It was the local Government Act of 1929 that put an end to the self-governing Urban District of Ham by decreeing that smaller districts should be absorbed into large adjoining boroughs. Richmond and Kingston divided the spoils of Ham with its abundance of fields and a relatively small population. During the 1930s there was a pressing need to clear the condemned housing in Richmond and provide good comfortable council housing, appropriate for the 20th century. The open land of Ham was the natural choice for Richmond Council. Yet the council houses built on this land were to prove *dream homes* for their new residents and give a great start to many young families.

By 1939 Keith George Clark, known locally as George or Nobby, had found work as an apprentice baker at Sadler's bakehouse in Petersham Road and was living with his grandparents Jesse and Beatrice at 13 Evelyn Road. By now, Beatrice was the go-to person in Ham, if you needed a collar starching.

During the Second World War artists were commissioned to make sketches of typical rural life throughout England as part of the Recording Britain Collection. The adjoining villages of Petersham and Ham were recorded more fully than any other plot in the country. This wonderful collection of 18 sketches is now held at the Victoria and Albert Museum. They represent the end of an era because within twenty years the farm and the cows would be gone and with them the last vestiges of an agricultural landscape.

1927 aerial view showing the workings of Ham River Grit Co. The railway line was a narrow-gauge 2 ft (610 mm) light industrial railway running along a half a mile of track, parallel with the towpath. © Historic England

London's Smallest Railway

Just below Teddington Locks writes Ralph Harold Brotherton in the "Evening News" where a lane turns off from the towpath towards Ham, you see behind a gate a notice which bids you beware of the trains. London's railway map at once jumps into your mind and you think wonderingly, "What trains?" But here, though you may not have known it, is London's smallest railway, a quarter or half a mile of track along the edge of the great ballast pits of Ham. Most of these pits have been worked so deep that they are full of water and bear fleets of dredgers. But some of the farther pits still have dry bottoms, and the little railway doubles down into the bed of one of these. The track is of the narrowest gauge. You step over it in the easiest of strides. The two little locomotives stand no higher than a horse. Their wheels look to be barely a foot in diameter. And you wonder that the whole engine does not tip up when the burly driver steps aboard. There are some scores of trucks rather like coal scuttles slung between arms rising from wheeled bases. The engines take the trucks down into the bed of the pit and bring them back laden with ballast to the dock, where the barges lie. About a yard of ballast goes into each truck. It is a rather untidy little line. Having no sidings to speak of, it throws its surpluses off the track. They lie scattered in all sorts of positions by the side of the rails, sometimes with their scuttles off the hinges. Yet there is a neat little shed that will take one locomotive at a time, and there is a loop which gives room for two engines to pass, for neither can be conveniently thrown off the track to make passage for the other. And there is a real junction, where the main line sends a branch down into the pit. It is the level crossing, perhaps, that impresses you most with the reality of the line. So many warnings are there that you cannot step across the track without a thrill. Suppose you met a train? Would it be bad for you, as Stephenson said it would for the coo! Probably it would. These little locomotives push as readily as they pull, and they have, you notice, good butting ends that would certainly hit you pretty hard. Trains are a common sight to the Londoner. He sees and, perhaps uses them every day. Yet Ham is the suburb most remote from the railway. There are people who live there and do not see an ordinary train all the week. All the same, in this no-man's land of London's railway map, two small locomotives busily jostle ballast trucks up and down a self-contained line over what is probably London's richest mineral field: a rather exotic looking region of deep pits, water, strange machinery and beautifully clean heaps of washed stone. So, Ham, less intimate than many a country village with the railway, has its level crossing. And there is no excuse for you if you charge into a train.

W.G. Bagnall Loco at Ham Pits in 1933. Courtesy of the Industrial Railway Society

A crane loading aggregate into a hopper with wagons below. Courtesy of the Industrial Railway Society

A close up showing the small train with the locomotives on the front and back in front of the sheds on the Ham gravel pit line. © Historic England

Ham River Grit Co. lorries DW

The Bakehouse in Petersham Road DW

13 Evelyn Road. GE

Avove left: The Royal Oak Pub in Ham Street. This later briefly became the Ham Village Centre.

Above: Edge of Manor Farm, Ham Street c1940

Left: Cows from Ham Manor Farm passing Ham House stables in Ham Street.

All images are part of the Recording Britain Collection ©Victoria and Albert Museum, London

Sylvia Percival comes to Richmond Park

For Sylvia Percival, life in Moss Side, Manchester was extremely frustrating. The aggressive German bombing campaign had devastated parts of the city and the shoe shop where she worked. She felt an overwhelming need to get away and do something positive. In 1942 Sylvia joined the Auxiliary Territorial Service, *the Women's Army*. After basic training she undertook more specialised training as a mess cook at the military garrison of Catterick in North Yorkshire, three miles south of Richmond. On the completion of her training, Sylvia was transferred south to an army camp in Richmond Park, three miles south of Richmond in Surrey. A strange coincidence!

Sylvia was based at the camp on the high ground above Kingston Gate. This was the same camp where Tom Sloan would later be based for his period of convalescence prior to the Normandy invasion (see A House in the Country). Sylvia was engaged as a cook in the mess but during the night-time bombing raids she and many of the other women soldiers helped operate and supply the anti-aircraft guns that were based in the park. She had originally been trained as an aircraft spotter but because of a defect in one of her eyes she couldn't easily identify the difference between the British and German planes. To her relief, she was quickly reassigned to helping with the supply of the ammunition to the guns.

Sylvia in 1942 having joined the ATS GC

With the large number of soldiers stationed in the park, there was a lot of cooking and at times the handling of the large pots was extremely tiring. Many years later she was telling her youngest son Graham about the time when she lost the top of her finger in the industrial meat mincer. Graham asked the obvious question, *what happened to the top of your finger?* Sylvia, matter-of-factly, replied, *a soldier must have eaten it*! Graham wasn't sure how to digest that piece of information!

Left: ATS (Auxiliary Territorial Service The women's army) operating a range finder on an HAA gun site

Right: 435 HAA Battery with 2/3rds of its personnel supplied by the ATS took over operational gun sites in Richmond Park IWM

Despite the long hours, Sylvia thoroughly enjoyed her active and positive role in the army, and she loved the camaraderie of the other women in the ATS. Here she established strong friendships that would endure a lifetime. These friendships also required that she become a prolific letter writer to keep in contact, albeit remotely, with all of her dear friends. She was going to need those close bonds of friendship in the difficult years ahead.

Ponds and Decoys

There were many soldiers based around the perimeter of the park. The large expanse of land was also ideal for positioning anti-aircraft guns. Pen Ponds was drained of its water to prevent reflected moonlight from providing the crews of German bombers with a very useful navigational reference. Starfish sites were established to the east of Pen Ponds to create the impression of burning towns and lure the bombers into prematurely dropping their bombs.

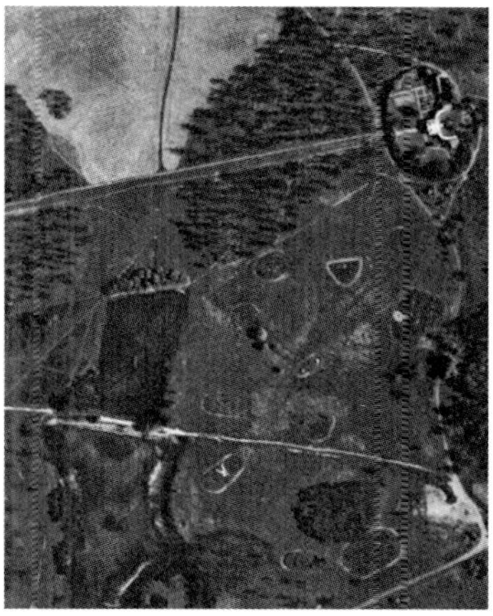

Middle to lower left shows the faint outline of Pen Ponds that had been drained of water to prevent enemy bombers from having a clear navigational reference. Bottom to centre right is the location of a Starfish decoy site. White Lodge is top right EH

Jesse Slatter died in March 1944 at the age of 74 and was laid to rest in the graveyard of St Andrew's Church. His wife, Beatrice, continued to live in 1 Tollemache Alms-house along with her grandson George Clark, who had now signed up and was working as a driver in the Transport Corps of the army. He would later drive an ammunition lorry down from Scotland in support of the allied invasion and follow the advance troops out of their Normandy bridgehead.

The Starfish (code for S.F Special Fires) decoys were intended to create an illusion of a burning town or city after a night-time bombing raid EH

It was at a dance at the Bute Avenue Hall next to All Saint's Church in Petersham that George met Sylvia. She was being bothered by some local men and George stepped in with a mate, who was an army boxer, to provide her with more courteous company. Sylvia was taken with his good looks and apparent gentlemanly behaviour and they began seeing each other regularly. Yet the allied invasion was still secretly being planned and the future remained very uncertain.

1944 RAF aerial reconnaissance photo of Ham showing clearly the extent of the gravel pits and the established roads. Note the concrete barges lined up in the lakes that had formed from the gravel pits © Historic England

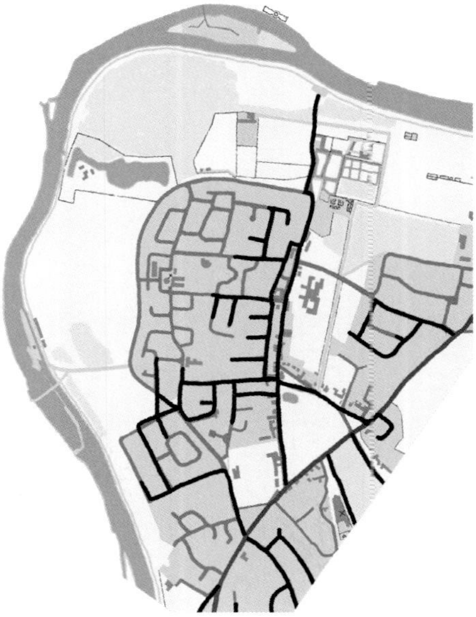

Modern day map of Ham with the established roads of 1944 shown in black. This shows the extent to which modern housing and roads have covered Ham Lands and the gravel pits since the end of the war GE

A close up of a concrete barge. They played a key role in the D-Day invasion of Normandy in June 1944. They were used to transport fuel to other ships involved in the invasion. Once emptied they were used to form parts of the Mulberry harbours and pontoon bridges that helped move men and equipment quickly to the shore

Sylvia and George Clark married in August 1946 at St Andrew's Church. They continued living at 1 Tollemache Alms-house with Granny Beat and it was here that Keith was born in August 1947. Sylvia considered herself extremely fortunate to be allocated a council house at 2 Murray Road shortly before Christmas that same year. With three bedrooms, a back boiler and instant hot water, an

1 Tollemache Alms-house. GE

inside bathroom and a garden, this was a perfect base to raise a family. Graham was born some six years after Keith, in June 1953.

Granny Beat died in 1950 and was also buried in the graveyard of St Andrew's, some 56 years after marrying a milkman from Ham at St Luke's Church in Canbury. She had in that time experienced two world wars and the great depression of the 1930s.

Filling the Pits

As soon as the war was over, housing development in Ham was renewed to alleviate the acute shortage of housing for Richmond residents. German prisoners of war were employed on the preparation of sites and prefabricated bungalows were erected in Ham Close, Back Lane, Hardwicke Road, Murray Road, Simpson Road and Latchmere Lane. This was gradually followed by more permanent housing and later, blocks of flats which made a greater impression on the waiting list.

1947 aerial view from over Teddington showing the extent of the new construction of houses in Ham. The prefab bungalows can be seen centre left below Ham House © Historic England

Left: By 1948 there was a concerted effort to build homes for the people on the Richmond housing list. The filling in of the pits was accelerated with debris brought from bomb sites in many different parts of London. One can't but help consider the settling time needed for such a vast amount of earth, concrete and other rubbish! Copyright of SHC

Below: Prefabricated bungalows in Ham Close RLS

Above: 1948 The relentless filling in of the vast gravel pits. The prefabricated bungalows can be seen in the background

The Stevens Family

Gerald Stevens was born in January 1942, the youngest of five with two older brothers and two older sisters. Yvonne his closest sibling was some 18 months older. They lived at 6 Mead Road in Ham, one of the original council houses in the village. When his mother first moved into the house, she could look out of the back windows and see across the fields all the way to the river. Gerald's grandfather, Frederick, had been a general trader in Ham and was the proud owner of a few cows that grazed on the Common and drank from the watering hole that is now the picturesque village pond. Fred's own personal watering hole was the Crooked Billet in Ham Street where over the years he downed many a gallon of ale. When the modern houses were built in Lawrence Road in the 1930s, he purchased Number One. Prior to the war, Gerald's dad, Stanley, who was employed as a fitter's mate at the National Physical Laboratory at Bushy Park, earned extra cash as a caddy at Richmond Golf Course in Sudbrook Park. During the war he served as an ARP warden and witnessed much bomb damage to local houses and the trauma experienced by the families involved.

Gas & Electricity

When Gerald was very young there was no electricity at Mead Road. Light was provided by gas lamps with very delicate gas mantles. When the mantle broke you had to carefully replace it. With its steady rush of gas, it was very soothing to listen to in the quiet of the evening. In the kitchen there was a slot meter to take coins for the gas. *We placed the coin in the slot and turned a metal ring until the coin dropped with a satisfying metallic clunk.*

Only when Gerald was seven years old, did the house get fitted with electricity. This required another slot meter which was installed in the hallway for electricity and was fed with shillings. The gas & electricity board men came round routinely to empty the meters. Some people in desperation, having run out of money, broke the padlocks on the meters to get to the money. Gerald recalls,

We'd be listening to something on the radio: "Oh, Christ the lights gone out", with which the radio also died: "Come on Dad you must have a shilling".

St Andrew's Primary School on Ham Common

Gerald went to primary school at St Andrew's from the age of five, in 1947, until he was eleven. There was an average of 30 children in each year, a total of about 180 local children attending the school.

1952/53 Teachers of St Andrew's Primary School Back Row: Miss Robinson, Mr Page & Miss Ray Front Row: Miss Webster, Miss Cox, Miss Herbert & Miss Ayres. GS

Some seventy years later, Gerald vividly recalls, *Mr Gomm, the headmaster, who lived at 3 Ham Street, was a truly horrible person and all the children were petrified of him.* The headmaster had a small office with a corrugated roof in the playground. In the summer it benefitted from the shade of the expansive canopy of the three London plane trees that observed the antics of all the children as they progressed through the school. Mr Gomm had a rule that from the age of nine boys could be caned to keep them in check.

Gerald remembers, *Mr Gomm took real pleasure in inflicting pain on the young boys. As soon as he walked into a classroom, a wave of fear swept through the room and we all dropped our heads to avoid his gaze. He would walk up behind us and then hit one of us in the back of the head with his knuckles. In those days, parents tended to give the teachers the benefit of the doubt when it came to dispensing discipline and the use of the cane was an accepted means of punishment. On one occasion, while playing flicks (cards) up against the playground dividing wall, a card disappeared behind Mr Gomm's hut. One of the boys endeavoured to retrieve it but got himself stuck behind the hut. Mr Gomm dragged him out and just laid into him.*

For trivial misdemeanours I seemed to have got on the wrong side of Miss Webster in my fifth year at the school. Over a period of a couple of weeks she sent me several times to Mr Gomm's office for punishment. Each time I was caned twice on my left hand. A splinter from the cane opened up the skin and the wound became infected. This was really painful and caused me a lot of discomfort. It was also a step too far for my mother. With the support of her sister, they went around to Mr Gomm's house in Ham Street and confronted him. The caning switched to someone else for a while.

Personal hygiene was taken seriously, and children were sent home if they had dirty shoes or dirty fingernails. Gerald further recalls, *Miss Herbert was the 1st year teacher when we were 5-6 years old. She was strict when she needed to be but otherwise, she had a gentle and patient way about her which the children appreciated. In the 2nd year, and bearing in mind we were only 6 to 7 years old, we had Miss Ayres who was a right dragon and used to hit us on the back of our bare legs with a white stick. That really stung and brought tears to our eyes. Furthermore, she wouldn't let us go to the toilet if we needed to between breaks. If we ended up wetting ourselves, she made us stand in the corner of the class with the curtain draped around us to hide us from view.*

In year three we had a very pleasant teacher, Miss Robinson supported by Miss Ray. That was an enjoyable year. Miss Cox who taught us in year four was also very nice. Things changed in year five with Miss Webster, who didn't appear to like me at all.

Fortunately, in our final year, we had Mr Page, who later became the headmaster. Though strict and firm, he was a really decent man. He took a genuine interest in us and showed us a collection of prehistoric flints and arrowheads that he had found in Ham Lands. With the use of a presentation that was shown on his large projector, he helped us visualise what Ham would have looked like during the prehistoric period. We were all captivated. Mr Page was also a very keen sportsman and a passionate cricketer. During the summer term he set up a wicket on the Common and placed either a thruppenny bit or sixpence on top of the stumps. If we could bowl down the wicket, we kept the coins. Everyone tried but very few succeeded. It was a great way of tiring us out and calming us down!

In the playground was a flagpole and the Union Jack was raised on both Ascension Day and Empire Day. During the winter, the classrooms were poorly heated by cast iron stoves fuelled with coke. *During each break we huddled around the stove to try and snatch a warm*. In the summer, a large clump of stinging nettles grew behind the east wall of the school. *Keith Shaw tumbled right in the thick of them and screamed his head off. He was rushed home and his mum covered him in a blue ointment.*

On leaving St Andrew's, Gerald went to Mortlake School. It was only in his last year in 1956 that he had the opportunity to transfer to the newly opened Grey Court School. Gerald recalls that Mr Calvert, who lived in Wiggins Cottages in Ham, was one of the most popular teachers at the school. He made teaching fun and Gerald has never forgotten one of the trips across the road to Secrett's Farm to watch the cows being milked. Many years later when Gerald was sitting in the Roebuck on Richmond Hill, having a quiet beer, a voice from behind him brought him upright, *Hello Gerald*. With pleasure he immediately replied *Hello Sir, how are you?* Such was the affection that the students had for Mr Calvert.

St Andrew's School in Ham Street now used as the Catholic Church of St Thomas Aquinas GE

Childhood Games

A favourite at school was playing flicks with fag (cigarette) packet picture cards: *We used to stack cards up against the wall and compete to knock them down. The person who knocked the last card down would claim all of the cards*. The objective of another game was to cover the flicked card of an opponent. If you did you claimed his card.

Marbles – Rules of the game

Marbles was a very popular game that was played in the gutters of the street and again it tended to be played by the boys.

Playing anybody alleys was an invitation to a game. The first player would roll a marble along the gutter. His rival would then roll another and endeavour to hit the marble. If he did, he kept both marbles. Some of the boys used ball bearings that they retrieved from the Ham Grit Co. maintenance yard near Hardwicke Road.

I ain't playing him. He'll dump me, meant that the chap was too good and would win all your marbles.

Tips & Re's, short for tips and rebounds. If declared at the beginning of the match it meant that if your marble slightly tipped or rebounded onto a marble, then you could claim it.

I'll have dumps, meant that if you lost all of your marbles during the game you would be given a marble to continue playing.

I've been dumped, meant that you had lost all of your marbles.

Collecting Birds' Eggs

Grey Court School was built on a small orchard within the land of Newman House (Grey Court House). Gerald spent many hours in this orchard searching for birds' nests and the eggs inside. It was a popular pastime to collect the eggs, then pierce them with a pin to drain out the yoke before keeping the intact egg, safe in a carton. Gerald managed to collect nearly 90 eggs. Even St Andrew's Primary School had a collection of birds' eggs in a showcase.

Football Teams

In the early 1950s Ham boasted two very good football teams, Ham Rovers who played opposite the New Inn pub on Ham Common and Ham F.C. who played at King George Sports Field near Ham House. For a number of years on Boxing Day there was a charity match on Ham Common between the two teams.

Ham FC in 1952 GS

The Gravel Pits

The children of Ham all spent a lot of time playing in the vast area of the gravel pits, many of which had filled with water to form deep lakes. Gerald remembers, *around the pits was an abundance of wildlife, especially birds: ducks, coots, moorhens, swans, willow warblers, skylarks and reed buntings. Kingfishers used to nest on one of the islands in the middle of the lakes. The water was very deep and shelved quite quickly making it a dangerous place for non-swimmers. To get to the island to find kingfisher eggs we built a raft out of old oil drums that we had found elsewhere in the pits. There was one green pool that had a wonderful assortment of fish: roach, bream, carp and rudd. We spent many a day fishing for eels.*

Gerald further reflects, *It took fifteen years for them to fill in the gravel pits. One of the gatemen at the Simpson Road entrance to the pits took many a back hander to allow lorries to dump stuff that they couldn't dump elsewhere. There were quite a few accidents at the pits with tipper trucks ending up in the water and one chap was decapitated by a tipper platform collapsing unexpectedly.*

By the late 1950s most of the gravel pits had been filled in. In 1963, after only a relatively few years of settlement, Wates, the builders, began the development of the new estate which would ultimately add some 704 dwellings to the village of Ham.

Bonfire Night

It became a local tradition to build a large bonfire on Ham Common for Guy Fawkes night on the 5th November.

18th October 1955 - Building the Guy Fawkes Night bonfire on Ham Common Photo by Hulton Archive/Getty Images

For up to a month before, the local people would collect all sorts of flammable material to put on the bonfire. Watneys, the brewery and Cellon, the local paint factory both provided material that would burn well! The bonfire which was normally located between the cricket pitch and the pond ended up being as tall as a house.

Children made a guy with a mask and some old clothing stuffed with straw or padding. Pulling the guy around in a cart or old pram, they would compete for a preferred pitch in Ham, where they would call out, *penny for the guy*. The money earned was then spent on fireworks: Penny bangers that would be fired out of bicycle pumps or dismantled for the powder to make magical genies. Tuppenny rockets launched from empty milk bottles or Catherine wheels, nailed to the fence post, which invariably promised much but fizzled to a halt prematurely and left a permanent scorch mark on the fence.

Memories of bonfire night are a heady mixture of excitement, discomfort and on occasion, acute pain. The irritation of eyes smarting from the smoke of the fire and streaming with tears. Potatoes and chestnuts being roasted in the embers of numerous fires, clothing permeated with smoke for weeks, a sparkler being held incorrectly or a firework going off prematurely or in the wrong direction.

In the grey light of dawn, the excitement of trawling the streets for the spent rockets and making a collection of the singed colourful casing of roman candles, jack in the box, golden fountain, silver tree, golden rain and numerous other exotically named fireworks.

The Final Days of the Manor Farm of Ham

Gerald as a child, loved to visit Secrett's Farm. He recalls the large yard with a row of milking sheds down one side. *You needed to be wearing wellies to negotiate the large amount of cow muck.* In a corner of the yard facing Back Lane was a drinking trough which strangely contained a lot of small fish, including sticklebacks. One of the sheds adjacent to Ham

Ham Street outside Secrett's Farm ©SHC

The main yard with the large barn centre left. The bull was kept in the shed on the far right that ran parallel with Ham Street ©SHC

Street housed a huge bull with a ring in his nose. Gerald recalls that when he went to Grey Court School, he and his mates often cut through the farmyard from Back Lane. However, before entering he always made a careful check because he didn't dare enter the yard if the bull was in it. On a few occasions Yvonne caught Gerald annoying the bull by rattling a stick on the gate. With her sibling seniority of eighteen months, she assumed the right to admonish him: *If you continue to do that Gerald he will break out and chase you all the way down the street.*

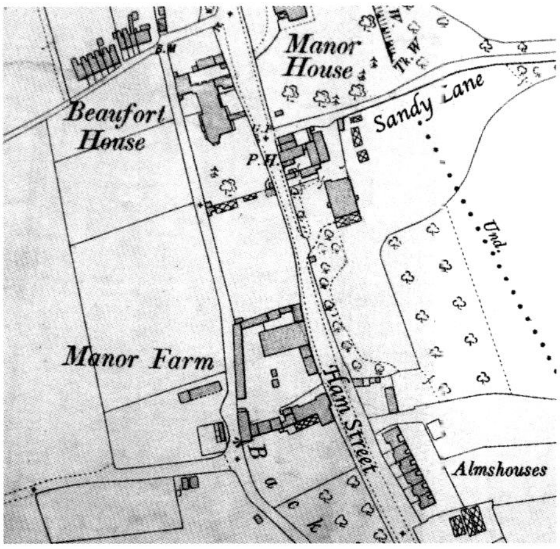

1913 Map: Location of the farm opposite what is now Grey Court School. Ham Library is now located opposite the Tollemache Alms-houses. Although the farm was locally known as Secrett's Farm it was still officially marked as Manor Farm NLS

The old barn was a fascinating place to visit with its ancient timbers supporting a steeply pitched roof. Gerald was a keen collector of birds' eggs. One day he and a mate went to the barn with the intention of getting an egg from the nest of a barn owl. They visited a small white shed in the farmyard where they paid three pence to Mrs Secrett, with her silver-grey hair, to fill a sack with straw to feed their rabbits. This was simply a ruse to get into the barn to collect the straw. Once inside, Gerald and his mate climbed up the hay bales to reach the timbers where the barn owl was nesting. Unfortunately, before they could reach the nest Mr (Louis) Secrett, who was nicknamed Lulu, came in and caught them on top of the hay bale. *Get out and take your straw with you*, he shouted. They departed rather quickly.

The ancient barn of Ham Manor (Secrett's) Farm © SHC

Despite this setback, Gerald recalls that Mr Secrett was a decent chap and well liked in the village. He was a tall man who wore gaiters and a trilby hat like the Pilgrim fathers. He rode around the village on a pale green BSA Bantam 125cc motorbike. If there were any complaints about the quality of the milk from his dairy, he would personally visit the household to apologise and put it right. Unfortunately, because he rode the bike through the farmyard it was invariably covered with cow muck. The local lads of the village, who prized their precious motorbikes and kept them spotlessly clean, would joke, *here comes old Lulu on the cowshit Bantam.*

Bert Gadd in the white coat loading the milk on the milk cart in the yard of Secrett's Farm. Napoleon, also known as Peter the Pole on the left. GS

Bert Gadd and Sylvia delivered the milk locally. They pulled a battery powered milk cart. When they lifted the bar on the front, the motor whirred and the cart moved forward.

The cowman was a chap who we called Napoleon, and every day he took more than forty cows up Sandy Lane to pasture. The cows left a terrible mess as they passed. Many years later, Gerald had to carefully weave his motorbike around the cow pats as he drove along the lane. Yet he couldn't resist opening the throttle to create a wonderful echo that rippled off the high walls either side of the lane. But an overzealous application of the brakes on a cow pat could easily have a very messy ending.

Gerald reflects, *it was terrible to see them demolish the farm and that wonderful old barn. It could have been a centre piece for any new development. What a lack of foresight!*

When they did finally demolish the farmhouse in 1958, they discovered at its core, a medieval manor house dating from the 15th century when King Henry V, hero of the Battle of Agincourt, owned both the Manors of Ham and Petersham. The manor house predated Ham House by two hundred years. **Truly a treasure lost!**

The milking sheds in Secrett's Farm facing onto Back Lane © SHC

1952 - Sandy Lane, looking from Ham Street, before it was widened

Gerald on his motorbike with his mate Mick Harrison outside Gerald's house at 6 Mead Road GS

Looking south along Ham Street at Secrett's Dairy and the farmhouse on Ham Street (1952) RLS

Looking south from Secrett's Farm that can be seen front right. On the left are the Tollemache Alms-houses. Jesse Slatter and his wife Beatrice lived in Number One after leaving 13 Evelyn Road DW

Graham Clark's Story

My Dad spent a lot of time away from home and I saw very little of him. In fact, he far too readily relinquished all of his responsibilities as both a husband and a father. My mum (Sylvia) was left to support us financially and emotionally. Yet she was stoic and resilient and always put on a brave face. Despite everything, she remained positive throughout. Goodness knows the turmoil that she went through quietly and alone, endeavouring to raise myself with the help of my 'big' brother Keith, so as to give us the best possible start in life. She certainly was a great mum and dad, all rolled into one.

Sylvia with Keith and Graham at Warners Holiday Camp GC

Appearances were all important

With my Dad's prolonged absence, it was essential for my Mum to keep the house running as well as she could. She lived in a continuous state of apprehension that the council could take the house away from us and maybe even put my brother and myself into care. For Mum, our house at 2 Murray Road was our sanctuary and she valued it enormously. Perhaps it was her time in the army, but my Mum was acutely aware that appearances were all-important and accordingly she was scrupulous in keeping the house looking trim and tidy. Our front step was meticulously cleaned with red Cardinal polish.

To ensure that she met the rent payments and made ends meet, Mum invariably had to work lunchtime and evening shifts as a cook at the The Café Continental on Hill Rise in Richmond. This meant that she had to prepare all our evening meals, though, being a cook, she did a great job and we simply had to warm up cottage pie, savoury mince, bubble and squeak, pasties…. She also taught us how to prepare simple meals. Nevertheless, with my brother only seven and myself having just turned one, Mum had to make arrangements for friends and neighbours to keep an eye on us while she was at work. We therefore had countless aunties in the neighbourhood, watching over us. Auntie Mary at 2 Stuart Road was one of our special aunts who remained a very close friend with my mum for over 60 years.

Mum then spent several years working as a cook and housekeeper for a diabetes specialist, Dr Butterfield and his wife, Elizabeth. Their home was at 3 Maids of Honour Row on Richmond Green, in the grounds of Richmond Palace. Dr Butterfield entertained a lot, and this meant that Mum had to prepare many luncheon and dinner parties at weekends. Mum became an indispensable member of their household and a very close companion of Elizabeth Butterfield (later to become Lady Butterfield). Every six months, Mrs Butterfield gave Mum an extra £50 as a contribution for Mum to take Keith and myself on special trips. On a couple of occasions, Dr Butterfield paid for Mum to take us to Warners holiday camp on the Isle of Wight for a week. These were thoroughly enjoyable and very memorable holidays. Even after Keith and I had grown up, Lady Butterfield who had by now moved to Cambridge to support her husband's role as Vice-Chancellor of the University, regularly sent Mum £50 (until Mum's death in 2010).

(When Dr Butterfield became Professor of Experimental Medicine at Guy's in 1958, he was the youngest medical professor in London. For the next 13 years he was increasingly absorbed by his research on diabetes. He ended his career as Regius Professor of Physic, Master of Downing College and Vice-Chancellor at Cambridge University).

With Keith being six years older, he naturally and very capably assumed the male role within our small household and my protector within the wider community of Ham. If I was ever subjected to any bullying, he would have a quiet word with the families of the bully concerned and "it would be sorted".

2 Murray Road

2 Murray Road

For Keith and myself, the back garden was both a learning and a work area. It was the space to shell peas and peel potatoes on a Sunday morning, to wait at the coal shed to count the sacks being delivered and pay the coalman his 7/6d, to chalk on the walls and paths, make a snowman, fix bikes and repair that chain again, make trolleys and maintain scooters, spray said items, do naughty things with magnifying glasses, along with swatting may bugs with a tennis racket, make stag hornies (beetles) fight, try to repair a burst Frido ball with a hot knife, build a bonfire for Nov 5th, water fights

Street Pals - Graham (right) with Paul Sossick (middle) and Julia Smith in Stuart Road. GC

on a hot day, put Dubbin on our football boots, hope that we were going to be on the team sheet that week, make the garden a football or cricket pitch, clean our school shoes, play darts on the shed door or test my William Tell crossbow, extinguish chip pan fires, the odd birthday parties with friends, family and relatives, play with fire, try smoking with rolled up paper or a fag end we had found, kick a ball against the shed, risk the odd broken window pane in the Crittals and keep a smelly rabbit as a pet. We laughed and cried over many things.

When Keith left school at the age of 15, I was increasingly 'home alone' for much of the time. Although I was comfortable with my own company, I do remember many a long summer night, being in my bedroom by 8pm, looking out of my window, watching the older kids playing in the street and wishing I could quickly get older!

I recall setting fire to the shed, burning my mum's new red melamine dropleaf table kitchen with a smouldering taper and helping Fred the milkman on his round without telling my mum where I'd gone. On one occasion, Keith ran through the house, with me on his back, and both my feet went through the windowpanes in the back door! On these occasions Mum employed the feather duster cane stick handle to administer a little bit of corporal punishment!

The council estates in Ham provided a great sense of community, supported by local schools, thriving parades of shops, six pubs and a working men's club all serving the needs of the local people. We all got on as neighbours, and fellow villagers. It was a great environment to grow up in. The youngsters at the time were imbued with respect for our elders and professional people.

Territories within Ham

Within the Ham community distinct territories emerged. Ours was the Woodville, Stretton, Murray, Stuart grid of roads that provided our own posse of lads, and sometimes self-invited girls. I grew up with my street pals, Peter Bush, Malcolm Gaines, Paul Sossick, Julia Smith, Robbie Good and his twin sister Irene. We were all armed with our own individual nicknames. Keith my brother had already been nicknamed Goober so I, a younger version of Keith, was called Gubba Clark. We saw the recreation ground on Sandy Lane as a defined border with Petersham and we crossed this border at our own risk. Another territory was made up of Back Lane, Lock, Lawrence and Ashburnham Roads and Beaufort Court. Yet if any of us got into trouble in Kingston, we would immediately become the H&P band of brothers!

The Gravel Pits

2 Murray Road on the north west edge of the council estate was literally a stone's throw from the perimeter fence of the pits! The fence had been worn down by constant use so we simply had to step over it to enter the original village theme park.

The Stuart and Murray Road posse could often be found roaming the wasteland of the pits, the surviving lakes and Apple Island, located between the rifle range and the Mariners, from breakfast till sunset. Our uniform consisted of T-shirts, shorts, and a pair of Clark's sandals or black Harry Harrison toe cap plimsoles. By the end of each day, our skinny frames were reluctant owners of scratches from vicious brambles, nettle and wasp stings, really irritating gnat bites, bruises and grazes to our knees, and an uncomfortable dose of sunburn. Calamine lotion, with its distinctive smell, was liberally applied by one of the aunties all over the reddening patches of skin.

In one of the lakes, we sailed oil drum rafts and fished for gudgeon, sticklebacks and other unrecognisable fish. Many of the fish were deformed, probably as a result of the toxic chemical drums that had been dumped in the pits over the years and had leaked.

In case we had to repel another posse, we were armed with our weapons: a whippy willow stick fitted with a ball of clay on the end ready to launch, homemade willow bows with arrows carefully whittled with our penknives. The most effective of all was a homemade catapult using a cut up inner tube to pull back and a pocketful of best quality Ham pit gravel. We all suffered the pain of getting hit by a piece of gravel or pebble in the back as we spun round to avoid getting hit in the face! The cost for these days of adventure, daring and thrills? Nothing! It was real Lord of the Flies adventure.

On those long lingering summer nights, after tea, we would congregate on the riverside rec to squeeze out the last rays of daylight for extra time on the swing or a final attempt on goal. The magic of my independence was invariably dispelled as the strident voice of my mother carried all the way from Murray Road across the wilderness, "Graham, time to come in now". So embarrassing!

The Big Freeze of 1963

With temperatures so cold the sea froze in places, 1963 is one of the coldest winters on record. Bringing blizzards, snow drifts, blocks of ice, freezing fog and temperatures lower than -20 °C, it was colder than the winter of 1947, and the coldest since 1740. It began abruptly just before Christmas in 1962.

Graham recalls the sheer excitement of the immense snow falls: *January brought a 36-hour blizzard with huge drifts of snow (homes opposite the open land of the pits really suffered). As the winter progressed, we experienced frozen pipes and a burst cold-water tank with water pouring through a bedroom ceiling (fortunately Keith who was now a trained plumber was able to quickly fix it). On cold mornings I avoided the lino in the house by jumping from rug to rug, on the way to a freezing bathroom. Here, I sparingly employed a flannel for a quick wipe. Downstairs we lit all the gas rings on the cooker to make a warm kitchen and made porridge for a solid breakfast. It was my job to clean the ashes from the fireplace and sprinkle them onto the garden path, so no one slipped. I vividly recall the constant smell of paraffin from the heaters in the house and jumping into a freezing bed. Yet, I have fond memories of the snow falling in winter and the Crittal window frames freezing with delicate patterns of ferns forming in the glow of the streetlight.*

We only moaned to ourselves, as we might have got a clip round the ear, if we said something in range of Mum. "Right! It's your turn to rake out the ashes, lay the fire with kindling and paper and go and get a bucket of coke from the shed!" "Ahhh Mum!"

The banks and shallows of the Thames and Ham Lands flooded and froze and we could skate on the frozen flood plains from Ham Street car park to The Mariners. The river iced up in some places so firmly that we could walk on it. Slides on Ham Pond and in the playground at Orchard School, which, I never remember closing. Steaming gloves, stinging fingers and sitting on a hot radiator to warm up after a bigger lad had put a snowball down my back.

Unbelievably the milk, the coal, the post and papers still got delivered! Oh, and for some reason we sang Beatles hits on the way back from Cubs as we were running through Cut Throat Alley on a Thursday night - Love Me Do, Please Please Me - they had arrived! No football for 10 weeks, Ham Lads went cold turkey!

The Ambush at the Dysart

Our standard early 60s snowwear consisted of a duffle coat or anorak, an itchy rollneck and a knitted balaclava on the top half. Thick shorts didn't quite reach our wellies that encased thin cotton socks. Unfortunately, on the trek pulling sledges to the Dysart Gate of Richmond Park, our socks would 'go to sleep' and peel off the front of our feet. With home knitted woolly gloves or mittens we flew again and again, down the long slope of the hillside below Pembroke Lodge. Yet the real excitement was in the final act of our winter campaign. Preparation, as my Mum drilled into us, was everything and with military precision we built our own individual piles of snowballs close to the wall inside Dysart Gate. Then, one of us in turn, went out of the gate to wait at the bus stop and put his hand out as the 65 or 71 buses came down the hill. As soon as the bus came to a halt our intrepid scout would dash back inside the gate and this would be the signal to launch a barrage of snowballs at the side of the bus. If we were lucky one of the snowballs would enter a window that had been slightly opened to clear the steamy windows. If we were very lucky, an irate conductor would descend to the open rear platform from where, hanging onto the white plastic coated pole, he would launch a volley of abuse at us. He was a prize target. Conveniently hidden by the eight-foot wall, we estimated his position and duly replied with another volley of snowballs!

These escapades became part of the folklore of the street kids of Ham.

Sledging in Richmond Park

February 1963 at the author's parents' home in Tudor Drive with a Morris 8 snowed in. GE

Christmas

My mum put a tremendous amount of effort into making our Christmas something very magical. She would begin preparing towards the end of the summer, buying small tins of ham and other treats then hiding them away. Being a very good trained cook, she would make the Christmas cake and pudding around two months before, to absorb the flavours. It was my job to wrap an old sixpence in a bit of greaseproof paper and drop it into the last stir of the pudding. Mum then boiled the pudding in a muslin cloth. Once the Christmas cake had been baked, she carefully iced it then decorated the snow scene with a little Father Christmas, a sledge, and a tree.

In December we made endless paper chains and put up other recycled decorations that we had retrieved from the loft. After untangling the fairy lights and keeping her fingers crossed that they would continue working, Mum then carefully dressed a posh tinsel tree that didn't drop needles and stood proudly before the living room window at the front of the house.

A visit to Santa's Grotto at Bentalls or Goslings was the best treat ever!!

The last week of the term at school was an easy week: read in class, pick up school report, nativity or school play, lunchtime record club in hall (who's got the mistletoe!), final assembly and a carol concert at St Andrew's or St Peter's. Whether it was Oakfield, Orchard or Grey Court, this was the best walk home of the year. Christmas excitement was upon me as I wondered what I would get. How slowly those days before Christmas Eve passed!

A couple of days before the 25th, I helped Mum make sausage rolls and mince pies. Once cooled we put them into old biscuit and chocolate tins.

In my head I can hear my mum on Christmas Eve morning saying, 'it's all about the preparation'. I have just finished prepping the swede, carrots, sprouts (don't put a cross cut, use a pointed knife in the stalk instead, they won't fall apart if slightly overcooked!). Potatoes (rinse to get rid of starch) and parsnips on Christmas Day morning, left in very cold water and pan ready to go, let your meats get to room temperature, cooks more evenly. "Timing, it's all about timing, make notes, what time are we sitting down?".

Best of all, I can see the image of Mum, looking out to the garden in one of those 1950s aprons/pinnies, the Light Programme on the radio playing either The Christmas Song by Ella Fitzgerald or Nat King Cole, her singing along and saying, "Graham come here and do some prepping!"

Oh, the anticipation and excitement, how hard was it, getting to sleep on Christmas Eve after being told not to get up before 6.30am: "keep your eyes shut, Santa's had a busy night, and he may be behind on deliveries!"

How did Santa get that sack to the end of the bed when I thought that I was awake all night?! Yet, he always managed to bring us presents that we really loved. I so remember my tin William Tell crossbow and a meths powered car! A set of dominoes, a Matchbox or Spot-On car and a selection box that was finished by Boxing Day.

Mum would spend Christmas morning in a very steamy kitchen with the back door open, making the final preparations for the Christmas lunch.

This was the best meal of the year and made all the merrier with cheap crackers, dreadful jokes, paper hats and finding that sixpence in the pud! Nothing was wasted and Mum would imaginatively use the scraps to make meals over the next few days, bubble and squeak with cold cuts and turkey fricassee and rice.

We were also lucky to have good neighbours to share the cheer. Snowball or Port and Lemon anyone? Merry Christmas to you all!

Adapting to change

In 1975 Sylvia received a letter from the council giving her notice on 2 Murray Road. Fortunately, she managed to get a top floor flat in Bowes Lyon House in Ham Close where she lived for the next thirty years.

Richmond Golf Club at Sudbrook Park

With both Graham and Keith well established in work and living elsewhere, Sylvia remarried in 1977. The pattern of her life changed once more, and she became a keen member of the ladies' section of Richmond Golf Club at Sudbrook Park. She loved the camaraderie at the club and had the ability and confidence, through her previous experiences and associations, to be both comfortable with, and interested in, all the individuals that she encountered. She continued playing golf for 24 years. Graham fondly recalls her enduring philosophy:

No one owes you anything so go and find it yourself

It's all about the preparation

Sudbrook Ladies – Sylvia 3rd from left. GC

It's strange how it all turns out! Graham left Grey Court in 1969 at the age of sixteen and managed to secure a much sought-after Telecommunications Technicians Apprenticeship with the Post Office. After five years he joined a little-known American company with the initials IBM. His role as a Customer Engineer was to support those leading-edge organisations which had invested heavily in IBM office equipment within London. Graham remained with IBM for 32 years, the latter part with a senior role in their UK sales mid-range/ commercial computing organisation.

Early in his career with IBM, Graham took up golf and his mum would occasionally invite him to join her for a round at Sudbrook Park. On one such occasion over lunch she introduced Graham to one of her golfing friends, another Clark, Fred Clark who just happened to be the Managing Director of IBM in the UK and lived nearby in Bute Avenue.

1948 aerial view of the golf course at Sudbrook Park, showing the route of the Sudbrook © Historic England

Graham is in the final stages of writing his own book with focus on his early life in Ham and his interest in music and clubs in and around London in the 1970s.

Ham Lands

In November 1983, Sir David Williams, leading the Richmond Council, brought to an end any future development of houses on Ham Lands. Thanks to the efforts of David and many other passionate supporters, 178 acres of Ham Lands has been designated as a local nature reserve by Richmond Borough Council. It is also designated as 'Metropolitan Open Land' which gives it the same protection as land in the Green Belt.

The Ham gravel pits had been filled with debris and topped off with soil brought from many parts of London and the South East of England. That soil carried, within it, samples of local seeds which have since flourished and created a botanical garden, a microcosm of the native wild plants of the south of England.

David Williams & Ham Lands
Imagery ©2020GoogleMaps

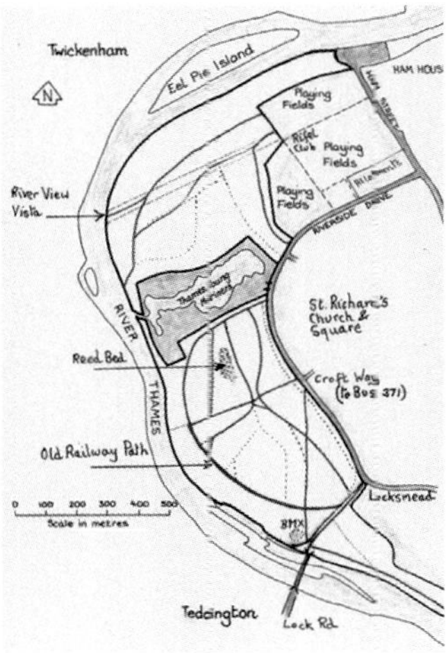

Map of Ham Lands today. HUG

Evelyn Pritchard, a local Historian who significantly improved our knowledge of Ham through her research, numerous articles and books. She is seen here walking her dog in Ham Lands RLS

The site is now a mix of habitats, mainly woodland, scrub, grassland and wetlands that contain a thriving and diverse mix of plants and animals including a number of rare species. There are meadow wildflowers that attract bees and butterflies, and the reserve is home to an abundance of bird life.

Sources:

Family history carefully researched by Mike Shaw
Pritchard Evelyn – A portrait of Ham in early Victorian times 1840-1860
Mulberry Keith – Various interesting & informative articles that can be found on Ham & Petersham History and Memories Facebook Group
Chave Leonard - The Growth of Ham in the 20th century
Berryman Ron – Saving the view from Richmond Hill (Journal of the Richmond Local History Society 2001)
Parker Eric - Highways and Byways in Surrey
Arcadian Times, May 7th 2011- The Ham River Grit Company & The Ham Lands
London's smallest railway – an article published in the Evening News and available in the Richmond Local Studies Collection
Day Martyn - Richmond Park - Starfish Decoy Sf8A - The Fires Burn On!
Surrey History Centre – 1911 CC28/68a Ham River Grit Co & 1948 C119/87 Filling in the pits
The Industrial Railway Society
Personal interviews with Gerald Stevens and Graham Clark
Graham Clark's personal blogs on the Ham & Petersham History and Memories Facebook Group
hamunitedgroup.org.uk/friends-of-ham-lands

Picture Credits

©SHC: Reproduced by permission of Surrey History Centre
RLS: Courtesy of Richmond Upon Thames Local Studies Library & Archive

NLS: Reproduced with the permission of the National Library of Scotland
©The Rayne family: Reproduced by permission of the Rayne family and Surrey History Centre
GE – Gordon Elsden
GC – Graham Clark
GS – Gerald Stevens
DW – Courtesy of Sir David Williams
EH - The photographs come from "Fields of Deception" by Colin Dobinson, an English Heritage publication covering the history of Britain's wartime bombing decoys
HUG – Ham United Group

Kingston's Theatre and Picture Houses

Side view of the Empire Theatre facing the Elite Cinema on the right

Programme for the Kingston Empire OW

As you drive around Kingston's one-way system past Wilkinsons (formerly C&A), you can see the last letters of the name of the Empire on the side of a building, above a pub. This forgotten theatre was an important and much-loved place of entertainment for the people of Kingston from 1910 to 1955. It was built on the site of an 18th century mansion owned by Dr William Roots, from a family of notable Kingston surgeons. Prior to that, the large house was owned by the Hardinge family, the Lords of Canbury Manor.

During its relatively short life, the Empire Theatre hosted nearly every celebrated music hall and variety artist of the period including; Gracie Fields, Jack Hylton, Max Miller, Florrie Forde, Flanagan & Allen, Marie Lloyd, Harry Champion, the Western Brothers, George Robey, Vera Lynn, George Formby, Tommy Trinder, Frankie Vaughan, Billy Cotton and his Orchestra, Louis Armstrong and many others.

In her comprehensive study of the Empire Theatre, Claire Jones draws us to the following appreciation of Variety Theatre by the Poet Laureate John Betjeman:

We can hear the swish of the bar doors, as people come out into the auditorium; we look up at the boxes and the plaster cherubs holding electric lights; we hear the crackle of peanuts in the pit; the stage is darkened except for a single flood light spotlighting the artist; excitement mounts as we reach the last big names on the bill who appear just before the interval, and last but one after it. The whole house rocks with laughter or waits in breathless suspense for a well-timed joke; the rapport is established between the artist and the audience – an intimacy and understanding which we remember all our lives. It is the true genius of music hall, and something that television can never give us.

Music hall was an affordable evening's entertainment and for a long while, one of the most popular ways of spending a night out with the family.

A mother of one of John Hayward's mates was an usherette at the Empire theatre and she quite often managed to get them cheap tickets up in the gods. John attended the last ever show at the Empire, starring the fabulous Billy Cotton band.

Eric Lavender remembers that the Empire *had twelve acts of two halves with all sorts going on. Comedy, dance, actors, bands and comedians, very vaudeville. There was truly a great variety of acts. I would go quite often and because my friend's dad was on the door, we were allowed to slide in free after the first act. Big bands came to the Empire and we were spoilt for choice. The top billed act would be the last to perform.*

The Empire Theatre

The entrance to the gods was down the side lane leading to the foundry. The doors and windows of the foyer looked on to the main street. The interior always looked plush and of a cold winter evening, it was especially warm and inviting. It's a great shame that such a venue, providing wonderful family entertainment, has ceased to exist.

After the war, Owen Walter's parents, who thoroughly enjoyed musicals, took him often to the Empire. He recalls that this was a very special theatre, with lovely comfortable seats, looking down to the stage. It provided great entertainment for all the family.

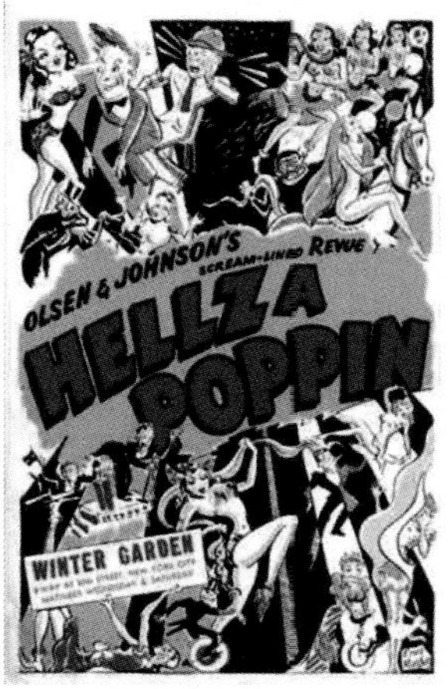

Bill Waddell's father was an avid music hall fan and also loved going to the Empire: *We would take 6d seats up in the gods. I remember chewing on the brass rail while I concentrated on the show. I clearly recall being entranced by the hit musical show, Hellzapoppin' that came over from Broadway in America. I also saw a young comic double act called Morecombe and Wise appearing on the Empire stage.*

Yvonne Clements fondly remembers the entertainment palaces of Kingston, true palaces with their sumptuous foyers, glittering lights and plush seats. The barely suppressed excitement that had to endure the long wait to the weekend when they would go and see one of the variety performances at the Empire. With a bill that presented both well established and up and coming artists. Musicians, singers, comedians, magicians, dancers .... some were brilliant, others not so great but loved and applauded just the same. *Yet up in the gods, the seating was stacked so steeply that if I leant forward, I would easily suffer from vertigo.*

Every Christmas, Yvonne and her mum took her younger brother Harry to the pantomime at the Empire. They had the cheaper tickets *up in the gods* with access via a door on the side of the theatre on the lane that led to the foundry. Near this door, stood a chap with a brazier holding red hot coals, on which he roasted chestnuts that he sold in a small bag for a few pence. When Yvonne was a child, they could not afford gloves so they had to toss the chestnuts from hand to hand, with much vocal exclamation, until the chestnuts cooled sufficiently to peel them.

In the dark and chilly winter evenings, Harry remembers how inviting the Empire theatre was with its richly decorated and warmly lit foyer: *Once inside, the staircase seemed to climb upwards forever. With little legs it was quite a journey. One year we watched Jack and the Beanstalk. From our lofty perch high up in the theatre, I watched with amazement as Jack climbed up the beanstalk*

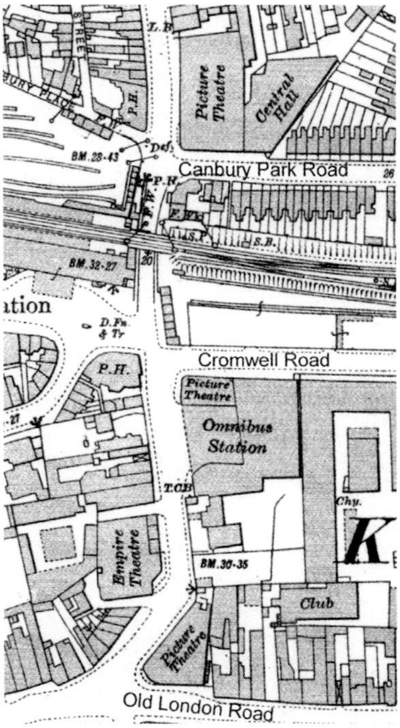

Above: 1928 aerial photo showing from left to right; Cinem Palace Picture House, The Kinema Picture House, The Empire Theatre and the Elite Picture House © Historic England

Far left: 1934 Map showing the concentration of Picture Theatres in Canbury. NLS

Left: The Elite Cinema

that grew out of the stage and reached a height, level with myself.

The Elite Picture Theatre, that opened in May 1921, was located on the corner of London Road and Richmond Road. It was considered at the time one of the most beautiful picture houses ever built. The foyer resembled the interior of an old mansion, with carved oak panelling that came from Preston House in Malling, Kent. A coal fire was kept burning throughout the winter months. Above the foyer were four tea rooms where a delicate afternoon tea could be enjoyed.

Bill Waddell agreed that the Elite was really something very special. Mike Eaton reflects, *the Elite Cinema was a really decent cinema in a beautiful building, but sadly demolished, then replaced by C&A and later by Wilkinsons in a functional inelegant building.*

Eric Lavender remembers that the Elite, *was policed by an immaculate Commissionaire in full regalia with a peaked cap descending over the top of his nose, just like a guardsman. He was a man of authority who impressed order on the queues leading into the cinema. The queue for the pricey seats,*

2 and 3 (2s 3d) & 2 and 9 (2s 9d) ran down the side of the cinema along the Old London Road. The holders of the cheaper 1 and 3 and 1 and 9 tickets queued along the opposite side of the cinema towards the Granada.

Kingston's first cinema, the Cinem Palace located on the corner of Richmond Road and Canbury Park Road was unknowingly built very close to where the ancient Latchmere Brook changed its south westerly course and headed directly west towards the river. It was replaced by the Regal Theatre, which opened on 15th February 1932. Seating 2,445 people, the Regal was fitted with a large stage, dressing rooms, a dance floor and a cafe. A huge Wurlitzer, originally designed for a Chicago millionaire's residence, was installed for the opening of the theatre. The organ had twelve ranks of pipes, cathedral chimes and a grand piano played from the keys.

The Cinem Palace on the corner of Richmond Road and Canbury Park Road

The huge Wurlitzer, originally designed for a Chicago millionaire's residence, was installed in the Regal Theatre for its opening in February 1932

In 1938 Associated British Cinemas (ABC) took over the cinema. The organ continued to play throughout the war except for a brief spell in 1940 when the cinema was damaged by bombs. The organ was removed from the cinema in October 1972 and taken to the musical museum in Brentford.

The Regal cinema which later became the ABC

Mike Eaton went to the Regal for Saturday morning pictures. Here he watched cowboy movies starring Roy Rogers and Gene Autry. Cowboy and Indian films later reclassified as westerns were very popular at the time.

Bill Waddell recalls that, in the late 1930s, there was a terrific choice of entertainment in Kingston: *I most often went to Saturday morning pictures at the Regal in Kingston. This featured the Mickey Mouse club with cartoons, a film, a serial (come back next week to see the next instalment) and a session to sing along with the organist. The words were put up on a screen and a ball bounced from word to word.*

In 1950, Yvonne Clements who was ten years older than four-year-old brother, Harry, accompanied him to ABC Minors. The programme would start with the organist rising from the pit with his mighty Wurlitzer and playing a tune that all the youngsters would sing along to:

We are the boys and girls well known as

Minors of the ABC..

And every Saturday all line up..

To see the films we like and shout aloud with glee..

We like to laugh and have our sing song

Such a happy crowd are weeeee…

We're all pals together

We're Minors of the ABC!

Next on was loony tunes before Flash Gordon made an appearance to save a desperate situation. Pathé News then introduced snippets of international news, though Harry recalls that at the time, despite the war having finished, there still seemed to be a lot of conflict all around the world. The morning's entertainment would conclude with a much-favoured cowboy movie.

The Granada Cinema

The Granada Cinema

In 1938 the Hyams Brothers were granted permission to build a cinema in Clarence Street, Kingston. It was only half built before being taken over by Granada Theatres in June 1939. The theatre was opened five months later by a film star couple Jesse Mathews and Sonnie Hale who lived locally in Hampton and had gained some notoriety in a divorce scandal.

There was a fully equipped stage and the screen was 30 feet wide and 24 feet tall, allegedly among the largest in the world. The theatre housed a Wurlitzer organ with a grand piano that had originally been installed in the Picture House, Edinburgh. On the entrance facade there were three large windows which allowed light into the foyer. Inside the auditorium there were three decorative grilles on the side splay walls which had the organ chambers behind. The entrance ceiling was highly decorated and boasted a 'Granada' chandelier.

Mike Eaton recalls that it was a real treat to go to this cinema with his mother, if she could afford it. They always took the 1s 9d seats. This was the one occasion when his mum truly relaxed:

They played the A film and this was followed by the Pathé News which was our only real means of getting information (albeit censored) about what was happening in the war. There were some adverts then the B movie. At the end of the day they would play the national anthem and we would all stand up as a mark of respect. We truly enjoyed ourselves and were in the cinema from about 5:30pm until 9pm before walking back home. Good times!

In his early years, Eric Lavender's mum preferred to take him to the Grenadier (Granada) as it was a little more up market:

The foyer of the Granada

The Granada was the swishest of them all with a massive stage that also hosted a lot of good shows. For 6d, Saturday morning pictures was great entertainment. We could see two or three cartoons, a serial and a film, normally a cowboy movie. We would watch the Back Street Kids, the Three Stooges and also sing along with the organist, with a bouncing ball guiding us along the lyrics, shown on the screen. The organists could get magical sounds out of the Wurlitzer. As we became a little older, we progressed from being a Grenadier to a Marshall where we were expected to watch over the youngsters.

During the intervals, usherettes would drill down from the back of the cinema holding a tray full of tubs of vanilla ice-cream. As the cinema darkened, following the interval, we could see them both on either side of the stalls, lit up by a small light, continuing to serve their last customers.

Carole Richardson recalls the Kingston Kinema that was located next to the bus station: *It was small, dark and a little grubby and commonly known as the flea pit.*

The Odeon Cinema in the High Street opposite the Police Station

The Kingston Kinema next to the bus station, known locally as the flea pit.

Eric commenting further on the Kinema, *it was a bit shabby. You went to the Kinema and came out with an itch.*

Carole Richardson reflects, *going to the cinema was a real outing. Films were played on a continuous roll so once you had paid your money you could stay and watch several showings if you wished. On one occasion I watched three successive showings of "Calamity Jane". I saw "It's Great to be Young" a total of 12 times, over a few visits, because I had a crush on Jeremy Spencer.*

Picture Credits

Every effort has been made to trace the ownership of the pictures used, though in many cases without success.
OW: Courtesy of Owen Walter
NLS: Reproduced with the permission of the National Library of Scotland
Pictures of the theatre and cinemas can be found on the two following sites:
Matthew Lloyd, www.arthurlloyd.co.uk
www.cinematreasures.org

Sources

Jones Claire – Remembering the Empire, Kingston's Variety Theatre 1910-55 held at Kingston History Centre
www.arthurlloyd.co.uk/Kingston
Sampson June – Kingston Past

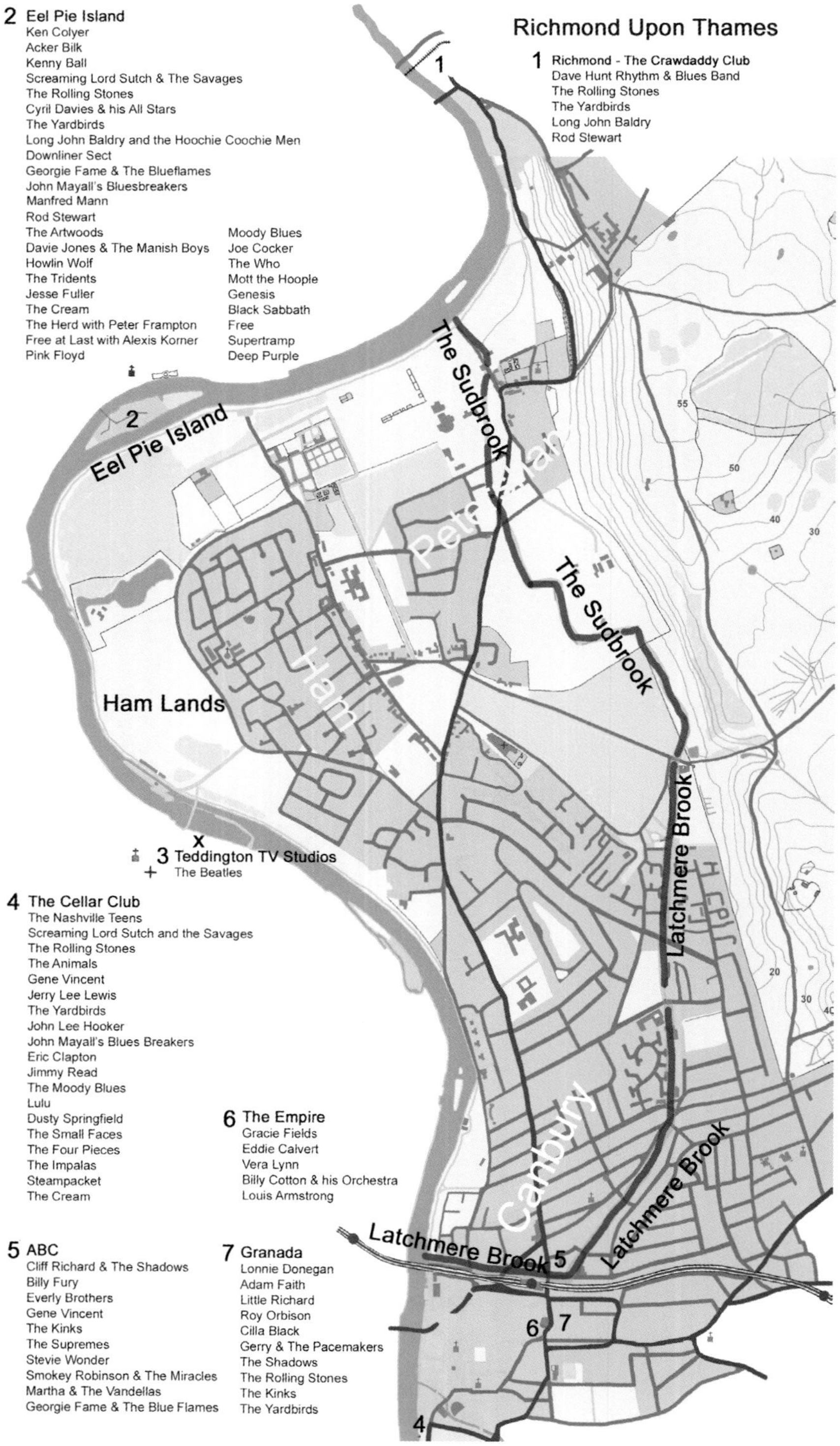

Musical entertainment in local Thames side towns in the mid 20th century

Into the Light

Setting the Scene

The austerity, the rationing and the general drabness of the war and post war years produced a generation of youngsters with creative minds and great energy but with few sources of entertainment. What they lacked in material possessions, they more than made up for with a fertile and resourceful imagination. This generation were receptive to new waves of music, introduced from the United States, beginning with Traditional Jazz and followed by bigger and more energetic waves of rock 'n' roll and Blues music inspired by Black American musicians. The Thames-side towns of Kingston, Twickenham and Richmond were to play a very important part in this musical revolution.

What was left of the Latchmere Brook, alias the Sudbrook, lethargically moved unnoticed through the middle of this landscape before quietly discharging into the Thames a short distance east of Eel Pie Island.

Bushy Park

Between 1942 and 1963 the US Army occupied a Military base in Bushy Park that was called Camp Griffiss. It was here that the Supreme HQ Allied Expeditionary Force, led by General Eisenhower, planned D Day and the invasion of German-occupied France. The base also played an important role in the Berlin airlift in the late 1940s.

American troops based at the camp visited the pubs and shops in Kingston and hosted dances, to which many local girls were invited. Glenn Miller and his band performed at the base. Many of the GIs brought with them Jazz and Blues records of very talented American musicians who were, at the time, unknown in the UK. On their departure, many of these 78 rpm records were sold to second-hand furniture shops in Fife Road and a narrow lane off Eden Street. To discerning local musicians, these records would soon become extremely valuable!

A Beacon for Change

The war imposed a period of austerity and rationing that continued well into the early 1950s. As the country slowly recovered, more jobs became available and very gradually, people had more money to spend. The Festival of Britain in 1951 celebrated British Science, Technology, Industrial Design, Architecture, Music and the Arts. With key exhibition areas on the South Bank of the Thames and Battersea Park, the Festival heralded an optimistic and fruitful period of recovery and became a "beacon for change" that resonated with many thousands of visitors. The Festival celebrated vibrant colour in place of soot stained, black and grey cities and the traditional brown and green country landscape.

Teenagers

In the early 1950s the British press began referring to youngsters from the age of 13 to 19 as teenagers. This gave them a separate identity distinct from their parents and younger siblings.

In February 1955, a worried mother wrote to Mary Brown's agony aunt column in the Daily Mirror, desperate to understand what it was that had turned her teenager bad:

My son, who was fourteen a month ago, used to be reasonably obedient and straightforward. He confided in me and we were best of friends. This last year he's been steadily changing. He's cheeky and he's sulky… Why should a boy change like this? Do you think he's got into bad company? I'm so worried in case he becomes one of the 'delinquents' we read so much about.

The genie was well and truly out of the bottle! Teenagers were desperate to be seen to be different from their parents and in many cases try things that their parents clearly disapproved of. Music, played on juke boxes in small coffee bars and by talented energetic musicians in nocturnal dens by the Thames, was a natural outlet for this rite of passage.

Art School

At the time there were generous grants from the Government that enabled students to take courses at the specialist art schools. These art schools would accommodate many students, from the age of 13, who spent their spare time both listening to American music in coffee bars and learning their craft as hopeful musicians. The art schools had a great influence on the youth of the Thames riverside towns.

Chris Archer, a long-term resident of Ham and Petersham, who studied at Twickenham Art School, recalls,

Looking back, the best thing that happened to me was that I failed my 11 plus. This enabled me at the age of 13, in 1955, to go to Twickenham Art School. I found myself on a fabulous course that as well as mainstream subjects of maths and English taught me life drawing, painting, plant drawing, technical drawing, historic ornament, lettering, typography and fine metalwork, including silversmithing. Most of the teachers were experienced practitioners in their various crafts and I was inspired by the lettering and typography teacher who worked in commercial art studios three days a week and taught for the other two. His extensive experience meant that he could teach us exactly what we needed to know to earn a living as a commercial artist. Art schools then had an atmosphere of relative freedom. It was all fairly laid back and we all loved the work we were doing. This course laid the foundation of a successful and thoroughly enjoyable career in graphic design. During this time, I worked for four large record companies to produce album cover designs and the creative material for advertising and promotional campaigns for large bands.

Radio

Few families could afford televisions and new records were still relatively expensive, so radio became a natural medium to hear the latest music from America. The BBC, which had a monopoly on radio broadcasting, was not so obliging with its selection of progressive popular music and at this time there were no commercial stations in the UK. Instead, many teenagers tuned into the American Forces Network AFN or Radio Luxembourg to hear their music. From 1960, Radio Luxembourg, which had one of the most powerful privately-owned transmitters in the world, broadcasting on medium wave, deliberately targeted the growing teenage market, with increasing emphasis on popular music. Many parents were bemused when their difficult teenagers showed a willingness to go to bed early. Little did they realise that they were tuning into Radio Luxembourg underneath the sheets. In 1964, Radio Caroline, a pirate radio station operating from a ship in international waters off the Essex coastline, was established to broadcast popular music and circumvent the BBC's broadcasting monopoly. The movie "The Boat That Rocked" amusingly covers this period. Pirate radio was extremely important for new bands. Regular airplay on pirate radio combined with an appearance on TV programmes such as Ready Steady Go would help a good single from an unknown band climb steadily up the music charts. By 1967, several pirate radio stations were broadcasting to a daily audience in excess of ten million. Influential pirate radio DJs included John Peel, Tony Blackburn, Kenny Everett, Johnnie Walker, Tony Prince, Emperor Rosko and Spangles Muldoon. Most of these DJs would later join a restructured BBC Radio when it emphatically embraced popular music.

Television

The new medium of television was an increasingly important conduit for introducing popular music. Stringent Government control, however, limited more radical and expressive music or musicians. Davie Jones (later David Bowie) was told to get a haircut when he first appeared with the Manish Boys.

Six-Five Special burst onto the television on Saturday nights from February 1957. The show was targeted at a young audience, *with plenty of music, in the modern manner, with rock'n'roll, skiffle groups, traditional jazz, featuring top music groups and soloists.*

Get your hair cut! Alamy stock photo

Juke Box Jury was a music panel show, based on the American show Jukebox Jury. The programme was aired on BBC Television on Saturday nights between June 1959 and December 1967. The show featured celebrity guests who were asked to judge the hit potential of recent record releases. By 1962 the programme was attracting 12 million viewers a show.

Thank Your Lucky Stars was a pop music show broadcast on ITV from 1961 to 1966. It was essential viewing for millions of British teenagers. As well as many of the top British bands, it also included visiting American stars.

Ready Steady Go! was a British rock/pop music television programme broadcast every Friday evening from 9 August 1963 until 23 December 1966 on ITV.

Top of the Pops was a British music chart programme, broadcast weekly on Thursday evenings on BBC 1 from the 1st January 1964. Finishing in 2006, it became the world's longest running weekly music show.

The Beat Room shown on BBC 2 in 1964-65 presented beat, rhythm and blues and other pop music.

The Empire Theatre

The Empire Theatre in Kingston

Since 1910 the Empire Theatre had provided live entertainment to the people of Kingston with an endless stream of accomplished entertainers and musicians. Those musicians performing on the grand stage included Gracie Fields (*Sally*), Jack Hylton (*the British King of Jazz*), Flanagan & Allen (*Underneath The Arches*), the ukulele playing George Formby, Frankie Vaughan (*Give Me The Moonlight*), Donald Peers (*In A Shady Nook By A Babbling Brook*), Vera Lynn, Billy Cotton & his Band and Eddie Calvert, the man with the golden trumpet.

George Birdsall, a long-term Ham resident, living in Lawrence Road, recounts that Vera Lynn, while performing at the Empire Theatre, used to stay at the Lawrence Hall Hotel (later the Cassel Hospital) on Ham Common.

In the early 50's Mike Eaton was heavily into jazz and he saw a number of acts at the Empire which included Ted Heath, Ronnie Scott, Terry Lightfoot and Humphrey Lyttlelton.

Shortly before lowering its curtain for the last time, the Empire hosted Louis Armstrong for a week in March 1955.

Louis Armstrong in 1955 - wiki

The Musical Revolution

1954 Onwards

The teenagers, growing up in Britain in the 1950s, were on an endless quest for excitement to relieve the monotony of their lives. Popular music remained the domain of the crooners and Jazz legends. A review of the top 100 singles in 1954 shows the continuing prominence of Perry Como, Frank Sinatra and Dean Martin along with Doris Day and jazz supremoes such as Eddie Calvert, Duke Ellington, Nat King Cole and Billy Cotton & his Band. This was also the year that Sally Clark, who at the age of seven in 1939 had made her first public performance as a singer in the entrance hall of Bentall's Department Store in Kingston, charted with her first UK hit, but now known as Petula Clark.

Lurking down in 75th position in the annual sales chart of 1954 is Bill Haley & His Comets with *Shake, Rattle and Roll.* Within a year Bill Haley & His Comets will enjoy a meteoric rise into the consciousness of a generation of youngsters with *Rock Around The Clock.* Used under the opening credits of the movie Blackboard Jungle, the song reaches number one in November 1955 and becomes the UK's first million selling single. Cinemas throughout the country will suffer an outbreak of young people jiving in the aisles. Some of the cinemas even get trashed. Rock 'n' Roll has arrived in the UK!

Rock Around The Clock heralds a popular musical revolution in 1956 as the traditional crooners are challenged by Bill Haley & His Comets with four singles, and a 21-year-old Elvis Presley who releases *Heartbreak Hotel* and *Hound Dog.*

Mike Eaton and his mates bought 78 rpm discs and they would pop round to each other's houses and listen to them on a gramophone. Mike bought one of the original Elvis LP's.

This was the period of the Teddy Boys, who prided themselves on being delinquent youths! They adopted an Edwardian era style of clothing which included drainpipe trousers, drape jackets with velvet collars and crepe-soled suede shoes, hence the name, Teddy Boys. In Kingston they had a reputation for gratuitous violence and the duffel coat wearing students in the area tended to avoid them for fear of being duffed up!

Closer to home, Lonnie Donegan was appealing to the younger generation to cast off their inhibitions and get directly involved in music. A traditional jazz musician by trade, he joined Ken Colyer's Jazzmen along with Chris Barber and Monty Sunshine. In their Dixieland set, he played guitar and banjo but during the interlude he introduced a "skiffle" break. With a washboard, tea-chest bass and a cheap guitar, Donegan and his two fellow musicians played folk and blues songs by American artists and released a fast version of Leadbelly's "*Rock Island Line*". This soared to Number 2 in the UK charts in April 1956 and immediately gained the attention of the youth of Britain.

John Lennon formed his skiffle group, the Quarrymen in March 1957. He was one of many talented musicians who were influenced by Lonnie Donegan.

Rock Island Line - The Singles Anthology by Lonnie Donegan records:

When I came along with the old three chords, people began to think that if I could do it, so could they. It was the reintroduction of the folk music bridge which did that. – Lonnie Donegan

He was the first person we had heard of from Britain to get to the coveted No. 1 in the charts, and we studied his records avidly. We all bought guitars to be in a skiffle group. He was the man. – Paul McCartney

I wanted to be Elvis Presley when I grew up, I knew that. But the man who really made me feel like I could actually go out and do it was a chap by the name of Lonnie Donegan. – Roger Daltrey

Skiffle was a DIY rock 'n' roll for many young aspiring musicians and enabled many teenagers to join the camaraderie of a band playing and enjoying a new energetic type of music. The main instrument in the group was a guitar and a player who knew at least three chords. This was accompanied by a home-made double bass and a wash board. The group were now able to copy all the latest hits and embark on a journey of creative expression, high energy and great fun. If they were confident enough, they could audition for a slot at a local pub or village hall.

Chris Archer: *Four or five of us formed a harmonica band at the Art School, I played the tea-chest bass. I was also a member of a skiffle group, that was called the Flophouse Five. It was great fun!*

Eric Lavender from Canbury Park Road was also a part of a skiffle band: *At this time the skiffle movement was coming in. As we didn't have much money, we made our own instruments. We screwed a small cymbal into the top of a washboard. With thimbles placed on fingers and scraped down the board, this created a percussion instrument. In place of a double bass we used a tea chest with a broom handle screwed in and a strong string to create the double bass sound.*

A few years later Eric progressed to the George Andrew's Six which played traditional jazz in the Fighting Cocks in London Road, a very popular venue with local youngsters.

Yvonne Stevens was at the time living with her family in Mead Road, Ham. She recalls, *In 1957 a skiffle band, that went by the name Rick Richards, played a number of gigs at the Crooked Billet Pub in Ham Street and the Ham Institute in New Road. Tony Makins, the bass player, had a bit of a crush on me and would walk for miles to come and see me. On one occasion Tony and Rick put up a tent in our back garden. My Mum was very anxious that they took it down before my father came home.*

Tony and Rick, being reasonably accomplished musicians, broke out of skiffle and went their separate ways. In 1958, Tony, who now went by the stage name Tex Makins, joined Marty Wilde's (father of Kim Wilde) backing band called the Wildcats. (In 1961, Tex played with Billy Fury and the Blue Flames then a year later accompanied Georgie Fame. In 1963, he supported the French Elvis who went by the name of Johnny Hallyday before returning to Georgie Fame from October 1963 until the end of 1965.)

Tex Makins (left) and Billy Fury Courtesy of Gerald Stevens

The Eel Pie Hotel & Ballroom © Dorothy

Eel Pie Island

It was the manager of an antiques shop in Kingston, Arthur Chisnall, who provided many youngsters of Richmond, Twickenham and Kingston with an unforgettable magical adventure. In late 1956 he hired the ballroom of the Eel Pie Hotel to host traditional jazz on Friday and Saturday nights. The official opening was Friday August 10th with Ken Colyer's Jazzmen performing New Orleans Jazz. Skiffle was played during the interludes.

Eel Pie Island Hotel was originally built in the 1830s as an elegant retreat for London's wealthier residents. In the 1920s the ballroom with its well sprung dance floor entertained the Quickstep, Charleston and Foxtrot. The lift and fall of the dance floor enabled elegant dancers to fly across the floor. It had been a wonderful ballroom with a riverside bar in a pleasant island hotel.

Aerial view, from above Ham, of the Eel Pie Hotel & Ballroom located in the centre of the south side of the island, © Historic England

Chris Archer was a visitor to the Island, shortly after the Eel Pie Jazz Club had opened: *My parents had visited Eel Pie Island Hotel in the 1930s when it was a popular venue for ballroom dances. I first started going to Eel Pie Island in 1956, of an evening after art school. At the time, the island was only accessible by a small chain ferry that was operated by a man who turned a handle to pull us across. The fare was 2d each way which enabled us to board the ferry and rattle our way the short distance from the end of Water Lane to the Island.*

We then followed the footpath through the trees to the other side of the island, overlooking Ham, to gain entrance to the hotel ballroom. At the time, I was probably one of the youngest members of the audience, though being relatively tall, I was able to buy myself and a friend from Art School a bottle of light ale. It was a wonderful atmosphere, being away from my parents, having a beer and listening to great jazz music being played by Ken Colyer's Jazzmen, the Crane River Jazz band …

Reading the following roll call of some of the more prominent and influential new wave musicians of the period will undoubtedly bring back vivid memories of pubs, clubs, boy and girl friends and a sense of occasion and nostalgia to many people who were teenagers during the late 1950s and early 1960s in this area.

Elvis Presley continues his rise throughout 1957. Little Richard first appears on the scene with four singles including *Long Tall Sally* and Jerry Lee Lewis introduces himself with two energetic singles. Lonnie Donegan maintains the skiffle crusade with two big hits and local boy Tommy Steele and his Steelmen announce themselves with three hits including *Singing the Blues*. His large 17th Century mansion inside the tight corner of the Petersham Road was known for decades by many local residents as the Tommy Steele house. The top deck of the 65 bus afforded a great view into the house! A band named The Crickets launch Buddy Holly on a tragically short but highly influential career and the Everly Brothers keep everyone dancing with *Wake Up Little Susie* and *Bye Bye Love*.

In early 1957, a bridge was installed to connect Eel Pie Island to Twickenham. It was just wide enough to take a Mini or an Austin 7. The toll fee was established at 2d each way. The bridge made life a little easier for the musicians carrying their instruments back and forth. Though, it remained a challenge when covered in ice.

Maggie, whose parents lived in one of the prefabs on Latchmere Recreation Ground, visited Eel Pie Island every weekend with her husband and brother-in-law, a clarinet player who played traditional jazz:

Saturday night was jazz night with more than a hundred people. The dance floor was heaving. The musicians all took their turns to play. None of them was famous. They were there for the love of music. There was no formality. There were other musicians who turned up and joined in. They all had something in common, they were all broke and they all loved music. My brother in law never travelled anywhere without his clarinet. I recall that Ronnie Lane had been told by his father: "If you learn to play an instrument you will have a friend for life". That is so true.

I have wonderful memories of everyone laughing, singing, dancing and generally having a great time. It was a very friendly atmosphere. The floor would bounce a lot with the stomping and dancing and the gigs would normally last until 1 or 2am.

Long John Baldry was a lovely man but permanently broke. I always thought that he would be very big but he never seemed to break through into the big time, despite being so talented. I bought a transistor radio off of him. My husband bought a leather jacket for £20 off another broke musician by the name of Reg Dwight. Some ten years later we bumped into Lonnie Donegan in Spain and spent a while with him, reminiscing about our marvellous evenings on Eel Pie Island.

I am now 82 (2020) but remember it all so clearly. We counted down the week to Friday evening and the anticipation of visiting the Island. It was all so exciting. It was wonderful.

During 1957, Eel Pie Island's Saturday night jazz aficionados were treated to Ken Colyer's Jazzmen, Mr Acker Bilk and His Paramount Jazz Band, Kenny Ball's Jazzmen, the Storyville Jazz Band starring Peter (Ginger) Baker on drums and a group called Merseysippi. The following year, Merseysippi would perform at the Cavern club supported by an enthusiastic skiffle group called the Quarrymen with John Lennon and Paul McCartney.

Throughout 1958, Buddy Holly and the Crickets give Elvis some competition with three hits including the sensational *Peggy Sue*. The Everly Brothers have a massive hit with *All I have To Do Is Dream* which remains at number 1 in the UK charts for 7 weeks. Jerry Lee Lewis's frantic performance of *Great Balls Of Fire* lights the place up and soars to No. 1 in the UK Singles Chart.

Despite the hotel's dilapidated state, Eel Pie Island soon began to attract some of the big names of British Jazz. Acker Bilk and his band were now Friday and Saturday night fixtures on the island. Other regulars were professional jazz musicians that included Ken Colyer, Alan Elsdon and Terry Lightfoot. Ken Colyer excelled at the trumpet and cornet and was a fervent disciple of New Orleans Jazz. Apparently, he had joined the Merchant Navy at 17, travelled around the world but jumped ship in Mobile, Alabama to go and play jazz with his idols in New Orleans. He was offered the job of lead trumpeter on a tour, but was caught by the authorities, put in prison for a month then deported.

An interview, conducted as part of the Kingston RFM project, informs us that in 1958, Top Topham transferred from St Paul's Junior School in Borough Road, Kingston to Hollyfield School. In the same year, after swimming twice across the River Thames he was accepted into Leander Sea Scouts near Canbury Gardens. At the time his family lived on the corner of Clifton Road and Canbury Park Road. When he was 12 his father made him a tea chest bass which was the beginning of his musical career. At the age of 13 he entered the art school of Hollyfield where he met fellow students Eric Clapton and Chris Dreja. By now Topham was playing the guitar and they started playing blues music together.

The 1959 UK Music Chart sees the arrival of home-grown stars Cliff Richard & The Shadows and Marty Wilde to accompany Lonnie Donegan who has a uniquely titled hit called *Does Your Chewing Gum Lose Its Flavour On The Bedpost Overnight?* Buddy Holly's *It Doesn't Matter Anymore*, backed with *Raining In My Heart* is Britain's first posthumous number 1 hit, released shortly after Buddy Holly was killed in a plane crash on the 3rd February.

On Eel Pie Island Ken Collyer, Kenny Ball and Terry Lightfoot continued to entertain their jazz disciples. Mike Eaton recalls that the Coronation Hall in Kingston boarded over one of its swimming pools in the winter to host jazz bands on Saturday nights. It was here that Mike saw Acker Bilk perform *Stranger On The Shore*. Being a great jazz fan, Carole Richardson went to the Coronation baths to watch Acker Bilk, Terry Lightfoot, Chris Barber and Kenny Ball. She clearly remembers the floor being very spongy.

Carole also remembers that Turks boathouse at the end of Canbury Gardens had a clubhouse upstairs with another springy floor where they put on jazz.

Coffee Bars

Students were drawn to the coffee bars in the area to listen to their favourite music on the resident juke box. At the end of Canbury Park Road was La Capone, a small coffee bar with benches and a juke box. The juke box was later replaced by a record deck which enabled the students to play their own records. This is how energetic American musicians such as Little Richard and Jerry Lee Lewis, in the absence of coverage by the BBC, were being introduced to a wider audience. This is also where those records that had been left behind by American G.I.'s were establishing a growing following for a new wave of Rhythm and Blues music, led by black American artists such as Muddy Waters, Howlin' Wolf, B.B. King and Chuck Berry. If a local band could cover an unheard hit by one of these musicians, they would gain an immediate following. The race was on!

L'AUBERGE Coffee shop near Richmond Bridge. RLS

The Kenco Coffee House was close to one of the lanes leading to All Saints Church in Kingston and frequented by black clothed beatniks *trying hard to look depressed*.

L'AUBERGE by the bridge in Richmond was another favourite haunt for beatniks, a good meeting place on the Pilgrims' Way to Eel Pie Island.

Record Booths

Carole Richardson, living at the time in Tudor Drive, recalls, *In the 1950s Maxwell Music shop was located opposite Marks & Spencer in Clarence Street. Upstairs they had record booths. With my friends, we would go in and request to listen to a favourite record. They would place it on a turntable and tell us the number of a listening booth. On Saturdays there could be as many as ten of us in a booth listening and singing along to the song of the moment. The first record I bought was a 78rpm, Tommy Steele, Singing The Blues.*

By 1960, the traditional crooners have been overwhelmed by Elvis Presley *It's Now Or Never*, The Everly Brothers *Cathy's Clown*, Roy Orbison *Only The Lonely*, Eddie Cochran *Three Steps To Heaven* and Duane Eddy. As for local bands, Cliff Richard and The Shadows *Apache* are in the ascendency along with Adam Faith, though Lonnie Donegan is beginning to fade. Johnny Kidd & The Pirates release their most memorable song, *Shakin All Over.*

Performing at Eel Pie Island

Eel Pie Island had now become the *go to* place, the most atmospheric student jazz club in London. The art college students, the bohemians and the beatniks came and danced on the magnificent sprung floor within the dilapidated ballroom. They drank Newcastle Brown Ale and cider, endeavouring to make it last as long as they could on their meagre budgets. They were entertained by an all-star cast of professional jazz musicians. Carole Richardson recalls that she never dared visit Eel Pie Island because her father disapproved.

In 1961 Elvis Presley with *Wooden Heart, Are You Lonesome Tonight* and *Surrender* is going from strength to strength trailing local boys Cliff Richard and The Shadows in his wake. The Everly Brothers enjoy further success with *Walk Right Back, Ebony Eyes* and *Temptation*. Billy Fury, *Halfway To Paradise*, is becoming more established along with Petula Clark. The Temperance Seven revitalise the 1920s Jazz scene with two big hits *You're Driving Me Crazy* & *Pasadena* and Kenny Ball scores a big hit with *Midnight In Moscow* that reaches 2nd position in the UK Charts.

Traditional jazz continued to have a huge following during 1961. Eel Pie Island, along with its normal cast of jazz stars, welcomed Alan Elsdon's Jazz Band and Temperance Seven (former Chelsea Art School students) on four Saturday nights. They were in the midst of enjoying their chart success of the above two hits which had been produced by George Martin. (He later helped out the Beatles!) In October, Adam Faith performed at the Kingston Granada Cinema.

1962 is a year of consolidation of the established rock 'n' roll stars with a new generation of bands waiting in the wings. Yet it is Acker Bilk, a traditional Jazz musician, very well known in Kingston and Eel Pie Island, who has a massive hit with his haunting *Stranger On The Shore*. This single occupies the UK charts for 55 continuous weeks and sells more than one million copies. Cliff Richard and The Shadows perform at the ABC Cinema in Kingston in March.

The Cellar Club overlooking the river reached down the lane on the right side of the Odeon Cinema in Kingston.

A swelling wave of rhythm and blues encouraged Hugh O' Donnell, a club owner with a reputation as a handy boxer, to open the Jazz Cellar in Kingston in July 1962. He engaged an up-and-coming R&B band, The Nashville Teens, to perform on three Saturday nights at the Club. Shortly after, the club moved to a first-floor room of a rickety old boat house overlooking the Thames: behind the Odeon Cinema in Kingston (opposite the Police Station) where it oddly became known as the Cellar Club.

Mike Berry & The Outlaws, heavily influenced by Buddy Holly, performed at the Club in September. By tapping directly into R&B and Rock and Roll, O'Donnell had stolen a march on Arthur Chisnall. Chisnall, however, was not slow to respond and on Wednesday 17th October, three bands performed on Eel Pie Island - Mike Berry & The Outlaws, Cliff Bennett & The Rebel Rousers and Screaming Lord Sutch & The Savages (with Ritchie

Blackmore on lead guitar). Music at Eel Pie Island would never be the same again and the bridge would be busy three nights a week.

The R'n'B wave flooded the Thames towns and Kingston was soon overwhelmed with musical talent. On Friday 19th October, Richard Penniman, otherwise known as Little Richard, supported by Jet Harris and the Jet Blacks and Sam Cooke made a triple bill at the Kingston Granada Cinema. Richard was supported by 16-year-old keyboard wizard, Billy Preston. While singing *Good Golly Miss Molly*, standing on top of the piano, Little Richard fell down onto the stage clutching his chest. He lay on the stage so long that the audience began to fear that he was having a heart attack. Then he quietly resumed singing his song and the audience realised that he had been playing with them.

On 1st November, Screaming Lord Sutch and The Savages performed at the Cellar Club: Billy Fury and Marty Wilde led the Mammoth Tour at the ABC in Kingston at the end of the month. The Everly Brothers were down to play at the Kingston ABC, but Don Everly was incapacitated. By all accounts, Phil Everly enthusiastically carried the show, alone.

Yvonne Stevens recalls, *I was at St Andrew's School in Ham Street, with Bobby Hemmings. He was another budding musician and took the stage name, Bobby Angelo. He had a backing group called the Tuxedos and released his biggest hit, Baby Sitting, in 1962. The band appeared on Juke Box Jury and the single reached number 1 in many European countries. The band played regularly in the Swan pub in Kingston as well as The Cellar Club where the manager, Hugh, engaged them as a warmup band to Gene Vincent.*

In 1963 an earthquake, with its epicentre in Liverpool, splits the established music scene wide open with aftershocks that will resonate for decades. The Beatles have four hits, *She Loves You, From Me To You, Please Please Me* and *I Want To Hold Your Hand.* Strangely they are upstaged by fellow Merseyside band, Gerry & The Pacemakers whose first three single releases all reach no 1 in 1963. Johnny Kidd and The Pirates enter the charts.

This was also going to prove a sensational year for music in the Thameside towns of Kingston, Twickenham and Richmond.

Not to be outdone by the club on Eel Pie Island and the Cellar Club in Kingston, Giorgio Gomelsky, a music promoter with a blues club in Piccadilly, opened a club in the back room of the Station Hotel in Richmond. The club later became known as the Crawdaddy Club after the Rolling Stones performed Bo Diddley's 1960 song *Doing The Craw-Daddy* in April 1963.

The backroom of the original Crawdaddy Club

Gomelsky's first house band was the Dave Hunt Rhythm & Blues Band with drummer Charlie Watts, and guitarist Ray Davies, who later formed the Kinks. According to local legend, one of the harshest winters on record prevented the Dave Hunt Band from getting to Richmond and this gave an up-and-coming band called the Rolling Stones (named after a track on a Muddy Waters album) the opportunity to play their first gig at the Crawdaddy on 24th February 1963. Having done a reasonable job, they became the Sunday house band on a five-month residency and shortly after they were engaged for another night at the club.

Meanwhile, on Sunday 17th February 1963 the Beatles visited Teddington TV Studios, beside Teddington Lock, to be filmed for an appearance on ABC's 'Thank Your Lucky Stars'. The Beatles returned to Teddington TV Studios on Sunday 14th April 1963 for another performance on 'Thank Your Lucky Stars'. Gomlesky met the Beatles in the TV Studios and invited them to the Crawdaddy Club at the Station Hotel that evening to watch and meet the Rolling Stones.

The Rolling Stones performing at Eel Pie Island

Arthur Chisnall was obviously monitoring the local music scene very closely and he had been made aware of this new band in town. On 24th April the Rolling Stones began a 24-week Wednesday night residency at Eel Pie Island.

Within a couple of months, the Rolling Stones became so popular that the small hall at the back of the Station Hotel was unable to accommodate their growing fan base. The Crawdaddy Club was forced to move to a larger venue, the Richmond Athletic Ground near the River Thames.

Dave Gearing who was raised at 57 Ham Close and now lives in Ontario remembers queuing up to see the Rolling Stones outside the Station Hotel: *It was jam-packed inside and they locked the back doors to stop people sneaking in. The venue in Richmond Athletic Ground had beams suspended below the low ceilings. We used to climb up and hang upside down from the beams. When the song finished, we would drop down and reclaim our pint. At times it looked like a bat cave!*

Chris Archer: *In the 1960s, with a group of friends, I regularly attended the Crawdaddy Club based at the Station Hotel, opposite Richmond Station. Here I saw the Rolling Stones. When I was 21, in the summer of 1963, I went to the Richmond Jazz Festival, held in the Athletic Ground. This was one of the Rolling Stones first big public performances and I was there!*

Terry Isted of Lovell Road in Ham: *I used to go to the Jazz Cellar (The Cellar Club) in 1962. The girls liked to dance and the best way to meet a girl was to dance with her. Hugh, the owner was a short stocky guy, but his reputation preceded him. Apparently, he had been a sparring partner of a famous boxer and was quite useful.*

I also went to the Station Hotel several times to see the Rolling Stones and the Yardbirds. Many years later I heard a Chuck Berry LP and then realised that most of the music the Stones had been playing at the Crawdaddy were covers.

From this moment on, Arthur Chisnall introduced new British R'n'B groups on Wednesdays and Sundays on the Island while retaining the Saturday night Trad Jazz tradition.

In the week commencing 8th September the Rolling Stones were seen locally at three venues;

Monday 9th	Their last performance at The Crawdaddy, Richmond on Thames
Wednesday 11th	Eel Pie Island, in The Thames
Thursday 12th	The Cellar Club, Kingston on Thames

Looking back on their 24th and last performance at Eel Pie Island on 25th September, Arthur Chisnall was reputed to have commented, *never mind the ballroom, the whole bloody Island was overflowing.*

At the end of this last performance, Mick Jagger told the audience that they were going on tour (with The Everly Brothers and Bo Diddley). If that didn't work out, he'd see them soon. They never came back.

From June to December, Cyril Davies and his select band of all stars, including Long John Baldry, commanded the Sunday night stage at Eel Pie Island with authentic rhythm and blues. Cyril Davies was a panel beater by trade but a dedicated R'n'B musician by night. With Alexis Korner in Blues Incorporated, Cyril Davies had introduced electric guitars and amplifiers to give their music a little more verve. Davies inspired a generation of up and coming R'n'B musicians.

Cyril Davies on harmonica with his all-stars. Long John Baldry stands out!

The *Kingston RPM* project interview with Top Topham, discloses that it was during the interval of the All Stars that the Yardbirds with lead guitarist Top Topham first took the stage at Eel Pie Island on 23rd June and performed material by Jimmy Reed. According to Topham, it was at this gig that they settled on the name Yardbirds after Charlie Yardbird Parker, a black American jazz saxophonist. They were warmly received by Cyril Davies and went on to accompany the All Stars on Sunday nights. At this time Eric Clapton was performing on Tuesday nights with The Roosters at The Cellar Club.

When the Rolling Stones went on tour the Yardbirds were invited to take a regular slot at the Crawdaddy Club at Richmond Athletic Club. This proved a pivotal moment for Top Topham because his father insisted that he continue his studies at Epsom Art School. Topham was replaced in the band by his friend from Hollyfield, Eric Clapton. It was the residency at the Crawdaddy Club that established the Yardbirds with Chicago blues music drawn from Howlin' Wolf, Muddy Waters, Bo Diddley, Sonny Boy Williamson II and Elmore James. A live album was recorded by Sonny Boy Williamson backed by the Yardbirds at the Crawdaddy on December 8th.

John Mayall - wiki

Recordings of Blues and R'n'B music originating in the black American South, and the clubs of industrial Chicago were now highly prized by white British suburban teenagers. Transformed with the energy of electric guitars and the vitality of rock & roll, the music was essentially repackaged by local bands for British youth. Ultimately, in its transformed state, it would be sent back to the United States and many of its new American followers would have no idea where it originally came from.

October saw the Downliners Sect performing for the first time at Eel Pie Island along with Georgie Fame and the Blue Flames and Jimmy Powell and the Dimensions. John Mayall's Bluesbreakers, another massively inspirational band, would appear at the Island in November. The band served as an incubator for more than 100 different combinations of musicians. Many of the best-known rock bands to come out of Britain in the 1960s and 1970s had members that gained experience at some stage in their career, through the Bluesbreakers.

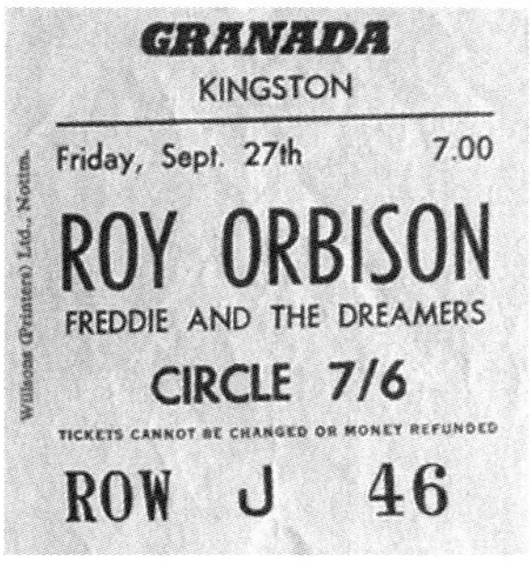

Meanwhile big promoters such as Brian Epstein and Don Arden were packaging big band acts and taking them on tour with venues that included the ABC and Granada Cinemas in Kingston. Roy Orbison performed at the Granada in September. Yvonne Stevens recalls, *he went on stage, just him and his guitar with the backing band concealed behind the curtains or in the pit. His amazing voice filled the whole of the theatre and captivated the audience.*

Gene Vincent replaced Little Richard, who had a twisted ankle, at the ABC in November. Cilla Black appeared twice in December at the Granada. First with Billy J Kramer & The Dakotas and Johnny Kidd and The Pirates and the second with Gerry and The Pacemakers.

1964 sees Roy Orbison come out from the shadow of Elvis Presley and receive well-deserved acclaim in the UK with massive hits *Oh Pretty Woman* and *It's Over*. The Beatles are on a roll with five chart hits and the Merseyside dominance is strengthened with the arrival of Cilla Black *Anyone Who Had A Heart* & *You're My World*. She is joined by female artists, Sandie Shaw *Always Something There To Remind Me*, Petula Clark *Downtown* and Dusty Springfield *I Just Don't Know What To Do With Myself* & *I Only Want To Be With You* and Lulu *Shout*. Lulu will perform with the Luvvers at the Coronation Hall in Kingston later in the year.

Cliff Richard and the Shadows have had a quiet year but London boasts the Rolling Stones *It's All Over Now, Not Fade Away* & *Little Red Rooster* and the Kinks *You Really Got Me* & *All Day And All Of The Night*.

The Supremes and Motown break though with *Baby Love* & *Where Did Our Love Go*. It won't be long before Kingston fans will be able to see them close up. Gene Pitney has two big hits including *Twenty-Four Hours From Tulsa*. Along with The Kinks and Gerry & The Pacemakers he will entertain a large audience at the ABC in Kingston in November.

The Kinks were invited to perform at the ABC in Kingston on 27th November. The Animals released *House Of The Rising Sun*. Their audience at the Cellar Club were blown away on first hearing this song.

Eric Burdon & The Animals - wiki

Sherry E remembers, *the Animals played quite a lot there, and sometimes played to only a few. Then they had the hit record (House Of The Rising Sun), and the queue to get in was all the way up the alley snaking round the corner as far back as the Ram. They must have been way over capacity in there that evening. Then they never played there again, sadly.*

Cyril Davies, who had apparently been suffering with pleurisy for some time, died at the age of 31 in early January 1964. He was a sorry loss to British R'n'B and never gained the recognition that he fully deserved. Baldry took over the All Stars and after their first gig renamed them The Hoochie Coochie Men.

After one late night gig, while waiting for a train at Twickenham railway station, Baldry listened to a chap on the platform playing the riff from Howlin' Wolf's Smokestack Lightnin' on a harmonica. Baldry introduced himself and invited the chap, named Rod Stewart, to join the Hoochie Coochie Men. At Eel Pie Island, Baldry provided Stewart with an ideal stage and helped shape him into both a singer and a performer.

The Eel Pie Experience - Tumbling into Wonderland (recollections)

We crossed the bridge and reached a tin hut by an open gate at the other end. Here we handed over 4d to the guardian of the bridge, masquerading as an elderly lady, to cover the two-way trip. We then walked along a winding track through the trees. The siren call of the saxophone or the electric guitar and the raw anticipation of wonderful music and the camaraderie of kindred spirits quickened our pace.

At the club entrance we paid 3s 6d and received, on the inside of our wrist, a stamp disclosing a mysterious geographical location. Each week, the stamp would have a different colour and a different location to render the previous week's stamp redundant. There was no benefit in not washing for a week!

The Eelpiland Club had a large ballroom with decorated arches down the side supporting dimly lit lamps. The area behind the stage was decorated with a cartoon featuring a jazz band in full session. The sprung floor was incredible. We went and bought our pints of Newcastle Brown Ale (the house ale) and ensured that we had drunk the top third before negotiating the dance floor. With people dancing and stomping on the floor it would rise and fall by up to two feet, just like a trampoline. If we were on it, trying to watch the band and drinking our beer we would dance whether we liked it or not. Many of the girls started off dancing around their handbags. There were some exceptional jivers on the floor.

Within the adult community of Twickenham, Richmond and Kingston the Island had a terrible reputation as a place that attracted undesirables and hooligans and where the young were led into moral danger. It was a veritable den of iniquity and parents forbade their teenagers to go there. Which simply meant that for many of us, it suddenly became one of the most desirable places to go.

Despite the tired décor and faded glory there was an overwhelming sense of warmth and belonging. It was like being in a wonderful story, following the winding road to Oz or tumbling down into Wonderland.

Arthur Chisnall had created a magical sanctuary on a remote island in the Thames for youngsters who needed space to breathe, be themselves and mix with kindred spirits. According to Don Craine of the Downliners Sect in the movie 'Clinging To A Mudflat', *Arthur with his glasses and pipe, resembling a nutty tutor, provided the youngsters with a reasonably safe environment without parental or adult supervision to do, within reason, what they wanted. Arthur kept a careful eye on them but in the main, he allowed them to get on with it. "Rarely was there any trouble at the club".*

Looking back, nearly 60 years later, those who were brave enough to defy their parents and go to the Island have very fond memories of experiencing something very special. Many of those who reluctantly complied with their parents' wishes look back, with more than a little regret, at what they missed.

Don Craine further recalls, *we played three times at the end of 1963 and once a month through 1964. It was fantastic, a really wonderful gig. You knew when you were playing here you were part of something special.*

In a documentary film called Rock & Roll Island, Rod Stewart commented on his experiences at Eel Pie Island: *When you dressed up in your finery and carefully arranged your hair and set off for Eel Pie Island, you had a palm tingling sense of anticipation. It was densely populated with music nuts, art students and pretty girls in short dresses. George Melly once said, 'You could see sex rising from Eel Pie Island like steam from a kettle.' For me, it was the place I began to understand the power of rhythm and blues.*

Rod Stewart with Long John Baldry

Yvonne Stevens: *One evening as we were crossing the bridge to the Island, we saw Elizabeth Taylor and Richard Burton on a houseboat moored to the Island and having a furious row. There was also a little dog rushing up and down, excited by the emotion.*

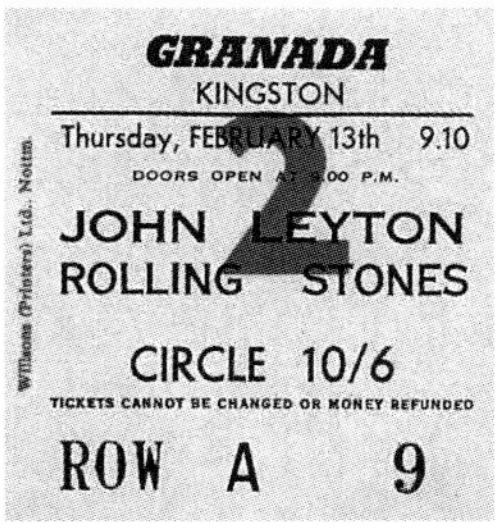

On 13th February the Rolling Stones performed as part of a package of bands at the Granada Cinema in Kingston.

On Sunday 23rd February, The Beatles arrived by boat at Teddington Lock for a recording session at Teddington TV Studios for ABC-TV's `Big Night Out'. The bridge was packed with screaming teenage girls. They would become regular visitors to the studios.

Above left: February 1964; The Beatles arrive at Teddington Lock. Photo courtesy of Linda Ikin, one of the many fans lining the riverbank

Above right: 11th July 1964 Featured in Teddington Hub News

Left: June 1964 -The Beatles at Teddington Studios to view a rough cut of Help Alamy stock photo

By February 1964, Hugh O' Donnell had arranged for The Yardbirds to perform on Monday nights at The Cellar Club in Kingston and The Animals to perform on Wednesday nights. He was prepared to spend good money to get top musicians to perform at the club alongside lesser known local bands.

The former boat house, overlooking the Thames, reverberated to the music and energy of Gene Vincent, Jerry Lee Lewis, The Nashville teens, Steve Marriott, The Stormsville Shakers, Mickey Finn & The Blues Men and The Tridents.

A Wednesday evening in May 1964 found Jimmy Page, Jeff Beck, Bill Wyman and Ian Stewart jamming on the Island. Shortly after, the legendary John Lee Hooker, over from America, headed an evening with John Mayall's Bluesbreakers and the Plebs at the Cellar Club. These were all intimate performances where the audience got close to the band to feel the blues. Top Topham remembered that after John Lee Hooker's performance, he came out of the club carrying his guitar and looking for a bus to take him into London. Topham pointed "The Great Man" in the direction of the railway station.

Keith Read, a student of Rivermead School on the Richmond Road in Kingston, was a guitarist in a local band called The Pieces Of Four that gained a slot at the Cellar Club. A little later, he joined the Impalas who played at both the Swan Pub and The Cellar Club before moving onto a bigger stage and supporting Gene Vincent at both the Coronation Hall in Kingston and The London Palladium.

The Pieces of Four performing at The Cellar Club in 1964. Keith Read (lead guitar), Ian Duffell (lead guitar), Robin Clements (bass) and Ian Clements (drums) garage hangover website

In August, the Artwoods led by Arthur Wood (older brother of Ronnie Wood) began the first of many performances at Eel Pie Island and Davie Jones stars with the Manish Boys. With the emergence of the Monkees in 1966 Davie Jones would quickly change his name to David Bowie.

In November the Cellar Club hosted the legendary Jimmy Reed, one of the most influential bluesmen of all time. He was supported by the Plebs and John Lee's Groundhogs while Eel Pie had a visit from Howlin' Wolf, whose influence was noted by the fact that this same year The Rolling Stones

Howlin' Wolf wiki

would reach number one in the UK charts with their cover of his *Little Red Rooster*.

On 14th November the Beatles returned to Teddington TV Studios for filming ABC-TV's 'Thank Your Lucky Stars'. The first two Beatles feature films *A Hard Day's Night* (1964) and *Help!* (1965) were both made at Teddington Studios.

Yvonne Stevens worked as a daytime nanny to Hugh O'Donnell's son. She recalls, *Shortly after opening The Cellar Club in Kingston, Hugh asked me to come along and help out. I was about 22 years old at the time. I helped out on various evenings, each week, for the next four years until the club closed. I was always accompanied by a friend, either Karen (whose real name was Betty) who lived in Hollybush Road on the Tudor Estate or another Karen who lived in Petersham Road. We all had club names, mine was Stevie.*

Yvonne Stevens Courtesy of Gerald Stevens

My father was very strict and forbade me from going out dressed indecently. The first time I wore a miniskirt my father stopped me "How dare you come down showing your knees!" I had to go and change. I would therefore leave the house in a proper long dress. But if I turned up at the club wearing my long dress, Hugh would say "What's that you are wearing?" So, I used to have a change of clothes round Karen's house in Hollybush Road and I would change there.

My father also insisted that I was always accompanied by a friend and I had to be back by 10:30pm. Hugh would normally arrange a car to take us home so that I didn't get into trouble. My father was short but very stocky and I was terrified of him. So, if I was late for any reason, I had to think of an imaginative excuse. One night I told him that a wheel had come off the bus.

The club used to open about 7:30pm. There was one large room with a stage. A DJ sat on the stage with his turntable and I often sat next to him passing him records to play. At the end of the room, through an archway, was a smaller room which contained a small bar and a few tables and chairs. Hugh would be behind it, though I am not sure if he ever had a licence to sell alcohol. A popular drink at the time was Babycham, though I invariably drank lemonade and orange.

The hall was always very full and, when not helping out, I loved to take to the dance floor and twist, jive and do the locomotion until I was quite worn out. Many was the time that I would say to my friend Betty, "I've overdone it tonight".

Hugh invited a lot of local bands to play at the club but occasionally he would splash out to get some big acts to perform such as the Animals and the Yardbirds. As soon as the Moody Blues hit number one with 'Go Now', Hugh got them in straight away. Hugh also managed to bring some of the great American artists like Gene Vincent and Jerry Lee Lewis to the Cellar Club, which looking back, was quite amazing.

I don't think that he actually advertised it very much. Everybody knew the Cellar Club. And everybody knew that if you went to the Cellar Club there would be good entertainment.

Gene Vincent with his dark curly hair always wore leather trousers. He asked me out, starting with the chat up line, "What's a nice girl like you working in a place like this?"

I'll never forget the energy of Jerry Lee Lewis, jumping up and down then leaping on the piano. My friend Karen (Betty) was astonished, "Crikey, he's gone mental".

Another singer with tremendous energy and enthusiasm was Lulu who performed Shout at the club and we all danced like crazy. She was great fun, very friendly and very young!

I clearly recall Dusty Springfield and The Springfields coming to the club for one gig. She had very thick orange make up, very thick mascara and a beehive hairstyle. She had an incredible voice but her appearance was well over the top!

The Rolling Stones performed once in September 1963 and a lot of the girls were clamouring to go home with them. I had already seen them earlier in the year at Eel Pie Island. They weren't really my scene.

Hugh was an ex-boxer and had a couple of low-profile bouncers at the club. We rarely had trouble in the club. This was a period when amphetamines were freely available, known as Purple Hearts and Black Bombers. Apparently, they helped you to keep going for the whole weekend, though I never tried them. I was too terrified of my father's reaction if I were caught. I'll never forget being in a pub in Richmond and this chap was on his knees, on the floor, barking. He banged into me and then a table and he apologised to the table.

At the time, I had long hair down to my waist. I finally got fed up with it and went to the hairdressers on Ham Parade and got a D.A (short for duck's arse because of its distinctive taper at the back). I'll never forget going into Mrs Dunckley's shop on the corner of Ham Street and the Bench Passage and Mrs Dunckley saying, " Oh my God! Has your father seen you? If I were you, I would hide".

Jennifer Stark in 1967

Jennifer Stark looks back at her evenings at the Cellar Club, *The Cellar Club was situated down an alley by the side of the Odeon, which led down to the River Thames. The club was actually elevated, so you reached it by stone steps which were on the outside of the Club. We think it was an old boat house because it was raised on stilts, may be the lower part was where the boats went out.*

I remember there were two guys on the door. The entry fee couldn't be very much because I was still at school. 2/6d rings a bell and we got a stamp on the back of our hands.

The bands were on a Saturday, but I also liked to go on a Sunday night as they played records to dance to. The dancing was very good and two or three of our best dancers were auditioned and actually appeared in Ready Steady Go. We all loved to dance to Woolly Bully sung by Sam the Sham and the Pharaohs. I loved El Pussycat by Mongo Santamaria and the night always ended with James Brown's Night Train. We all loved the Black American music, which then got emulated by the English bands. We also loved Motown, that's why so many of us love Northern Soul as it's now called. It brings back so many memories and the dancing of course.

I remember seeing an original line up of the Small Faces playing there. I also saw an American singer, Sugar Pie Desanto. I remember Long John Baldry and John Mayall's Bluesbreakers with Eric Clapton, I actually had a chat with Eric Clapton as he was sitting on those stone steps outside the club.

We were all very young, I was 15 in 1965. The club was not licensed to sell liquor. There were pills being popped, (Purple Hearts, Black Bombers), though I managed to steer clear of ever taking any there. The all-nighter people would dance all night because they were on pills.

We don't remember there ever being any real trouble there, though unfortunately I was at the Cellar the night of one of the police raids. It caused so much trouble at home, we didn't have a phone and I had to give the number of our prim and proper next-door neighbours, who then had to go and ask my Mum and Dad to arrange to collect me from Kingston Police Station. They didn't have a car of course.

There wasn't much money around. I think I used to make my clothes or adapt them from my Mum's, she had taught me to sew. I know I had a navy-blue reefer jacket but the boys used to have nice long leather coats. It was Pop Art at the time, so bullseye design and Mary Quant fashions. Black and White short mini dresses for girls. My hair was home done bleached blonde in a short bob style. I remember wearing a perfume called 'Intimate'.

The boys took a lot of trouble with their clothes, if they could afford it of course. The best boys coat at the time was a full length claret coloured leather coat with a mustard-coloured collar. The boys wore loafers and brogues. Levi's were a must along with Sta-Prest trousers and button-down collar Ben Sherman shirts. Parkas for the scooter boys with blue beat hats (small brimmed). There was a shop in Richmond called the Ivy, where they bought some of the boys' clothes.

I can remember hitching a lift home many times and once being picked up by a couple in a large van and they had a 'live bear' in the back, probably from a circus or something. Imagine if my Mum had known all this.

I've got a couple of good friends from that era and we often reminisce. It was just magic, looking back through our rose-tinted glasses. I think that was the lasting memory - the atmosphere – it was a lovely warm feeling".

Jacqui Fogarty: *I do recall the Cellar Club as I was arrested when it was raided by police. Being only 15, I didn't have a chance really! But I was thoroughly enjoying everything prior to the raid!*

Michael Blandford: *I was a Cellar regular from late 1963 till summer 1965. I loved the place and the anticipation of walking up the steps before waiting to go in. I worked in the same factory as the bouncer during the day and he always let me in without paying. All of our scooters would be parked outside. On some nights as many as 100. If it was wet, you could always shelter under the side canopy of the Odeon. I mostly mixed with lads from the Kingsnympton Estate on Kingston Hill. We had a routine, Monday - Hammersmith Pally, Tuesday, Wednesday, Thursday and Friday – the Cellar Club. Saturday night - Richmond Community Centre or Kingston Coronation Hall. Sunday – the Crawdaddy Club. We would meet up outside the Druids Head and then head off.*

My first scooter was a Vespa GS 150 series 2 that was stolen (how I wished I had it now). I then had a Lambretta LI 150, wide line series 2 in black and chrome. I sold that mid-1965 and then got a Vespa GS 160 series 1. I still own it and love riding it.

Clothes were suits or smart jackets and trousers or sometimes Levi jeans (from Jack Brendon in Richmond Road, the only place in London you could buy them). Over the top, I wore a U S Army parka. We were always smart. I never wore check shirt and desert boots.

James E *As a mod, I remember my first Saturday all-nighter was at the Cellar. I don't know what band was playing though I do recall a lot of records being played through the night and a lot of pills being popped. I can't remember much except it was a regular venue after that night and I spent many a Sunday morning watching the sun rise over the river after dancing or talking the night away. I remember this venue with a genuine fondness and would love to experience it all over again. It is a great shame that this simple, intimate type of club no longer exists.*

The picture of The Roosters that appeared in a newspaper cutting. Pete is standing on the right and his brother Ron, is sitting with his guitar on the left.

In the late 1970s and early 1980s there was a chap by the name of Pete Jefferies who lived in Broughton Avenue and ran the laundromat in Ham Street opposite Grey Court School. Pinned on his noticeboard in the shop was a yellowing newspaper cutting dated March 1964, from the Surrey Comet. A closer look disclosed a youthful band called The Roosters that Pete had been a member of with his brother Ron.

The band achieved some fame, recording tracks that were shown on a Sunday evening in October 1964 on BBC 2's Beat Room. They were also profiled by Jackie magazine which enjoyed a sizeable young female readership. The band played regularly at Richmond Community Centre and the Cellar Club. The big time beckoned … Pete later played in other bands where lead guitarists had moved on, including John Mayall's Bluesbreakers.

Pete was a regular customer of the Water Gypsies pub in Ashburnham Road opposite the church (where the nursery is now located). He died some time ago but is not forgotten.

Chris Archer's younger brother Don visited Eel Pie Island in the 1960s: *I hadn't gone there necessarily for the music. It was just a good place for the cycle club members to meet up on a Sunday evening after competing in one of the local cycle races.*

Neither the ballroom nor the hotel had seen a coat of paint in a while and there was a general air of dilapidation. Mind you if it had been in good order we wouldn't have been welcome there.

Having merged with fellow members of the cycling group and exchanged a greeting, we weren't able to talk. The music was too noisy for that. We simply gave way to that pleasant euphoric state following a day's strenuous physical exercise followed by a few pints. Mind you, the beer was pretty good, Newcastle Brown, if I recall, recently introduced to the area. We therefore enjoyed the camaraderie of being together, enjoying a good pint of beer and simply letting our minds go with the flow.

It was really dark. Only the bar on the far side of the dance floor was discernible. When it was my round, I made my way cautiously across the heaving dance floor guided by the light of the bar. I could feel the bounce of the sprung floor arising from the gyrations of the massed dancers. Coming back would be a lot trickier with glasses full of beer.

One of the regulars on stage was a chap by the name of Long John Baldry. He was a fair bit taller than the other musicians on the stage. On this same evening he invited one of the members of the audience by the name of Rod Stewart up on the stage to belt out a few numbers.

Just like the narrow bridge over the river to Eel Pie Island, the stone steps up to the Cellar Club were not popular with the band members having to carry their kit into the club. Few of them had burley roadies to help out.

In 1962, at the age of twelve, Paul Keyes moved to 6 Latchmere Road with his parents. His new home was one of nine prefabs built on Latchmere Recreation Ground directly opposite the entrance to Latchmere School. Paul was one of the first students at Rivermead Boys School on the Richmond Road which took boys from the Richmond Road School and St Luke's School in Elm Road. When they initially merged there was a lot of fighting between the boys of the different schools, but it soon calmed down.

Paul recalls, *I used to go to the Coronation Baths on Saturday nights to watch the Downliners Sect, an R'n'B and blues-based rock band and one of my favourite bands. My Mum used to work at the Granada in Kingston, and she managed to get tickets for me to see The Shadows and Billy Fury. She even managed to get The Rolling Stones' autographs.*

At this time a lot of bands were emerging from Richmond and Kingston. Danny Jones and myself formed a band called the Pepper Ghosts. We spent a lot of time writing music and rehearsing. On one New Year's Eve we played at the Odeon in Kingston in front of 200 people. There was such an explosion of new music at that time that we devoted a lot of time to song writing. We genuinely believed that we were going to be another Beatles. If it could happen to them, it could happen to us. We very nearly got a contract with EMI. It was a period of new horizons after the doom and gloom of the war. I still have three good friends from my time living in Kingston and (nearly 60 years later) I continue to write music waiting for that big break…

In 1965 The Beatles release *Help, Ticket to Ride, I Feel Fine* & *Day Tripper.* The Rolling Stones vent their frustration with *I Can't Get No Satisfaction, The Last Time* & *Get Off My Cloud.* The Yardbirds raise their profile with *Heart Full Of Soul* & *For Your Love.* The Kinks who will appear at the Granada with the Yardbirds in May grow *Tired Of Waiting For You.* Manfred Mann relents with *If You Gotta Go, Go Now* and the Who embrace the growing mod movement in Britain with *My Generation* & *I Can't Explain.* The Moody Blues announce themselves briefly with *Go Now* and Georgie Fame has his first of three No. 1 hits with *Yeh Yeh.*

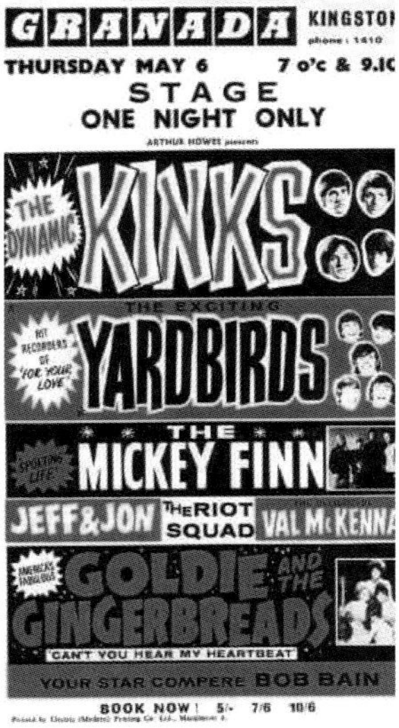

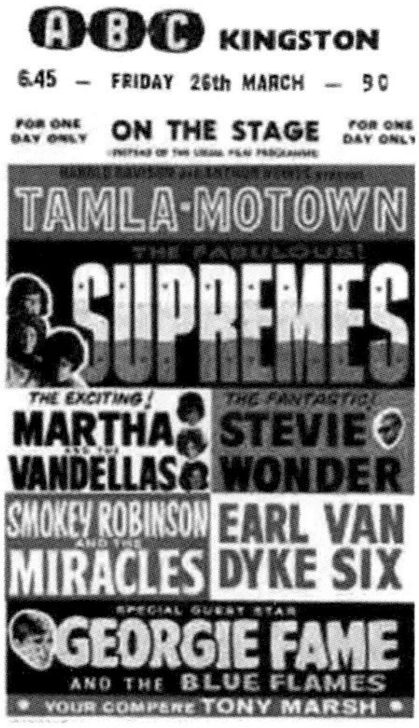

In March 1965, Tamla Motown came to Town. The Supremes, Stevie Wonder, Smokey Robinson & The Miracles, Martha Reeves & The Vandellas and a sole UK group, Georgie Fame and the Blue Flames all performed on the same night at the ABC in Kingston.

Through 1965, both the Cellar Club and Eel Pie Island hosted John Mayall's Bluesbreakers, The Alex Harvey Soul Band and Steampacket with Long John Baldry, Rod Stewart and Julie Driscoll. Regular fixtures at the Island were The Artwoods, and The Tridents with Jeff Beck and Rod Stewart was also performing with The Soul Agents. Two American legends Jesse Fuller, a one-man band musician and Champion Jack Dupree, a New Orleans Blues and boogie-woogie pianist, spent some time on the Island. The Small Faces and The Moody Blues performed at the Cellar Club but the Crawdaddy Club closed in July 1965.

The Beatles returned to Teddington Studios in late November to shoot clips for *I Feel Fine, Ticket To Ride, Help!, Day Tripper* and *We Can Work It Out.*

Regulars at Eel Pie Island were The Artwoods, John Mayall's Bluesbreakers, The Graham Bond Organisation, Champion Jack Dupree and The John Dummer Blues Band. The Cellar Club hosted The Small Faces, The Nashville Teens and Screaming Lord Sutch with Jimmy Page on guitar.

Since the summer of 1964 John Lennon had been living at St Georges Hill in Weybridge, a leafy rural town in Surrey. On Monday 30th May, autograph hunters, in a Mini, chased John in his Rolls Royce through Teddington. Both cars were stopped by police and the drivers fined for speeding. The autograph hunters got their autographs after the police finished with John.

1966 sees Frank and Nancy Sinatra bucking the trend with '*Strangers In The Night* & '*These Boots Are Made For Walkin*'. The Beatles are consolidating their legendary status with '*Yellow Submarine*', '*Eleanor Rigby*', '*Day Tripper*', '*We Can Work It Out*' & '*Paperback Writer*'. Competition arrives from the sunshine coast of America with The Beach Boys and '*Good Vibrations*', '*God Only Knows*' & '*Sloop John B*'. The Rolling Stones release '*Paint It Black*' which would become part of the dark folklore of the Vietnam War. The Kinks are a little more optimistic with '*Sunny Afternoon*', though The Walker Brothers ruin it all with "*The Sun Ain't Gonna Shine Anymore*". The Troggs can't control themselves. Perhaps it's a "*Wild Thing*"?

The Cream starring Eric Clapton, Jack Bruce and Ginger Baker did one of the last shows at the Cellar Club on a Friday in August and five days later appeared at Eel Pie Island. In September a youthful 16-year-old Peter Frampton was fronting *The Herd* on the Island. The Cellar Club had now closed its doors for the last time after one drug raid too many, leaving Eel Pie Island to continue promoting R'n'B along this stretch of the river. It is here in November that Alexis Korner and his new band *Free At Last* played one gig.

In 1967, Scott McKenzie gives advice on what to wear in your hair *If you go to San Francisco* and Procul Harum appear *A Whiter Shade Of Pale*. The Beatles maintain their musical crusade with *All You Need Is Love, Penny Lane, Strawberry Fields Forever* & *Hello Goodbye*. The Monkees have three hits and assure everyone that they are all believers. The Kinks enjoy the *Waterloo Sunset* and The Small Faces visit *Itchycoo Park*. Meanwhile The Rolling Stones want to *Spend the Night Together* while The Tremeloes assure everyone that *Silence Is Golden*. Stevie Wonder, Diana Ross & The Supremes keep the Tamla Motown flag flying and Jimi Hendrix has three edgy hits including *Purple Haze* & *Hey Joe*. Despite his undoubtable musical accomplishment and reputation Long John Baldry has a rare commercial hit but he isn't happy about it! *Let The Heartaches Begin*.

One by one, the intimate R'n'B Clubs along the river had closed. First the Crawdaddy then the Cellar Club in Kingston and finally Eel Pie Island, under the management of Arthur Chisnall, because he was unable to afford the repairs to the buildings demanded by the local authorities. This was a very sorry loss for many of the younger generation in the area.

The Artwoods

Nevertheless, the Island in its last eight months had a full programme with Saturday Jazz nights and a selection of R'n'B favourites on Wednesdays and Sundays. The Artwoods became the longest serving band with the most performances yet Island stalwarts such as John Mayall, Graham Bond and Alex Harvey were still performing. Alexis Korner with

Free at Last made two appearances and David Essex made his debut with *Mood Indigo*. Pink Floyd had three performances during which time they launched their debut single *Arnold Layne*. Although, the gig was sold out, one enthusiastic fan rowed a small boat round to the Surrey side of the Island. From his undisturbed seat on the river he could clearly hear both the music and the lead singer, Syd Barrett.

Elise M *My brother who used to go to the jazz venues told me about Eel Pie in the early days. My Dad forbade me to go, so I started going on Wednesday and Sunday from late 1964. My friends and I loved the Artwoods, but to see Pink Floyd and so many more groups was incredible. The amber, Newcastle Brown and cider were great. I was bereft when the Club closed. There will never be another place like it.*

In 1968, Louis Armstrong, some 13 years after spending a week performing at the Empire Theatre in Kingston, reminds everyone *What a Wonderful World* we live in. This remains at number 1 in the UK charts for a month. The Beatles introduce us to *Hey Jude, Lady Madonna, A Magical Mystery Tour* and forewarn us of their musical mortality with *Hello Goodbye*. The Small Faces enjoy a *Lazy Sunday Afternoon* while The Rolling Stones liven things up with *Jumpin Jack Flash* and Joe Cocker is about to make the big time *With A Little Help From His Friends*. The Herd, starring 18-year-old Peter Frampton, assure us that they *Don't Want Their Loving To Die* but within months Frampton has left to form Humble Pie with Steve Marriott. The Crazy World of Arthur Brown give us *Fire* and Manfred Mann warn us that we have not seen nothing like *The Mighty Quinn*.

On Wednesday 4th September, the Beatles returned to Teddington Film Studios to make a promotional film for *Hey Jude*. An introduction for the clip of `Hey Jude', was later presented on `Frost On Sunday'. They also used the studios to rehearse for their album *Let It Be*.

The Yardbirds under the lead of Jimmy Page evolved into the New Yardbirds and with a complete change of personnel renamed themselves Led Zeppelin. They would become one of the most innovative and influential rock groups in history.

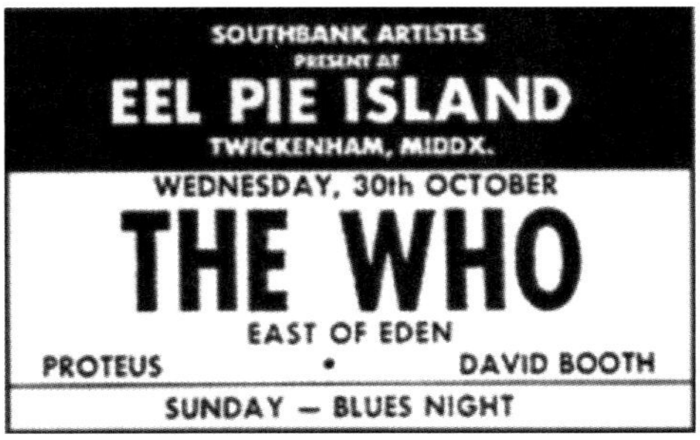

The owner of Eel Pie Island Hotel, Michael Snapper, allowed the hotel to be used for community and Arts projects. 1968 saw occasional gigs but jazz was now relegated to memory. The Downliners Sect appeared twice in the Autumn and a revamped Moody Blues performed in September. Joe Cocker performed in October. In the same month The Who finally appeared at the Island and Pete Townsend used the venue to try out some material for a Rock Opera named *Tommy*. The God of Hell Fire, Arthur Brown, entertained the audience with his *Crazy World* and John Mayall reminded everyone of what has been lost with a final performance in November.

The Beatles continue to develop their craft in 1969 with an eclectic mix of hit songs including *Get Back, The Ballad Of John And Yoko, Something* & *Come Together*. This same year, two exceptional performers, Frank Sinatra and Elvis Presley slow things down with reflective ballads *My Way* & *In The Ghetto*. The Rolling Stones maintain their edge with *Honky Tonk Women* and Fleetwood Mac, formed by former members of John Mayall's Bluesbreakers, enjoy three hits. David Bowie launches *Space Oddity* five days ahead of the Apollo 11 launch and is finally destined for stardom as Bob Dylan is taking it easy with *Lay Lady Lay*. Tamla Motown stars sweep into town. Marvin Gaye *Heard it Through the Grapevine* while Stevie Wonder, *For Once In His Life* has three hits including *My Cherie Amour* as Martha Reeves and The Vandellas *danced in the street* and Smokey Robinson wipes *the tracks of his tears*.

In contrast to their enthusiastic and playful visits to Teddington Film Studios some six years earlier, the Beatles returned at the beginning of 1969, divided and acrimonious. They begin rehearsing and filming a documentary on the making of the final Beatles album, *Let It Be*. When the film was released in May 1970, much of the internal turmoil has been edited out to focus on the creative genius of the band.

9th April 1969 Penultimate photo session. BB

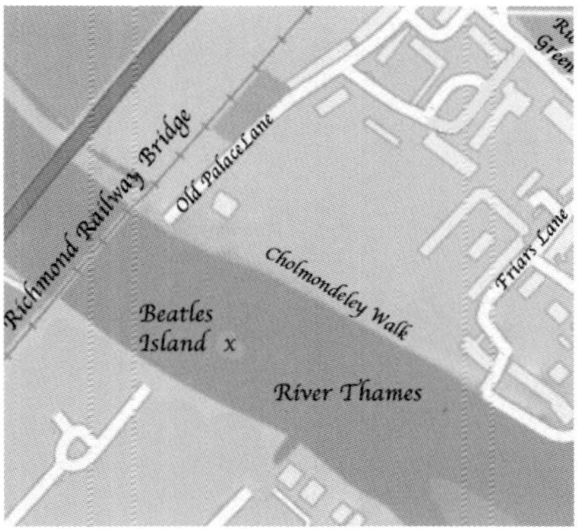

Map showing the location of the Island

Beatles Island between Twickenham and Richmond. BB

On Wednesday 9th April, the Beatles took part in their penultimate photo session besides the Thames at Twickenham. They boarded a rowing boat just upstream from Richmond Railway Bridge and rowed out to a small island in the Thames between Richmond & Twickenham. Here, they went through the motions of waving to the photographer on the riverbank before rowing back.

Eel Pie Island Hotel hosted a few progressive groups including Edgar Broughton, Van Der Graaf Generator, Stray and Hawkwind Zoo. In September the hotel was recast as Colonel Barefoot's Rock Garden with further performances by the above bands and Wishbone Ash.

Let It Be, the final single to be released by the Beatles, reaches No.2 in the UK Charts and No.1 in the US in 1970.

The magical decade of the 1960s was over. The incredible wave of R'n'B music had swept over and through the Thames-side towns of Kingston, Twickenham and Richmond. Eel Pie Island was the last survivor of the intimate R'n'B clubs but was now very much on borrowed time. The final roll call was impressive with Mott The Hoople, Genesis, Black Sabbath, Edgar Broughton, Free, Supertramp and Deep Purple. The last documented gig on the Island took place on 21st November but within a year, the Thames witnessed its own fire in the sky and *Smoke on the Water* as the Eel Pie Hotel with its legendary ballroom, burned to the ground.

Author's note; *One Friday, in the summer term of my final year at Latchmere Junior School in 1970, my father who was a sound engineer with BBC Radio took me to experience the Radio One Club which he was directly involved in broadcasting throughout the UK. I managed to watch the show backstage and met the DJ, a friend of my father, and the live bands who were performing. During the lunchtime show, the DJ called me out for a brief chat on air. It was a little difficult to refuse, being enthusiastically encouraged by the musicians. The following Monday, Miss Tilbury, one of my form teachers, asked me if I was feeling better after my day off. I confirmed that I was, with which she smiled and mentioned that it was strange because the younger teachers had all been listening to the Radio One show at lunchtime on Friday and someone who was on it, sounded a lot like me. What a coincidence!*

The Carnabys, a local Thames-side band with songwriter and lead singer Jack Mercer, all met at the Twickenham jam sessions that still run now, did their musical apprenticeship in school fetes including the Russell School in Petersham, Gfest at Grey Court School in Ham and local pubs such as the Swan in Twickenham. In 2013, they won the Hard Rock Rising competition, contested by 12,000 bands from 94 countries. This rewarded them with an appearance at the Hard Rock Calling Festival held at London's Olympic site, supporting Bruce Springsteen and Paul Weller. They then went on a world tour sponsored by Hard Rock Cafe. On their return to the UK they continued to tour, supporting Blondie, Patti Smith amongst others and enjoyed a regular slot at the Eel Pie Club (at the Cabbage Patch) in Twickenham.

Several of the band members are still playing today. Jack Mercer is currently performing as VC Pines at festivals such as Reading and Leeds on the BBC stages. The early days of performing in and around Twickenham and Richmond, honing his craft, were instrumental in creating his success today.

Having known them for many years and followed their progress through the local school fetes and Twickenham pubs, I took the opportunity to spend a few days with them in Hong Kong, where I had some knowledge and experience of the local night scene as a result of several years' service with the Royal Hong Kong Police!

After two energetic and very well received performances at the Hard Rock Cafe in Lan Kwai Fong, they took the overnight flight to Tokyo for the Japan leg of their tour en route to Sydney, Australia then the West Coast of the USA… Quite a journey!

Sources

Many thanks to Celia Holman of Eel Pie Island Museum for taking the time to patiently work her way through the draft manuscript and make important corrections.
www.eelpiemuseum.co.uk/roll-call
www.uk-charts.top-source.info/top-100
www.garagehangover.com
kingstonrpm.org (featuring an interview with Top Topham)
www.visitrichmond.co.uk/events/music_heritage
www.surreylife.co.uk/out-about/rock-n-roll-history-at-eel-pie-island-twickenham
www.sandybrownjazz.co.uk/Features/JazzOnEelPieIsland.html
Rock Island Line - The Singles Anthology by Lonnie Donegan
Kingston Upon Thames Past and Present Facebook Group
Ham & Petersham History and Memories Facebook Group
Video extracts: Look at Life Eel Pie Island 1967 by the Rank Organisation &
Clinging to a Mudflat – Eel Pie Island

Picture Credits

Every effort has been made to identify the owners of the images used in this chapter. Many images are now seen on numerous sites and their ownership can't be traced.
Wiki - Several of the pictures of the bands and artists are public domain images obtained through Wikipedia
BB - www.beatlesbible.com
The posters and tickets have been found on the sites of various Facebook groups

History in the Making

These very personal stories have highlighted the immense change that has affected both the landscape and the people, living on the Latchmere Terrace, through the early to mid-20th century.

Change continues apace, yet within this growing and diverse community of residents, schoolchildren, shopkeepers and tradespeople, there is a treasure trove of engaging and heartfelt stories. These stories, in turn, will become part of the fabric of local history and will continue to inspire and entertain future generations.

We simply now have to make sure that they are recorded…

Ham Parade

Ham Parade

Some of the local shopkeepers, restaurant staff, inn keepers and library staff who work hard, week in, week out, to serve the community around them

Park Road

Tudor Parade

Ashburnham Road

Back Lane

Ham Street

Petersham Road

Surprise at the Brook's End

During the COVID-19 outbreak, on a very early morning dog walk by the river, I encountered a local fisherman, Peter Paul. He was fishing in the Thames from a concrete platform right above the outlet of the Sudbrook where it finally reached the river.

From this very spot, he was delighted to catch a very rare sea trout weighing in at a little below 4lbs.

Having weighed and measured the fish, Peter then returned it to the river to continue its journey…

About the Author

Gordon was raised on the Tudor Estate, within the Parish of Ham. He attended Latchmere School and Rivermead Secondary Boys School: at the same time, he gained an important part of his education while roaming the vast landscape of Richmond Park and Ham Common and playing on the banks, and on occasions, in the River Thames.

Following his graduation from Loughborough University with a degree in economics and mathematics and the benefit of two fabulous years with the Officer Training Corps of the British Army, he became an Inspector in the Royal Hong Kong Police. Several very exciting and action-packed years later, faced with the imminent handover of Hong Kong, Gordon returned to the UK. Here he embarked on a career in international business with multinational companies that included Racal Electronics, 3M and Marley Floors. In 2005 he began his own trading business, based in Shanghai, with his home and family in Ham.

His extensive travelling in China, Central Asia, the Far East and the Middle East has presented him with the extremes of human habitation: densely populated urban cities and nomadic landscapes that have changed little in a thousand years. This has given Gordon a greater appreciation of the settled and secure environment of Ham and Kingston and the wonderful natural landscape embraced by the River Thames only a short walking distance from his home. It has also prompted him to look a little closer and ask a few questions!

Armed with a greater understanding of the special nature of this landscape, Gordon was motivated to write his first book, *Remarkable Ham – The Untold Story*. It was during a subsequent presentation in Tudor Drive Library that his audience, mostly retired, began relating their own stories. Another project beckoned: to fill a gap in local history shaped by the stories of the people who had personally experienced them.

The COVID-19 outbreak effectively grounded Gordon, preventing any means of travelling to China. Instead, he used his time to interview, by telephone, many remarkable people and shape their fascinating stories with a few supportive pictures and maps into this book, *People of the Latchmere*.

Hopefully in reading these very personal stories, you will find some interest, some inspiration and more than a little entertainment.

A Very Big Thanks to:

Sandra Baker who published, on Kindle, the diary of her great aunt, Connie Webb. Sandra allowed me to include extracts from this diary and these have helped give us an illuminating and very personal account of Harry Hawker and the Sopwith team at the riverside during the First World War.

Lindsay Birch for her patience, creativity and professionalism in the creation of a book that complements the wonderful stories of People of the Latchmere.

Betty Bore for her support and foresight at putting me in contact with the Dicks family.

Eel Pie Island Museum for all the great information held at the museum and on the website. Also, thanks to Celia Holman for personally taking the time to patiently work her way through the draft manuscript and make important corrections.

Eileen & Richard Elsden, my parents, for establishing a comfortable and secure home in Tudor Drive in 1960 that gave myself and my two younger sisters easy access to a wonderful natural playground and great foundations for adult life.

Nicola Elsden for her patience and support in keeping the family boat afloat and on course during my numerous business trips overseas and my long hours focused on this project.

Tim Everson for his help in reviewing and correcting the chapters on the East Surrey Regiment and his great help in clarifying the origin of many Kingston pictures.

Friends of Ham Lands, a local community group that works hard to preserve this wonderful and very sizeable natural landscape for the benefit of local residents.

Friends of Latchmere Rec. (FoLaR) for their hard work and commitment to the ongoing care and maintenance of Latchmere Recreation Ground.

The Ham & Petersham Association for their vision and hard work in creating and maintaining an attractive natural environment around the Latchmere Brook, just outside the Ham Gate of Richmond Park.

David Hassard, a key player in the Hawker Association and the Kingston Aviation Project, for his great help and support in the writing of the chapter about the pioneers of aviation.

Andrew Smith and John Hutchings of the Industrial Railway Society for providing me with extremely rare photographs of the Bagnall locomotives that operated on the Ham Railway Line.

Cam Dunn, Angus Dunn and Brent McDonald of Intafloors, Australia for their commercial support that helped to finance the production of this book. Cam and Angus come from the same neck of the woods as one of the stars of this book, Harry Hawker!

Carolynne Cotton and the staff of Kingston History Centre for their patience and help.

Jessy Jin, my business partner at Phoenix Ryzing in Shanghai who so adeptly kept the business running in China, throughout lockdown, while I concentrated on this project.

L'amandine – Alina Cazamir and Izabela Krawiec who kept the coffee shop on Ham Parade open for take-aways throughout the coronavirus outbreak. That daily shot of coffee and their warm welcome was very much appreciated. Not forgetting Peter Shyjka, Vivien Sunlight, George & Julia, Ian & Tricia, John & Bev, Barry and Roger, all members of the L'amandine faithful, for their interest and support in the progress of this project.

Janine Stanford, the very capable archivist of the Richmond Local Studies in the Old Town Hall, for her continuous enthusiasm and prompt and comprehensive replies to all my requests for help. Thanks also to Lara Bond for sorting out all the photographs that I needed. Richmond Local Studies were very generous in their provision of the images.

Mike Shaw for his expertise in researching the family history of many of the characters in this book. He also provided very valuable assistance in proof-reading the draft text and critically advising on necessary corrections. A big thanks also to his wife, Elizabeth, for her input.

Gerald Stevens for his invaluable knowledge of the local area. He is always a useful and very helpful source of information and amusing tales about life in Ham. He has also published his own book, recounting growing up in Ham, from the late 1940s to the early 1970s.

George Stirling for his very necessary proof-reading of the entire draft manuscript. He is another compatriot of Harry Hawker who has settled in this area, just along from the spot by the river where Hawker test flew those early Sopwith float planes.

Surrey History Centre – Julian Pooley and the staff of the centre who were extremely helpful and supportive during the research stages of this project. They were also very generous in the provision of images to support the stories.

Tudor Drive Library – Cesar, Cecilia and Alice for their assistance in providing a forum for the initial audience in the library and conveying details of people interested in contributing to the stories.

Owen Walter for his great knowledge of north Kingston, his detailed information on Latchmere School and his comprehensive collection of photographs and newspaper articles connected with this area.

Kip Waddell – nearly ten years ago Kip, who was serving as the warden of St Andrew's Church in Ham, gave me a tour of the graveyard with a tantalising insight into the lives of some of the people buried there. When this project began, he was the first person that I wished to interview. Unfortunately, he became very ill and I was unable to document his story.

Mike Watson – having assiduously helped me in the proof-reading of *Remarkable Ham - The Untold Story*, Mike was good enough to volunteer to proof-read the manuscript of *People of the Latchmere*.

Index

People